THE FLOWER GARDEN

THE FLOWER GARDEN

Roy Genders

WARD LOCK · LONDON

CONTENTS

Chapter 1

FLOWERS THE WHOLE YEAR ROUND

Flowers in the garden. Flowers in the home. Everyone likes to have them. And with a little care in selection and siting they can be grown in colourful abundance the whole year round no matter how small the garden.

Flowers are not nearly so exacting in their demands as vegetables. You may not have the time to grow vegetables, but you can almost certainly fit in a few flowers. The hybrid tea rose has a life of at least twenty years, given only a small amount of care in its pruning and culture whilst the paeony may be left unattended for a century or more! Many other plants are either almost as durable or very simple to raise: a perennial by definition should bloom year after year, if not for ever; whilst annuals flower for only one season though there are those which do better if given a winter's start. These are called biennials.

PRELIMINARY CONSIDERATIONS

For flowering plants to have a long life and to bloom to the maximum of their capabilities, they should be selected according to their suitability for the particular soil of one's garden and the prevailing climate. For a cold wind-swept garden, low-growing plants of extreme hardiness are best, and in gardens which suffer from late frosts (perhaps on the banks of rivers), the half-hardy plants should either be omitted or planting delayed until June. Yet much may be done to provide protection from cold winds by planting a colourful hedge of escallonia or shrub roses, or erecting interwoven fencing or wattle hurdles on the side of the prevailing wind (usually north or east).

To be efficient, a fence should be 5–6 ft tall, and so that it is not easily blown over by strong winds the panels should be held in place by 3×3 in posts driven at least 15 in into the ground and preferably cemented in.

Grow climbing roses against the fence; the thornless 'Bourbon', 'Zephirine Drouhin', is admirable for this purpose for it bears its bunches of silvery-pink flowers from June until October and their perfume will reach to all parts of the garden.

Grow climbing plants on all those unsightly walls of house or outbuildings. There will be at least one suitable for every aspect and every type of soil,

7

providing the maximum of beauty for the minimum of labour; all that is necessary is to tie in the shoots. No part of the garden should ever be bare of flowers; every piece of fencing and every wall should be a blaze of colour for many months of the year; even the paths, made of old bricks or paving stones, should carry carpeting plants which bring an old-world charm to the most modern town garden.

Permanent paths are important for the full enjoyment of the garden and should certainly be made alongside the herbaceous border, which will also be permanent. It has been said that the permanent border is dying out because it demands too much time in its upkeep. But really it is the most labour-saving part of the garden; only those plants of tallest habit require staking and tying and this may be reduced to a minimum by planting the more compact varieties. There are now lupins which grow no more than 2 ft tall and delphiniums which grow to less than 3 ft and these need staking only in the most wind-swept garden. Many perennials require no staking at all and require neither lifting nor dividing for many years. All they ask for is an occasional mulch of humus-forming manures to maintain food requirements and improve the texture of the soil.

There are flowering plants for every purpose in the garden: to make a permanent border or shrubbery; for the alpine garden; to make a colourful dry wall; to fill tubs; to beautify a sunless corner; for winter, spring and summer bedding; for cold gardens and those that are rarely troubled by frost and cold winds. There are plants for all types of soil: for acid soils and calcareous soils; for heavy soils and light soils. And all that is necessary by way of tools is a good border

fork, a spade of stainless steel, a rake and a hoe, and a trowel for planting, again preferably one of stainless steel to which the soil will not adhere—it makes for greater ease in working.

RAISING ONE'S OWN PLANTS

When gardening becomes a hobby, a small greenhouse, frame and propagator will provide much enjoyment and interest. Summer bedding plants can be raised, cuttings propagated and the range of plants available greatly extended. It is surprising just how many plants may be raised from seed, using only a simple propagator and the sunny window of a warm room. Exotic wall-covering plants like *Campsis radicans*, with its flowers of geranium red, may with a simple propagator readily be raised from seed. The popular scarlet bedding zonal pelargoniums, still popularly known as geraniums, too, may be raised in this way and though not coming true from seed, many plants will bear flowers the equal of the best named varieties.

The Propagator There are a number of highly efficient propagators on the market now made with either a galvanized or plastic base and a high polythene cover. These stand over reliable hot-plate-type heating elements. They usually have accurate rod thermostats built into the base for efficient use. When the seeds have been sown or the cuttings of shrubs, miniature roses or geraniums have been inserted, all that is necessary is to connect to the mains, set the thermostat control to 70 °F (20 °C) and await results. Almost any temperature may be maintained, and a warm, moist atmosphere ensures rapid germination and rooting.

Where a greenhouse is available but is not heated, a propagating unit will enable those half-hardy annuals such as lobelia and petunias to be raised from seed by sowing in February and pricking off the seedlings in March when there will be sufficient warmth during daytime to grow on the plants without check. This will enable the varieties of one's choice to be grown (for nurserymen rarely grow the best of the newer introductions on account of the cost of seed), and give control of the conditions under which the plants will grow throughout their life.

The Cold Frame Seeds of certain annuals and biennials requiring winter protection may be sown directly into a cold frame. A frame should also be available in spring for the hardening of summer bedding plants which must not be planted out until fear of frost has vanished. If buying in one's plants, a frame will enable them to be kept growing without exposure to cold winds and frost which may be experienced at the time, and planting to be delayed for perhaps a few days when this will be advantageous.

The Greenhouse A warm greenhouse will not only enable many plants to be raised from seed and propagated, but plants can also be brought into bloom during winter. Late chrysanthemums may be grown outdoors and lifted in during autumn to bloom at Christmas, and lily-of-the-valley and snowdrops, lifted when just showing above ground and grown on in small pots indoors, will bloom at a time when flowers are most appreciated. A lean-to greenhouse, erected against the wall of one's home and perhaps also used as a garden room, is ideal for plant propagation and for the winter protection of dahlias, geraniums and other tender subjects, especially

A cold frame, essential for starting many annuals and tender bedding plants

A lean-to greenhouse or room extension–an ideal place for over-wintering tender plants

in the colder areas. A lean-to may also be erected against a garden wall, but wherever it is to be built, an open sunny situation is essential so as to trap as much natural warmth and light as possible. If electric heating and lighting are available, greenhouse chores and plant activity can continue during the coldest and darkest days of winter.

Where space is at a premium, one of the circular greenhouses of more revolutionary design may be erected in a sunny corner. These are usually 7 ft high and 8 ft in diameter, with a dome which lifts to allow top ventilation in addition to an all-round intake of air at ground level. Heating costs are reduced by the elimination of unnecessary headroom. Heating consists of a close-coiled, mineral-insu-

lated, copper-sheathed cable operating at a low surface temperature and providing an even distribution of heat which will raise the temperature at least 25 °F (14 °C) above outside temperatures.

When taking the electricity supply from the home to a greenhouse, it is preferable to do so by underground cables which should be placed at least 18–20 in below ground. Unless one is a qualified electrician one should either have the cables laid and the connections made by someone who is qualified to undertake the work or, if one does the work oneself, it should be thoroughly checked by an electrician before being used. A water supply may be taken to the greenhouse by the same trench and if the pipes (now mostly of plastic material) are at this depth, there is little likelihood of the water freezing in winter.

To calculate the amount of heat needed to raise the temperature of a conventional greenhouse to 25 °F (14 °C) above that of the outside temperature, the total area of base and glass must be obtained. For a house 12 ft long and 8 ft wide, with a 2 ft base of brick or wood, and a door 7 ft high, the area will be approximately 284 sq ft, made up as follows:

2 sides with glass 12 ft × 3 ft	72 sq ft
2 roof sections 12 ft × 4 ft 6 in	108 ,, ,,
2 ends, glass 8 ft × 4 ft	64 ,, ,,
2 sides, brick 12 ft × 2 ft ÷ 2	24 ,, ,,
2 ends, brick 8 ft × 2 ft ÷ 2	16 ,, ,,
Total area	284 sq ft

This is multiplied by 10 to give the number of watts required, which to be on the safe side should be 3000.

The most economic and efficient way of heating a greenhouse is with a greenhouse fan heater; domestic fan heaters are not safe when used in greenhouses. The advantage of these heaters, from the plants' point of view, is that they circulate the air, and air-movement is important in preventing the incidence of disease in the greenhouse. A good greenhouse fan heater is one that has a built-in thermometer and a temperature control knob for setting to the degree required. Accurate thermostatic control means no wasted heat and low running costs. The sensitive element is usually placed behind the dial where it is unaffected by the radiant heat of the sun and where it can measure with accuracy the intake air temperature. The heater can be instantly connected to the mains and may be stood on a wooden block or on bricks where used for heating a Dutch-light house.

Tubular heaters are also effective and may be fitted to the wood- or brick-base walls. Where wall mounting is not practicable, the tubes may be held in place by spikes of galvanized iron inserted into the ground. The loading is 60 W per ft of tube and additional lengths can be added should higher temperatures be required. The tubes may be tucked away beneath the staging and provide effective heat for the minimum of care and expense. With thermostatic control, these heaters may be left for weeks unattended.

Where no electric supply is available or where the greenhouse is too far from the home, thermostatically controlled, oil-fired paraffin heaters will prove invaluable. These need no wick-trimming and are usually supplied with 5 gallon oil storage tanks, requiring only monthly filling. Fuel is metered into the vaporizing burner by two orifices. When the supply is turned on sufficient oil flows continuously through the smaller of these to maintain the flame in the burner at a low level. The thermostatic valve controls the fuel through the longer orifice, so that when the valve opens, fuel flows through both orifices and the flame burns at a higher level.

The unit is installed on bricks at the end of the greenhouse, with the oil storage tank on the bench for it must be no more than 3 ft nor less than 2 ft 6 in higher than the orifices as its height determines the fuel rate. The fuel line is clipped to the staging. To connect it to the burner, push the nipple into the fuel inlet, then turn on the tap and when the wick is moist, apply a light. In about half an hour adjust the thermostatic valve and the levelling screws so that the flame is even.

To heat a greenhouse 12 ft long and 8 ft wide to a temperature of about 50 °F (10 °C) during the winter, will require about 30 gallons of oil.

A greenhouse will usually require shading during summer. Hessian canvas or tinted polythene sheeting may be tacked to the outside of the roof. A less expensive method is to spray the outside of the greenhouse with a proprietary shading mixture. At the end of summer it is readily removed with a brush and warm soapy water.

To reduce the inside temperature of a greenhouse an air intake–extraction system should be installed, one ventilator introducing fresh air, the other removing the stale air, thus maintaining the house in a fresh, buoyant condition during the warmest days. The ideal position for these fans is above the door and in a corresponding position at the opposite end of the greenhouse.

Cloches Where no cold frame is available (and it may be quite inexpensively made), a greater use of annuals can well be made by raising plants under barn-type cloches in the open. Cloches may be used with great effect both for bedding plants and for flowers for cutting. Indeed, the seed for the latter can be sown where the plants are to bloom, and wintered in an exposed garden under cloches and the same cloches used to cover boxes of seed sown late in March for bedding out in June.

Tunnel cloches made with hoops and waterproof polythene sheeting or with PVC sheeting are an admirable substitute for glass cloches. The hoops are skewered into the ground to prevent wind damage and they are light and easy to move about.

WATER IN THE GARDEN

An efficient water supply is essential for flowering plants. The mist-spraying of roses for regular periods is known to keep them free from mildew and from many pests, as well as providing the plants with necessary moisture at the roots. It also prevents the transpiration of moisture from the foliage in hot weather and thus helps to maintain the health of the plant. Delphiniums, paeonies and chry-

santhemums are great moisture-lovers and require copious amounts during their growing season. Plants which lack moisture not only finish flowering prematurely but the quality of bloom suffers.

Labour saving and especially useful for those who have to be away from home during the daytime are the oscillating sprinklers which give adjustable watering over circular or rectangular areas, and the gentle swaying action ensures correct irrigation. The sprinkler may be set in the morning, possibly to take in parts of the lawn and flower border and there are several models which can water an area of 2000 sq ft or more.

If watering plants in dry weather and with the sun on them, it is necessary to give the ground a thorough soaking otherwise the roots will turn towards the surface in search of moisture (where only a sprinkling has been given) and more harm will result than if no watering had been done. For this reason where possible, water in the evening for this will give time for the moisture to reach down to the roots during the hours of darkness when there will be little or no evaporation.

A good hosepipe is essential in the large garden, to take water to the sprinkler or to use for hand watering when an automatic lever-spray nozzle will enable the jet to reach greater distances. For the small garden, a can with a long spout and fine rose sprinkler will make for efficient watering.

GENERAL PREPARATION OF THE SOIL

The aspect of one's garden cannot be changed, but the soil should be brought into as rich a state as possible so that almost all plants will grow well in it. Gardeners who are ready to take some little care in the preparation of the ground will be astonished at the increased

vigour and freedom of flowering of the plants. Most plants require a soil that is well drained in winter but which is retentive of summer moisture.

To take the new garden first. Here the soil is often of a heavy clay nature, the top soil having been removed, either sold off or used elsewhere, when the foundations of the house were made. First, it will be necessary to provide drainage, making the soil as porous as possible by incorporating crushed brick, often to be found about the garden of a newly built property, or old mortar, gravel or grit. Each or all of these materials should be thoroughly worked into the soil to open up the clay particles.

Lime should also be used in quantity to open up the sticky, clay soil that is to be found so often around a newly built house or estate. Caustic lime, which has

Bedding schemes. The tulips can later be replaced by colourful summer bedding

not been hydrated, is the most effective form, for the action of the moisture in the soil will generate considerable heat from the lime, causing it to expand and break up and in so doing will break down the clay particles in the soil. It should be applied to the soil at the same time as the drainage materials are incorporated, which is best done in late autumn before the soil becomes sticky. If left all winter the soil will, after the action of the lime and frosts, become friable. (Town soils, which are frequently of a sour nature, should be given a liberal dressing of hydrated lime in alternate winters.)

Then in March dig in as much humus as it is possible to obtain: clearings from ditches, decayed leaves, peat, used hops, shoddy (cotton or wool waste, readily obtainable by northern gardeners) and decayed manure, though this may be almost unprocurable for the townsman. A light, sandy soil also requires humus, though not for the same reason. Here it is required to hold summer moisture which will make artificial watering except during a very dry season almost unnecessary. Too much nitrogenous manure must be avoided, otherwise tall, lanky plants will result, making excess foliage to the exclusion of bloom. Should the soil be seriously lacking in humus, then plants will make little growth and though they may smother themselves in bloom, they will be short lived. There are exceptions to this, of course, but in general soil preparation it is best to try to strike the happy medium.

A chalk-laden soil, generally a shallow, hot, dry soil will respond to liberal applications of humus-forming materials, also by green manuring, digging in rape when it is about 2 in high. Such a soil cannot be given too much humus, but here again the nitrogenous manures should be used sparingly. Peat is an excellent material to use in a chalky soil, for it will neutralize some of the alkalinity.

PLANTS FOR A CALCAREOUS SOIL

Though the soil may be brought into as neutral a condition as possible to enable the largest number of plants to grow well in it, gardeners working over chalk or limestone would be advised to concentrate on planting subjects that are known to grow well in calcareous conditions:

Trees and Shrubs

Abelia	Ceanothus
Berberis	deciduous spp.
Buddleia	Cistus spp.
Clematis s	Lavender
Cornus mas	Lilac
Cotoneaster	Osmanthus delavayi
Cydonia japonica	Prunus
Cytisus	Pyracantha
Daphne	Pyrus
Forsythia	Ribes sanguineum
Genista	Rubus
Helianthemum	Sorbus
Hypericum	Tree paeony
Jasmine	Viburnum
Kerria japonica	Wistaria sinensis

Herbaceous Perennials

Acanthus spinosa	Iris germanica
Achillea	Kniphofia
Aconitum	Linum perenne
Aethionema	Lunaria biennis
Alyssum	Lythrum
Anchusa	Madonna lily
Anemone coronaria	Michaelmas daisy
Aubretia	Oriental poppy
Betonica	Ostrowskia
Campanula glomerata	Pentstemon
Centaurea	Phlox
Cyclamen (hardy)	Potentilla
Dianthus	Poterium
Dicentra spectabilis	Pulsatilla
Echinops	Salvia patens
Eremurus	Scabious
Eryngium	Senecio
Geranium	Statice
Gypsophila	Verbascum
Hesperis matronalis	Veronica spicata

Annuals and Biennials

Antirrhinum	Mignonette
Canterbury Bell	Nigella
Clarkia	Pansy
Cornflower	Poppy
Cosmos	Scabious
Dianthus	Stocks
Godetia	Sweet Sultan
Kochsia childsii	Viscaria
Larkspur	Wallflower

PLANTS FOR AN ACID SOIL

Some plants will not tolerate lime in their diet; rather do they thrive on quantities of peat and leaf-mould to provide humus and the acid conditions they enjoy. The following plants prefer an acid soil:

Andromeda	Gaultheria
Arbutus unedo	Halesia
Astilbe	Hamamelis mollis
Azalea	Kalmia japonica
Calluna	Ledum
Camellia	Lilium sargentiae
Crinodendron	Lithospermum
Epigaea	Magnolia
Erica (except E. carnea)	Pieris
Exochorda racemosa	Rhododendron
Fothergilla	Spiraea

So that a wider variety of plants may be grown, a part of the garden may be brought into a more neutral soil condition by treating with hydrated lime or by incorporating liberal quantities of mortar. In this way, though the genuine lime-loving plants would not flourish, those growing well in a neutral soil would give a good account of themselves.

PLANTS FOR A HEAVY CLAY SOIL

For a heavy, not too well-drained soil, those plants of the New World, which possess extreme hardiness, are to be recommended:

Chrysanthemum maximum	Lavatera
	Oenothera
Echinacea	Ranunculus acris
Helenium	Rudbeckia
Helianthus	Solidago

PLANTS THAT DO WELL IN SEMI-SHADE

For those out-of-the-way corners which receive little sunshine, and to plant in the shade of a wall or building, there are numerous hardy perennials which will flourish under such conditions:

Astrantia	Omphalodes
Digitalis	Paeony
Hosta	Polyanthus
Hypericum	Primrose
Lily-of-the-valley	Pulmonaria
Mahonia	Scilla
Muscari	Snowdrop
Narcissus	Solomon's seal

SOWING AND PLANTING

The flower-lover who may wish to raise his (or her) own plants from seed or by cuttings should be familiar with modern equipment.

Pots Clay pots have been superseded by new and lighter materials. There are black polythene pots which can be bought very cheaply by the thousand and can be washed and re-used numerous times. Then there are Jiffy pots, manufactured from 75 per cent wood pulp impregnated with essential nutrients. Made square or round, in a range of sizes, these also can be bought economically in large quantities.

Thin-walled tray containers divided into compartments which are easily separated at planting time, are now popular. The compartments can all be filled with compost in the same operation. The 2 in size is obtainable in units of 24 and exactly fits into a standard 2 in wooden seed tray. There are also thin-walled pots made to take a dozen plants, the compartments being held together by a strip of waterproof tape which is removed when the plants are set out in the ground. Individual seeds may be sown, one to each 2 in pot, and there is no root disturbance, for transplanting is eliminated, thus saving considerable labour. Rooted cuttings of carnations and geraniums may be planted in the pots and planted out with the soil ball intact when the compartments are filled with roots.

Ideal for raising sweet peas and lupins are cubes based on vermiculite and perlite and containing fertilizers to promote healthy plant growth. The young plants may be moved to larger pots for growing on, the cubes also being planted so that there is no root disturbance.

Where sowing in boxes or pans, sow thinly or space out the seeds to 1 in apart to allow the seedlings room to develop. Overcrowding at this stage results in a drawn, 'leggy' plant which will never recover. Obtain the best seed from growers with a reputation to maintain. It will cost rather more but will amply repay its cost in reliable germination.

Composts Sowing composts may vary slightly but, as a general rule, the John Innes compost is to be recommended. It may be purchased from most garden stores but should be in a fresh condition. If made up for any length of time it can become contaminated with disease spores while the superphosphate used in its formula, and so valuable in promoting vigorous root action, will have lost its strength. The John Innes compost consists of:

2 parts loam (sterilized)
1 part peat
1 part sand   per bushel
$1\frac{1}{2}$ oz superphosphate
$\frac{3}{4}$ oz ground limestone

Introduce the sowing compost to the greenhouse several days before sowing, to enable it to absorb some of the warmth of the house. Line the boxes or pans with moist moss or damp peat before covering with compost to a depth of 2 in. The compost should be in a moist, friable condition and, after sowing, the seeds are lightly covered with additional compost and watered in before being placed in the propagator.

After germination, transplant the seedlings into boxes or pans containing the John Innes potting compost:

7 parts loam (sterilized)
3 parts peat
2 parts sand   per bushel
$\frac{3}{4}$ oz ground limestone
$\frac{1}{2}$ lb JI base

The John Innes base is made up of:

2 parts hoof and horn meal
2 parts superphosphate
1 part sulphate of potash

In place of the limestone, crushed chalk, or limestone flour as used for poultry, or whitening scraped from outhouse walls, can be used; they are forms of the same ingredient. Upon analysis, the JI base provides approximately 10 per cent potash, 5 per cent nitrogen, 7.5 per cent phosphates, each of which is so important for healthy plant growth. If making up one's own composts, do not exceed the amounts stated for it has been established that seedlings grow better in a slightly acid compost than in one of an alkaline nature.

Drills Seeds of those plants treated as biennials, eg wallflowers and forget-me-nots and hardy annuals, may be sown in drills outdoors in a prepared bed. First make the soil friable by breaking down lumps and remove all stones, then work into the top 2–3 in some peat or leaf-mould and give a sprinkling of super-phosphate of lime to encourage root action. Take out drills 6 in apart and 1 in deep with the back of a rake and sow

Paeonia '*Bowl of Beauty*', *one of the new race of stunning single peonies*

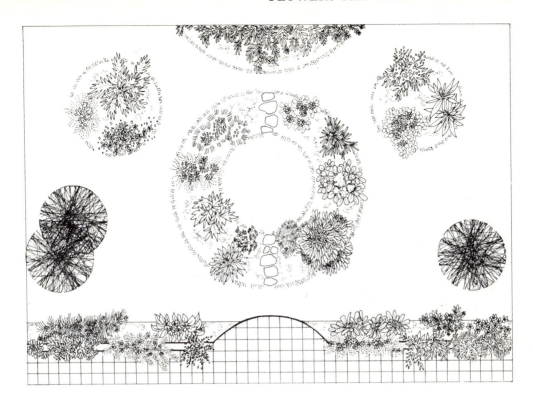

thinly. Keep the soil moist and, when the seedlings appear, keep the hoe moving between the rows to suppress weeds and aerate the soil. If the plants are to remain in the rows through winter, it may be advisable in exposed gardens to cover the rows with cloches.

Planting and Staking If possible always plant on a dull day and when the soil is nicely moist. When planting an herbaceous border, follow no regular pattern, but plant in groups of two, three or four for maximum effect. Make sure that each hole is large enough to accommodate the roots of the plants with room to spare, that the bottom of the hole is flat and that the plant's roots are spread out evenly across the bottom of the hole.

The taller-growing varieties of delphinium, eremurus and michaelmas

Left Desfontainea spinosa.
Above right Rosa 'Lafter'.
Below left Rosa 'Eleanor le Grice'

Curved steps lead down through retaining wall to the flower garden

daisy may require staking when they come into bloom for the stems have to carry a considerable weight, especially when the flowers are wet. Pea-sticks are the traditional mode of supporting such plants, but where these are unobtainable metal tripods will serve as well. The important thing is to put the supports round the plants when growth is only 6 in or so high.

PLANNING THE FLOWER GARDEN

Unlike the vegetable garden, the flower garden follows no definite pattern. Flowering plants may be used wherever colour is desired, but they should be sited where they will grow best and where they may be seen to maximum advantage.

The average garden is small and

rectangular and it is usually desirable to have some part of it down to lawn, which will be green all the year, and provide playing space for children as well as somewhere for grown-ups to sit and relax when the day's chores are finished. One's pleasure will be increased if on one side of the lawn there is an herbaceous border of generous proportions and if a corner at the end of the garden is made into a small spinney, with flowering trees, beneath which may be planted bulbs of all sorts to give colour throughout the year. Or a rockery may be made in the corner where two walls or lengths of interwoven fencing meet. This, too, may be planted to give year-round colour and will be a garden within a garden; for continuity, a small alpine lawn would merge rockery and lawn. Along the side of the garden opposite the border, flowering trees and shrubs can be planted in small groups, and here may be placed a garden seat in a small area of paving stones with carpeting plants growing amongst them.

The herbaceous border will be more pleasing if made in gentle curves with flowering trees at the corner farthest from the house. Always plant in small groups of one species or variety for maximum effect, taking care to avoid straight lines.

At the bottom of a low wall, separating the paved terrace from the garden, a lavender hedge may be planted or a bed of scarlet bedding pelargoniums ('geraniums') or salvias, broken by steps leading down to the lawn. To give height to the border, climbing roses (shown red in the diagram) planted 8 ft apart may be grown up rustic poles to 7 ft above soil level. Plant 'Zephirine Drouhin', 'Danse du Feu', 'Golden Showers' and others noted for their freedom of flowering over as long a period as possible. If planting ornamental trees and shrubs, remember to

put in those that bloom in winter and spring as well as the summer- and autumn-flowering varieties, and beneath them plant bulbs which will bloom at the same time. Or one may prefer to plant a border of roses, using the vigorous old shrub roses at the back to hide the fence and in front planting the more vigorous of the floribundas and hybrid teas, with the most compact varieties to the front. Such a border, or one filled with herbaceous perennials, will last for at least 20–25 years with the minimum of attention and no further outlay and each year will provide a mass of bloom for weeks.

Those who are retired and have more time for their gardening may prefer to plant a border of dahlias instead of shrubs or roses, here again using the taller-growing cactus dahlias and decoratives at the back and with the less tall semi-cactus varieties and pompons at the front. For brilliance of colour during late summer and autumn dahlias have no equal. However, there are now so many wonderful varieties of the Korean and Pompon chrysanthemum, in addition to the early autumn-flowering varieties of the large-flowering chrysanthemum, that a small border could be devoted entirely to these flowers.

For an acid soil, or for a neutral soil that has had plenty of peat incorporated in it, the heathers provide brilliance of colour throughout the year with their foliage and flowers. Use them in a part of the garden which the sun can reach; this is particularly necessary in winter when the heathers will make more than their expected contribution to the garden display. Heathers should be used like alpine plants, and set out in generous drifts by planting six or more of one variety.

The site should first be laid out by inserting a group of rocks into the ground

A rock garden should look like a natural outcrop, with plants growing in the crevices

with their flat surface showing just above soil level, like a natural outcrop and about the stones the heathers are grouped. Limestone rock should be avoided since it will, in time, kill many lime-hating plants. Plant crimson next to white, and group the salmon and pink shades together. Make use of heathers with golden foliage such as 'John Eason' and 'Golden Drop' which turn deep bronze in winter, both of them varieties of bell heather *E. cinerea*, which comes into bloom late in June and remains colourful until September when the winter-flowering species begin to bloom. *E. carnea* and its many varieties are happy in a soil containing lime. They bloom through winter and spring, 'Eileen Porter' bearing its crimson spikes until Easter. Shortly after, *E. tetralix albamollis* begins to bloom, a symphony in white with its elegant spikes and silver foliage. These heathers spread rapidly and are excellent ground-cover plants. They are also long lasting and entirely labour saving.

Where the garden is exposed to the sun and the soil is of a dry gravelly nature, often experienced where gardening over chalk or limestone, dianthus and irises should be planted, making full use of the wide variety of pinks and carnations, planting the Allwoodii and border carnations in beds to themselves, edged by pinks of dwarf, compact habit of which there are many. Irises enjoy the same conditions and may be planted in a border to themselves, whilst beds of the summer-flowering zonal pelargoniums ('geraniums')—those with handsome leaf variations as well as those bearing large flower heads of vermilion, pink and

A plan of an asymmetrical garden viewed from the house

mauve—will add splashes of brilliant colour over the garden canvas from June until October. In formal beds, which may be made to a pattern in a lawn, use pelargoniums with calceolarias and marguerites, heliotrope and verbenas, so beloved of Victorian gardeners who preferred the ordered symmetry of the formal bed to the happy abandonment of cottage-garden planting.

At the centre of a small lawn, a circle filled with dwarf plants will provide colour and interest for several months of the year.

In the layout shown here a colourful effect will be obtained by filling the circle (a) with scarlet geraniums and (b) with golden-leaved featherfew, 'Golden Moss'. In the space (c) white alyssum will quickly form a carpet completely hiding the soil, and will be in striking contrast to the other plants. Equally effective would be the use of pansies or violas, a yellow-flowering variety for (a), crimson for (b), and a carpeting (c) of white or blue lobelia.

The richness of tulips in spring and early summer may be accentuated by planting them in circles of contrasting colours, using the single early-flowering varieties which do not grow too tall. The planting area need not be more than 4 ft in diameter and can be edged with winter violas in mixed colours. Inside a circle of red tulips can be followed by one of yellow, then purple, pink and crimson. If the bed is raised slightly at the centre it will display the tulips to advantage.

Where planting tulips or gladioli or any of those plants which bloom at the end of an almost leafless stem, the display will be enhanced by using ground-cover plants such as forget-me-nots and cheiranthus of contrasting colours; their use will also reduce the number of bulbs needed and so keep costs to a minimum.

Bedding schemes are more effective if foliage plants of varying heights are incorporated. One or two plants of the almost black-leaved *Lobelia cardinalis* with its spikes of brilliant red on 3 ft stems will add an exotic touch to a bed of yellow calceolarias or dwarf yellow dahlias.

There are now many wonderful annuals of compact habit for small beds and of such freedom of flowering that a garden may be made colourful for a very small outlay. The 'Little Gem' antirrhinums grow only 6 in tall and make a delightful carpet for beds of gladioli, and the 'Floral Cluster' strain, raised by Sakata & Co of Japan and obtainable in all the antirrhinum colours, is admirable for massing in small beds. These plants make a bush 12 in high and the same in width, bearing as many as a dozen spikes at one time. The multiflora begonias are equally valuable for small beds, the 'Fiesta' strain producing on each plant masses of small double blooms, replicas in miniature of the greenhouse varieties.

The petunia is another plant which has been improved out of all recognition since the time when those dark purple flowers were borne on weak, lanky stems. The recently introduced 'Circus' bears large fully double blooms of salmon-red edged with white, whilst 'Pinwheel' bears a large scarlet trumpet striped with white.

So greatly has the dwarf marigold been improved of recent years that beds may now be planted with them, to the exclusion of all other plants. 'Red Brocade' makes a dwarf bush 8–9 in tall and bears fully double flowers of rich mahogany-red whilst 'First Lady', raised by Burpees in the USA is a dwarf African marigold covering itself for weeks with double yellow flowers of the size of tennis balls.

Chapter 2

FLOWERING SHRUBS

Trees provide the framework for the garden picture. They give it height and provide colour where no other plants can provide it, whether they act as a screen or serve as a focal point in the garden.

After the trees, perhaps the most important plants in the garden are the flowering shrubs which, because they are so labour-saving, are more widely planted each year. A border of small shrubs to provide colour from flowers, foliage or fruit the whole year round may be made in the smallest of gardens, possibly at the side, along the length of a neighbouring garden, or to provide shelter where the garden is exposed to prevailing winds. Or there may be a corner which receives only a limited amount of sunlight, or a stretch where draughts make it difficult for anything but the hardiest of shrubs to survive, and these may be beautified by shrubs which will give colour the whole year round.

Requiring neither staking nor tying, and the minimum of pruning and cultivation, shrubs are not only labour saving but are also permanent. Once planted into soil brought into as friable a condition as possible and where the ground is well drained, they should remain healthy for at least a lifetime before they require replacing.

PLANTING AND ROUTINE CULTURE OF SHRUBS

It is important that, before any planting is done, the ground is cleared of all perennial weeds, and if the soil is of a high clay content then drainage materials should be incorporated. These may take the form of boiler ash and clinker, grit from the seashore or river bank, together with humus-forming materials such as peat, used hops or seaweed.

Where the ground is light and sandy it will be necessary to use only humus-forming composts, together with some manure, for a light soil (and particularly where it is overlying chalk) will generally be a hungry soil, and most shrubs are gross feeders. Old mushroom-bed compost, decayed farmyard manure, used hops and bonemeal will provide the plants with an adequate diet. Whatever the manure used, and this will depend upon what is most readily obtainable, it should be worked deeply into the soil to feed the roots over the years.

To provide the plants with a yearly mulch is of even greater importance than the cultivation of the soil at planting time, for this will enable them to form continuous new wood by regular feeding in addition to preserving moisture in the soil during the summer months. In this way, the shrubs will remain healthy and vigorous almost indefinitely. The mulch, which may be of clearings from ditches, decayed manure, peat or used hops, should be spread around the plants as they come into new growth in spring, but before it is applied the ground around the plants should be forked over so as to aerate the soil.

Evergreens are best planted in early spring; deciduous shrubs may be planted at any time between November and March when soil conditions permit. Do not plant too close together. The shrubs quickly grow bushy and if they are deprived of air and sunlight they will gradually form an excess of dead wood and eventually die back. Also, it is important to make the planting hole sufficiently large, so that the roots are not crowded together. Spread them well out and as the soil is replaced, tread it quite firm.

Where planting a shrub border, plant shrubs of more vigorous habit at the back and the more dwarf to the front. Plant for all-the-year-round colour rather than for a concentration of summer blossom, giving particular attention to those plants noted also for their colourful fruit and foliage.

Routine culture consists of the removal of any dead or overcrowded wood each year, keeping the soil aerated and providing an annual mulch. If planted firmly, no staking will be necessary.

WINTER-FLOWERING SHRUBS

(*denotes evergreen*)

Azara* *Azara microphylla* is a most pleasing evergreen shrub from Chile,

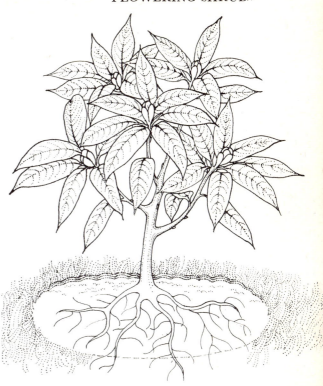

Planting a shrub. Always see that the hole is large enough to take the roots easily

bearing sprays of small shiny leaves. During late winter and early spring it produces tiny pale yellow vanilla-scented flowers, which are followed by bright orange berries in autumn. The plant appreciates some protection, for it is not completely hardy and should be sheltered from cold winds.

Corylopsis There are two delightful forms of this February- and March-flowering shrub, which make compact plants 4 ft tall. *Corylopsis spicata* is first to bloom, bearing in February its pendant sulphur-yellow flowers which carry the delicious perfume of cowslips. Then in March blooms *C. pauciflora*, which also bears yellow, sweetly scented flowers. In both cases the blooms appear before the heart-shaped leaves, which in autumn turn brilliant golden-yellow.

Daphne Being slow-growing, the daphnes are ideal small-garden plants,

Daphne mezereum, *whose richly scented mauve flowers withstand the winter weather*

probably the best form being *Daphne mezereum*, which blooms during February and March, its leafless stems being covered with purple-pink blossom which possesses a sweet perfume. The flowers are followed by scarlet fruit. There is also an attractive white form, *D.m.* 'Alba', the grey-white flowers of which are followed by yellow fruit.

The excellent hybrid *D.* × 'Somerset' should also be grown, for it bears its highly scented rose-pink flowers from the end of April to the end of May. Almost no pruning is advisable for any of the daphnes.

Garrya* The Californian tassel bush, *Garrya elliptica*, which is fully evergreen, is one of the most valuable shrubs in the garden. It has handsome dark green leaves, grey on the underside, and from November until March bears clusters of long drooping greenish-yellow catkins. The plant does well in a sunless position and requires little pruning, for the 6 in catkins are borne on the previous season's wood.

Mahonia* The well-known *Mahonia aquifolium*, with its glossy dark green leaves, grows in the form of a low bush and bears its trusses of tiny brilliant yellow flowers during February and March. The plants will flourish under town conditions and in a shaded position.

Rhododendron* Provided the plants can be given a lime-free soil and peat is packed around the roots at planting time, several of the rhododendrons are valuable plants for a small garden. *R. praecox*, with its lilac-pink flowerheads in February, is one of the few winter-flowering plants bearing pink flowers. It is so slow growing that pruning will not be necessary.

Viburnum* The winter viburnum, *V. tinus*, is a most valuable evergreen, for it will flourish in a sunless garden. It has large oval glossy green leaves and bears trusses of white flowers from October until March. Also evergreen but in bloom during May, when it bears fragrant white flowers, is *V. chenaulti*, which makes a small compact plant.

One of the best deciduous forms is *V. fragrans*, now properly called *V. farreri* but usually still sold under the old name, making a compact little plant of vigorous upright growth, and bearing fragrant pink and white flowers from Christmas until the end of March. A hybrid of this species is *V. bodnantense*, which also bears pink and white flowers in winter. Do no pruning apart from the removal of dead branches.

V. burkwoodii should not be neglected. It is semi-evergreen and bears its large fragrant white flowers in spring.

Winter Heather There is no better plant for the front of a shrubbery than the winter-flowering heather *Erica carnea*, together with its numerous varieties. This is one of the few heathers that grow quite happily in a soil containing lime, and it blooms from November until early April. Varieties of *Erica carnea* should be placed at the front of the border in groups of three, in those spaces which are difficult to fill with other plants. There they will quickly grow into colourful mounds, remaining in bloom even when the snow lies deep around them.

One of the best varieties is 'Loughrigg', which comes early into bloom and bears sprigs of bright crimson at a height of about 12 in. Also early is 'Winter Beauty', which bears rose-pink flowers. For mid-season, 'Ruby Gem' and 'C. M. Beale' (pure white) are excellent; and for late blooming try 'James Backhouse' (deep pink), 'Vivelli' (deep crimson) and 'Springwood White'.

Wintersweet *Chimonanthus fragrans* is a valuable winter-flowering shrub, for though deciduous it bears during the coldest days of winter its sprays of purple-yellow wax-like flowers which possess a strong perfume. Several sprays taken indoors and placed in damp sand will scent a large room. The plants appreciate some protection from cold winds, which may cause them to die back when young. Almost no pruning will be necessary.

Witch Hazel *Hamamelis mollis* likes a rich, deeply worked soil but will flourish under town-garden conditions. From December until March it bears fragrant golden flowers along its branches, if in a sunny position. The flowers have narrow, twisted petals and a delicious fragrance. The plants possess an additional attraction in that their hazel-like leaves turn brilliant crimson before they fall in autumn. Another form is *H. vernalis*, which during winter bears small pale yellow flowers, whilst *H. brevipetala* bears its straight-petalled golden flowers during January and February.

SPRING-FLOWERING SHRUBS

Azalea This shrub prefers light shade, and a soil free of lime and well enriched with peat. Beds of six or more planted together will provide a brilliant display during April and May. The Kurume hybrids are fully evergreen and make dwarf plants 18 in tall. The foliage is box-like, and the plants are covered in numerous small flowers. 'Esmeralda' bears double flowers of soft apple-blossom pink, whilst 'Benekirin' bears blooms of deep salmon-pink. 'Hinodegiri' (bright carmine-red) and 'Orange Beauty' are also lovely. With these evergreen azaleas the flowers tend to fade in strong sun.

Plant with them the semi-evergreen *A. malvatica* hybrids which grow to 2 ft and bear larger flowers, whilst the foliage takes on glorious tints in autumn. Of the numerous varieties available 'Fedora' (deep rose), 'Adonis' (white), 'Addy Wery' (scarlet), and 'Zampa' (orange-rust) are outstanding.

Berberis* For planting beneath trees or in shade cast by buildings, *Berberis darwinii* is one of those almost indestructible plants with dark foliage and bearing masses of orange flowers throughout spring, followed by jet-black fruit in autumn and winter. *B. sieboldi*, which also blooms in spring, is noted more for its brilliant foliage which in autumn turns vivid crimson before it falls.

Broom In addition to the large-flowered hybrids (described later), there are several species which will provide colour during April and early May. They like a dry soil of a poor nature and preferably free from lime. They should also be given a sunny situation.

Corylopsis pauciflora: *primrose yellow flowers with cowslip scent in early spring*

Of extreme hardiness is *Cytisus praecox*, which comes into bloom early in April to make a fountain-like plant of pale yellow flowers. In bloom at the same time is *C. albus*, the Portugal broom, its slender stems smothered in white blossom. Established brooms should never be pruned. Always obtain pot-grown plants.

Flowering Currant Tolerant of every soil and of every situation, with its attractive pale green pungent foliage and flowers like tiny bunches of grapes, this is one of the brightest plants of the garden. *Ribes sanguineum* 'Pulborough Scarlet' bears numerous crimson flowers in April and May; whilst 'King Edward VII' bears flowers of deep crimson-red. As a contrast the less hardy buffalo currant,

R. aureum, bears fragrant yellowish buff-coloured flowers in April. Each grows to about 4 ft and may be clipped into whatever shape is required. The plants may be used to form a colourful hedge.

Flowering Quince *Chaenomeles japonica*, formerly known as *Cydonia japonica*, and popularly known simply as 'Japonica', a most beautiful flowering shrub; may be grown against a wall as a specimen bush or it may be trained as a hedge. It bears its camellia-like flowers during March and April, and these later form greenish-yellow fruits which make excellent jelly if removed at the beginning of September. The cydonia is a hardy plant which grows well in any soil.

To form a hedge, 'Snow', with its large pure white flowers, and 'Rowallane', pure scarlet, make a most arresting picture when planted alternately with the shoots trained along wires. Also excellent are 'Falconet Charlotte', which bears double salmon-pink flowers, 'Elly Mossel', rich crimson flowers, and 'Boule de Feu', semi-double flowers of brilliant orange-scarlet.

To encourage the flowers to appear in profusion on short spurs, the ends of the shoots should be pruned back immediately after flowering each year.

Fothergilla Related to the witch hazels, these shrubs require a shaded position and a soil containing plenty of peat or leaf-mould. The 'flowers' appear as thick white stamens during April before the arrival of the leaves. *Fothergilla gardenii* is possibly the best form, growing only 3 ft tall, and in addition to its attractive 'flowers' its leaves turn brilliant scarlet in autumn.

Golden Bell Bush There are several delightful forms of this so rightly popular shrub which bloom through March and April, bearing their golden bells along the stems before the leaves are formed.

Of great hardiness, the plants will grow almost anywhere and rarely become too large for a small garden.

The first to bloom is *Forsythia giraldi*, which produces its yellow bells on long arching stems. Its leaves are of a shade of olive-green and bronze. Excellent is *F. spectabilis* of upright habit, which bears its golden bells along the whole length of the stems, whilst *F. suspensa atrocaulis* forms arching sprays of primrose-yellow bells on black stems.

Osmanthus* Prefers a soil containing some peat and is quite happy in partial shade. *Osmanthus delavayi* grows only 3 ft tall with arching branches clothed in box-like leaves. It is a most valuable small-garden plant, and during April and May bears masses of tiny fragrant white flowers.

Pearl Bush In April and early May this most beautiful shrub bears drooping racemes, the round, pinky-white buds of which have given it its popular name. *Exochorda racemosa* makes a plant of about 6 ft and requires a sunny situation and a rich loamy soil.

Pieris* Members of this delightful family must have a lime-free soil containing plenty of peat; they enjoy partial shade. *Pieris forresti* is perhaps the best form, but it is not quite hardy and does require shelter in sites exposed to cold winter winds. Its foliage opens as a brilliant scarlet, and during the last weeks of spring it bears panicles of fragrant white heather-like flowers. *P. taiwanensis* is also striking, with its foliage opening coral-red in April, in contrast to pure white flowers borne in drooping panicles.

SUMMER-FLOWERING SHRUBS

Beauty Bush *Kolkwitzia amabilis* is a graceful hardy bush, growing up to 4 ft and bearing throughout June small pink

trumpets with yellow throats. It will only bloom freely if given a sunny situation where its wood will ripen, and it is worthy of some care in siting.

Broom For a dry sandy soil and a position in full sun, the modern large-flowering Cytisus hybrids are outstanding. 'Lady Moore' bears flowers of a lovely shade of pinky-mauve, and with it one should plant the crimson-flowered *C. burkwoodii* and the rose-pink 'Enchantress'. Or plant together the lovely yellow 'Diana' and 'Cornish Cream'. Always remember to obtain pot-grown plants.

Bush Honeysuckle This is the weigela or diervilla, a hardy, deciduous plant closely related to the honeysuckles. They have oval leaves and bear long tubular flowers right through summer. The plants grow well in sun or partial shade and in any well-drained soil, but they do appreciate some manure. They grow about 4 ft tall, one of the best being 'Newport Red', which covers itself in clusters of ruby-red trumpets. For contrast, plant near it 'Alba', which bears snow-white flowers.

Chilean Gum Box* The escallonias with their glaucous-green foliage and wax-like tubular flowers are most suitable plants for a small garden, and particularly for one situated near the coast. Apart from the removal of dead wood, these shrubs require little pruning to keep them in shape, for most of them make compact plants growing to no more than 5 ft. They prefer a well-drained sandy soil.

There are many excellent hybrids, amongst the best being 'C. F. Ball' with its bright scarlet flowers right through summer, and 'Glory of Donard', which bears a profusion of cherry-red tubes. 'Peach Blossom' with its rich pink flowers and 'Donard Brilliance', bearing its crimson blooms in arching sprays, are also beautiful.

Cornish Heather* *Erica vagans grandi-flora* makes a plant nearly 3 ft tall and bears long spikes of clear pink during the early weeks of summer. The varieties 'Lyonesse', which has white flowers and attractive brown anthers, and 'Mrs D. Maxwell', which bears strawberry-pink flowers, both bloom during August. These heathers grow well in ordinary soil but not in one of chalky content.

Deutzia Native of China and the Himalayas, the plants have oval saw-edged leaves and bear their flowers during June and early July. *Deutzia campanulata* makes a compact plant covered in pure white flowers, whilst *D. gracilis rosae* bears its rose-pink flowers in clusters. *D. macrothyrsa* is also good, being of upright habit and bearing spikes of pure white blossom.

Forsythia spectabilis has by far the richest yellow of any spring-flowering plant

After flowering, weak and old wood should be cut away to prevent overcrowding.

French Honeysuckle *Hedysarum multi-jugum*, a native of Mongolia, is a most interesting hardy shrub which grows to about 4 ft and through summer bears its spikes of purple vetch-like flowers above attractive blue-green foliage. The plant likes a sunny position and a well-drained soil.

Golden Ball Bush* *Buddleia globosa* is a native of Chile and except during severe weather is evergreen with attractive grey-green foliage. During May and June it bears orange flowers, which are the size of small golf balls and sweetly scented. *B. globosa* requires almost no pruning and is one of the most attractive plants of the shrubbery.

Hydrangea No plant has a longer season of flowering; from August until November there is a wonderful succession of blooms until they finally fade on the approach of winter; and there is little exaggeration in saying that hydrangea blooms are as colourful in autumn as in summer. The plants appreciate some protection when young and are best planted from pots in May. The blooms will turn blue in an acid soil and where this is desired peat should be packed about the roots. One of the best varieties of *Hydrangea macrophylla* is 'Carmen', coming early into bloom and bearing deep crimson flowers which are an attractive shade of wine-purple when in an acid soil. For late flowering, 'King George V' is excellent; normally the flowerheads are rose-pink, but when the plants are in an acid soil a deep clear blue is produced.

Jew's Mallow *Kerria japonica* is one of the most pleasing shrubs of the garden. It makes a slender spreading bush only 4 ft tall with attractive pale green foliage, and during May and June bears small, golden-orange, rose-like blooms. There is also a double form. The plant is extremely hardy and does well in all soils.

Lilac Everybody's favourite for May and June flowering, and rightly so, for with its huge, sweetly scented flower trusses an established plant will provide lasting beauty. Of all shrubs, lilacs respond most to liberal manuring. It is also essential to keep the plants free from suckers, which readily form with grafted plants. The dead flowers should also be removed, but little pruning will be necessary apart from the occasional removal of dead wood.

The modern lilacs are hybrids of *Syringa chinensis* and *S. persica*, and are now obtainable in a wide colour range. The variety 'Primrose' bears large spikes of primrose-yellow; a most attractive result is produced when 'Primrose' is planted intermingled with 'Souvenir de Louis Spath', with its spikes of claret-purple. 'Sensation' is most lovely, its rich purple flowers being edged with white. Also outstanding is the new rose-pink-flowered variety, 'Esther Staley', and the white-flowered 'Monique Lemoine'.

Mock Orange No shrubs are of more easy culture than the philadelphus hybrids with their long arching sprays of rich orange-scented blossoms. They are completely hardy and will grow well in all soils. They make an abundance of cane-like growth, which should be thinned where there is overcrowding.

One of the finest is 'Belle Étoile', the arching branches being crowded with single white flowers which have a distinctive pineapple perfume. Of the doubles, 'Dame Blanche' makes a small, neat bush covered with clusters of tiny double flowers, whilst 'Virginale', of more vigorous habit, bears flowers like tiny double Bourbon roses.

Periwinkle *Vinca minor* or the lesser periwinkle takes its name from the Latin *vinca pervinca*, of which it is a contraction, the name apparently being derived from *vincio*, to bind, to wind around, an allusion to the long, flexible stems being used in making wreaths and garlands. As it flourishes in partial shade, it is a useful plant for ground cover, to plant on dry banks and in unsightly corners. But with its glossy evergreen foliage and mauve-coloured flowers it is attractive about a shrubbery, between other plants, and not least of its many virtues is that it blooms almost the whole year.

The plant enjoys a moist friable soil and is propagated by removing pieces of the trailing stems which root at the nodes. The double form 'Azurea Flore Pleno' is lovely and also the pure white, 'Alba', discovered in a Chiltington cottage garden.

Rhododendron With the large-flowering hybrids which bloom during May and June some well-decayed manure should be incorporated in the soil together with some peat, but no lime should be present. Modern varieties are outstanding, particularly 'General Eisenhower' (brilliant scarlet), 'Lady Mitford' (peach-pink), 'Goldsworth Yellow', and 'Mme Carvalho' (white with green shoots).

Rock Rose* Cistus is able to survive the poorest of soils and once planted requires little attention. All species are evergreen, with small, narrow leaves, and remain in bloom from early June until mid-August. They make rounded bushes 2 ft tall and the same in width.

One of the best is the hybrid 'Sunset', which bears bright rose-pink flowers all summer. Also striking is 'Wintonensis', the large white flowers having a wide chocolate zone at the centre.

Rose (shrub) See Chapter 3.

Rose of Sharon Like the periwinkle, the native British St John's wort is found in deciduous woodlands and enjoys semi-shade. In ancient days it was associated with the mystic rites of midsummer's eve. It enjoys a loamy soil and if plants are set 20 in apart they will quickly cover the ground between with dark evergreen foliage which remains attractive throughout the year.

The loveliest species is *Hypericum calycinum*, the large-leaved St John's wort or the rose of Sharon, a shrubby plant 15 in high and native of the Near East, introduced to our gardens by Sir George Wheeler in 1686.

Tree Paeony The tree paeony is one of the most beautiful of all shrubs, and contrary to popular belief is extremely hardy. It should, however, be given protection from cold winds in spring for it comes early into leaf and bears its blooms during May. Do not plant it facing east, where the early morning sunshine may damage the shoots whilst they are covered with frost. The plant likes a well-drained soil containing some decayed manure.

The blooms of *Paeonia suffruticosa* are often as large as dinner plates, and one of the best is 'Comtessa de Tudor', which bears double blooms of shell-pink. Also bearing double blooms are 'James Kelway' (vivid crimson) and 'Louise Moulchelet' (rose-pink shaded salmon).

Veronica* The shrubby hebes with their neat glossy green leaves and bearing their short, fat flower spikes throughout summer and autumn are indispensable shrubs for a small garden. They are completely hardy and flourish in any ordinary soil. One of the best is 'Bowle's Variety', which remains like a cloud of pale lilac from July until November and grows only to 2 or 5 ft. Also lovely is 'Warley Pink', which bears its rose-pink

Hypericum polyphyllum, *a small trailing St. John's wort with yellow flowers all summer*

flowers in similar profusion. They require little pruning.

AUTUMN-FLOWERING SHRUBS

Butterfly Bush *Buddleia alternifolia*, so much frequented by butterflies and bees, is one of the most beautiful shrubs of the garden with its grey-green leaves and long flower spikes in graceful arching form It makes an abundance of cane-like growth which should be cut back after flowering, and is hardy anywhere and in all soils. 'Royal Red' (purple-red) and 'White Profusion' make a striking display when planted together. Another excellent combination is 'Empire Blue', with its spikes of powder-blue, and pink-flowered 'Fascination'.

Clematis There is a form of this popular climbing plant which is of quite different habit from those we know so well. This is the variety 'Côte d'Azur', which makes a spreading bush 3 ft tall and in autumn covers itself in masses of pale blue flowers rather like hyacinth bells. The plants require a sunny position and a light, well-drained soil.

Colletia* This interesting autumn-flowering shrub is a native of South America where it flourishes under desert-like conditions. It therefore enjoys dry sandy soil and a sunny position. *Colletia armata* is an almost leafless spiny shrub which most unexpectedly bursts into a mass of tiny almond-scented white flowers in late September.

Desfontainea Chilean holly. This interesting shrub is almost hardy, and well worth the little trouble it requires. It needs a cool, shaded position, a light well-drained peaty soil and no pruning. It does well against a north or west wall in cold districts. *Desfontainea spinosa* is slow-growing to 8 ft, has holly-like leaves, and bears its attractive tubular flowers of red and yellow from July till September.

Fuchsia Coming into bloom mid-July and continuing until first frosts, the fuchsias are excellent plants for a small garden and beautiful with their unique drooping flowers. So that the plants will be untroubled by hard frost, ashes should be placed around the crowns. No wood should be removed until early June, when they may be cut hard back.

Of fuchsias suitable for a border on account of their hardiness and height (up to 4 ft tall), 'Dr Foster' is one of the best, with violet-purple flowers and scarlet wax-like sepals. 'Chillerton Beauty' bears a flower with pink sepals, whilst 'Mme

Viburnum macrocephaleum, *a useful all-purpose shrub thriving in almost any soil or site*

Corenillison' has pretty red-and-white flowers.

Ling *Calluna vulgaris*, the wild heather or ling, greatly dislikes lime and must be given a peaty soil. Most of the varieties bloom during early autumn but 'Goldsworth Crimson' (2 ft tall) comes into bloom at the end of September and continues until early November, bearing pointed spikes of deep crimson. Of the others, 'H. E. Beale' is a lovely double pink and 'Alba Blena' double white.

Potentilla With flowers like those of the strawberry plant, the potentillas are extremely valuable for a dry sandy soil, making compact bushes of 2–4 ft tall and remaining in bloom through summer and autumn. In most instances the foliage is silver-grey, affording a striking contrast to the dark green foliage plants of the shrubbery. Almost no pruning will be necessary apart from the occasional removal of dead wood.

Amongst the best potentillas are *Potentilla moyesi*, having grey leaves and large golden flowers; 'Moonlight', bearing pale

Pyracantha gibbsii, the firethorn, brilliant scarlet fruits through winter

primrose flowers; and 'Purdomi', with masses of lemon-yellow blooms.

Shrubs with Scented Flowers

Azara microphylla
Buddleia globosa
Buddleia hybrids
Chimonanthus fragrans
Colletia armata
Corylopsis pauciflora
Corylopsis spicata
Daphne mezereum
Hamamelis mollis
Osmanthus delavayi
Philadelphus hybrids
Syringa (lilac) hybrids
Viburnum tinus

Shrubs with Colourful Autumn Foliage

Azalea malvatica
Berberis sieboldi
Cercidiphyllum sinense
Corylopsis pauci flora
Corylopsis spicata
Euonymus latifolius
Fothergilla gardeni
Hamamelis mollis
Mahonia aquifolia

Shrubs Requiring a Lime-free Soil

Azalea hybrids
Cytisus (broom) hybrids
Desfontainea spinosa
Erica vagans
Erica vulgaris
Pieris forresti
Rhododendron hybrids

Rosa 'Gail Borden', a lovely deep rose flowering in summer and again in autumn

Flowering Shrubs to Give Colour All the Year *(* denotes evergreen)*

Botanical name	Popular name	Height	Colour	Month
WINTER				
* Azara microphylla	Azara	8 ft	pale yellow	March–May
Chimonanthus fragrans	Wintersweet	6 ft	purple-yellow	Dec–Feb
Corylopsis spicata	Corylopsis	4 ft	sulphur	February
Corylopsis pauciflora	Corylopsis	4 ft	yellow	March–April
Daphne mezereum	Daphne	3 ft	purple-pink	Feb–March
Daphne 'Somerset'	Daphne	3 ft	rose-pink	April–May
Erica carnea	Winter heather	1 ft	red/pink	Nov–April
* Garrya eliptica	Californian garrya	8 ft	yellow catkins	Nov–March
Hamamelis brevipetala	Witch hazel	5 ft	yellow	Jan–Feb
Hamamelis mollis	Witch hazel	5 ft	yellow	Dec–March
Hamamelis vernalis	Witch hazel	5 ft	pale yellow	Dec–March
* Mahonia aquifolium	Berberis (Oregon grape)	2½ ft	yellow	Feb–March
* Rhododendron praecox	Rhododendron	3 ft	pink	Feb–March
Viburnum bodnantense	Viburnum	5 ft	pink-white	Dec–March
Viburnum fragrans	Viburnum	5 ft	pink-white	Jan–March
* Viburnum tinus	Viburnum	4 ft	white	Oct–March
SPRING				
Azalea, Kurume hybrids	Azalea	1½ ft	orange-pink	April–May
Azalea malvatica	Azalea	2 ft	various	April–May
* Berberis darwinii	Berberis	2 ft	orange	March–May
Cydonia japonica	Flowering quince	3 ft	crimson/pink	March–April
Cytisus albus	Portugal broom	5 ft	white	April–May
Cytisus praecox	Broom	4 ft	yellow	April–May
Exochorda racemosa	Pearl bush	6 ft	white	April–May
Forsythia giraldi	Golden bell bush	4 ft	yellow	April–May
Forsythia spectabilis	Golden bell bush	5 ft	yellow	April–May
Forsythia suspensa	Golden bell bush	5 ft	primrose	April–May
Fothergilla gardenii	Fothergilla	3 ft	white	April–May
* Osmanthus delavayi	Osmanthus	3 ft	white	April–May
* Pieris forresti	Pieris	4 ft	white	May
* Pieris taiwanensis	Pieris	4 ft	white	May
* Ribes aureum	Buffalo currant	4 ft	buff	April–May
Ribes sanguineum	Flowering currant	4 ft	crimson	April–May
* Viburnum burkwoodii	Viburnum	5 ft	white	April–May

Above   the Pasque flower Anemone pulsatilla.
Below   the Auricula, Primula auricula

Botanical name	Popular name	Height	Colour	Month
SUMMER				
* Buddleia globosa	Orange ball bush	4 ft	orange	May–June
* Cistus 'Sunset'	Rock rose	2 ft	rose-pink	June–Sept
Cytisus hybrids	Broom	5 ft	various	June
Deutzia campanulata	Deutzia	3 ft	white	June–July
Deutzia macrothyrsa	Deutzia	3 ft	white	June–July
* Erica vagans	Cornish heather	3 ft	pink/white	August
* Escallonia hybrids	Chilean gum	3–5 ft	rose/red	June–Aug
* Hebe hybrids	Shrubby veronica	2–3 ft	purple/pink	July–Nov
Hedysorum multijugum	French honeysuckle	4 ft	purple	June–Sept
Hydrangea macrophylla	Hydrangea	3 ft	blue-red	Aug–Nov
Kerria japonica	Jew's mallow	4 ft	orange	May–June
Kolkwitzia amabilis	Beauty bush	4 ft	pink	June
Paeonia suffruticosa	Tree paeony	5 ft	pink/crimson	May
Philadelphus hybrids	Mock orange	8 ft	white	August
* Rhododendron hybrids	Rhododendron	3 ft	various	May–June
Syringa hybrids	Lilac	8 ft	various	May–June
Weigela hybrids	Bush honeysuckle	4 ft	pink/crimson	May–June
AUTUMN				
Buddleia alternifolia	Butterfly bush	8 ft	purple/pink	Aug–Sept
Calluna vulgaris	Ling	2 ft	crimson/pink	Aug–Oct
Clematis 'Côte d'Azur'	Clematis	3 ft	blue	Aug–Oct
* Colletia armata	Colletia	4 ft	white	Sept–Oct
* Desfontainea spinosa	Desfontainea	6 ft	red/yellow	Aug–Sept
Fuchsia hybrids	Fuchsia	2–4 ft	red/purple	July–Dec
Potentilla hybrids	Potentilla	2–4 ft	yellow	July–Oct

Chapter 3

THE ROSE GARDEN

The rose is England's national emblem and has been since Tudor times, when the marriage of the Lancastrian Henry Tudor and Elizabeth of York united the country after the Wars of the Roses, thus joining the White Rose with the Red.

The Reverend S. Reynolds Hole, Dean of Rochester and founder of the Royal National Rose Society, said: 'There should be beds of roses, banks of roses, bowers of roses, hedges of roses, edgings of roses, baskets of roses, vistas and alleys of roses.' Indeed, no other plant may be used in so many ways about the garden. The rose is the complete flowering plant; there is a species or variety for every purpose and no flower has ever been more popular. It is estimated that in the British Isles alone, more than 50 million roses are sold each year—one for each member of the population.

ROSES FOR A HEDGE

Roses for a windbreak may be preferable to privet or thorn, for a rose hedge will not only give protection to plants but also against intruders, as well as being colourful through summer and autumn. Roses for a hedge may be planted 3–4 ft apart and grown as shrubs, or they may be planted 6–8 ft apart and the shoots trained along strong galvanized wires fastened at 15 in intervals to stakes about 8 ft apart. Roses require sun and never grow well in shade, but they are not particular as to soil. For a hedge, the vigorous modern shrub roses may be used, and these of course may also be planted in the mixed shrub border or in a border devoted entirely to the old and new shrub roses which will be described later.

For a hedge, 'Chinatown', a modern floribunda of vigorous habit, 5 ft tall and almost as wide, with glossy foliage and bearing its golden-yellow flowers in generous trusses, will give satisfaction. To alternate with it choose 'Prestige', of similar habit but bearing flowers of pillar-box red, or the equally vigorous hybrid musk rose 'Penelope', its shell-pink blooms shaded with salmon. Another good choice would be 'Ballerina', untroubled by rain or wind, its single flowers of pink and white (rather like apple blossom) borne in large trusses throughout summer.

The hybrid tea rose 'Uncle Walter', of vigorous growth and producing a never-ending series of deep crimson-red flowers,

Climbing roses make attractive features when grown on tripods of rustic poles

is also ideal for a hedge, as is 'Fred Loads', raised by a Cheshire gardener and Gold Medal winner, Mr Robert Holmes. Its vermilion flowers open to reveal attractive golden stamens and can be seen from afar.

ROSES FOR WALLS AND SCREENS

These are the climbers and ramblers, which will cover a wall more quickly than any other plant and provide a longer period of colour too. They may be grown against trellis or rustic poles placed at intervals around a lawn or dividing one part of the garden from another. They may also be used to form a screen, or to hide an unsightly building or view. The pillar roses, as the less vigorous of the climbing roses are called, are grown up a 7–8 ft post and can serve as an alternative to standard roses to give height to a rose bed. Use them in any sunny position to break up the uniformity of the garden; they are especially attractive planted at intervals of 10–12 ft at the back of the herbaceous border when from early July they will take over the display from the lupins and delphiniums.

One of the best of modern pillar roses is 'Golden Showers', raised in California by Dr Lammerts who introduced the 'Queen Elizabeth' rose, that vigorous floribunda which is so often grown as a hedge. Also for a pillar is 'Autumn Sunlight', with bronzy foliage and orange-scarlet flowers, whilst 'Morning Jewel' bears clusters of hybrid-tea-shaped blooms of deepest pink and sweetly scented. Nor must 'Zephirine Drouhin' be omitted, for this thornless rose is at its loveliest against a pillar or post, its rich pink flowers with their unusual silvery sheen having the sweetest perfume of any rose. This rose, now more than 100 years old, is unsurpassed when used for a hedge or to cover a wall, making rapid growth and flowering profusely from its very first season.

Climbing Roses

'Allen Chandler' (12 ft) A vigorous rose, bearing its clusters of bright shot-scarlet during early summer and again early in autumn.

'Cramoisie Supérieure' (10 ft) Possibly the finest of all red roses, but because of its name is not as well known as it should be. The rich blood-red blooms are produced throughout summer.

'Cupid' (12 ft) Makes a superb wall plant. It is of vigorous habit, bearing early in June large clusters of shell-pink blooms with attractive golden anthers. In early autumn the blooms turn to huge vivid orange hips which remain colourful into winter.

'**Danse du Feu**' (8 ft) This is a new perpetual flowering variety, bearing its bloom right into autumn. The double orange-scarlet blooms are held in large trusses.

'**Elegance**' (20 ft) The most vigorous of all the yellow roses, bearing long tapering shoots which cover themselves with clusters of double golden-yellow blooms.

'**Gloire de Dijon**' (10 ft) Quite the best of all roses for a cold, northerly wall. It does, in fact, hate sunshine. The double creamy-yellow blooms are attractively shaded with orange and carry a delicious fragrance.

'**Handel**' (12 ft) The first true climbing bi-colour, the attractively shaped blooms being cream and plum-red.

'**Lady Waterlow**' (12 ft) A valuable variety in that, like Allen Chandler, it blooms profusely in early summer and again in September. The bloom is borne in clusters and is a lovely shade of soft pink.

'**Mme G. Staechelin**' (15 ft) One of the earliest climbers to bloom. Of vigorous habit, it comes early into bloom, the bright rosy-pink flowers carrying a rich fragrance. The foliage is completely mildew resistant.

'**Mermaid**' (20 ft) When once it gets going it is of vigorous habit, and, like Elegance, will often reach a height of 20 ft or more. Also like that variety, it grows well in poor, light soils. It bears its small primrose-yellow blooms, with their attractive golden stamens, right through the season amidst glossy foliage, that is evergreen in mild winters.

'**New Dawn**' The beautifully shaped blooms of blush pink are carried in elegant trusses from June until September whilst the glossy foliage stays on all winter. It will cover the wall of house or outbuilding in two years.

'**Pink Perpetué**' A clear pink climber

of vigorous habit, the blooms being held in large clusters from June until autumn.

'**Royal Gold**' The best yellow climbing rose, the large fragrant blooms of hybrid tea quality being of deep golden-yellow and produced all summer.

'**School Girl**' One of the loveliest of climbing roses, the blooms being of brightest apricot and carried in large clusters right through summer.

'**Souvenir de Claudius Denoyel**' (10 ft) The blooms are almost blackish-crimson, produced through summer, and carry a delicious perfume.

'**William A. Richardson**' (6 ft) Almost a century old and, like Lady Hillingdon, will stand up to the hottest conditions. In bloom throughout summer, the flowers are of a rich apricot and are richly fragrant.

'**Zephirine Drouhin**' (8 ft) Its great value is that it bears its double vivid pink blooms over a period of about twelve weeks, and their perfume will permeate a garden.

Rambler Roses

Several of the ramblers are valuable in that they come late into bloom, when many of the climbers are past their best.

'**Alberic Barbier**' (14 ft) Extremely vigorous and free-flowering. The pale cream blooms are very fragrant and the foliage glossy, being free from mildew.

'**Albertine**' (10 ft) One of the finest ramblers for a wall, the richly fragrant bloom is of an unusual coppery-pink colour, the foliage bright and glossy.

'**American Pillar**' (9 ft) A grand rose of great vigour and extreme hardiness. The deep pink blooms have an attractive white base.

'**Carpet of Gold**' (8 ft) Resembles Mermaid with its large single yellow blooms and their golden stamens, and its dark shiny green foliage.

'**Chaplin's Pink**' (10 ft) Bears large double pink blooms with a striking golden centre. A strong, healthy grower.

'**Dr Van Fleet**' (10 ft) A grand vigorous rose, bearing large double silvery-pink blooms over a long period.

'**Easlea's Golden Rambler**' (9 ft) A fine variety, with its glossy foliage and clusters of warm yellow flowers.

'**Emily Gray**' (14 ft) Extremely vigorous, the foliage is of a strikingly glossy bronze-green colour; the blooms are cream, flushed with orange.

'**Félicité et Perpetué**' (10 ft) The double blooms are blush-white, but its value lies in its glossy foliage, which is almost evergreen.

'**Orange Triumph**' (8 ft) A polyantha rose, with dark glossy green foliage and orange-red flowers, borne in large clusters throughout summer.

'**Sander's White**' (8 ft) Late to bloom, the double pure white flowers are a pleasing contrast to its bright green foliage.

PLANNING THE ROSE GARDEN

Roses never look lovelier than where massed together in beds, especially the hybrid teas and floribundas. The size of bed will be governed by the size of garden. They may be made to a symmetrical design but each should accommodate 10–20 plants, either of one variety only or of two with similar colouring. For the maximum amount of bloom it would seem that hybrid teas with their flowers of exhibition form, together with floribundas, noted for freedom of flowering, will provide the finest possible display. 'Piccadilly' and 'Pineapple Poll', which is a bi-coloured floribunda of similar colourings to 'Piccadilly' and of the same vigour, may accompany each other. The

golden-amber blooms of 'Whiskey Mac' blend admirably with those of the floribunda 'Redgold', whilst 'Princess Michiko' blends admirably with 'Super Star'. Some roses such as 'Elizabeth of Glamis', with its gorgeous salmon-pink flowers, and 'Violet Carson', biscuit and peach, should be given a bed to themselves, but two or three hybrid teas will often complement each other. For example, the handsome blooms of 'Wendy Cussons' and the crimson flowers of 'Alec's Red' look exactly right when planted together, presenting a picture of old-world charm. Hybrid teas of different shades of yellow, such as 'Sunblest', 'Super Sun' and 'Grandpa Dickson', will in no way clash where they are grown together; and those two glorious pinks, 'Femina' and 'Blessings', so attractive

A sunken rose garden surrounded by compressed stone walls with both grass and stone paths

A formal rose garden with symmetrical beds set in an area of crazy paving

under artificial light, seem exactly right in each other's company. More than one variety to a bed will add interest to the garden but take care that colours do not clash.

Roses look so right where the beds are surrounded by paths of paving stone or flagstones. There are no grass edges to cut and the roses can be enjoyed even when the ground is wet. The use of stone adds to the expense of making the rose garden but will be as permanent as the roses and saves hours of labour over the years. Gravel paths also blend admirably with roses.

Here is a simple method of making a paved path for rose beds, and less expensive than using the familiar York stone. Make a mould of wooden strips 2 ft square and 2 in deep. Remove the soil on the proposed pathway to the same width as the mould and 3 in deep. Lay a clinker base 1 in deep and place the

frame over it. A cement mortar mix is then poured into the mould over the clinker and when almost dry and frame is removed. A hundredweight bag of ready-mixed cement will be sufficient to make a section of path 6 ft long by 2 ft wide.

A paved path may be made with a lawn on either side and half-moon beds for dwarf roses cut into the lawn. Use standard roses to give the beds height and provide a pleasant rose 'walk', which will be particularly enjoyable if the roses are scented. The edge of the beds nearest the path can be planted with pansies and violas, which seem to associate so well with roses. The dwarf pinks may also be used.

Dwarf roses may also be planted on a low wall, possibly made on either side of semi-circular steps leading to a sunken rose garden.

For a wall, which may have aubrietias and other alpines trailing over the sides, one may use cement blocks with a stone finish and with ornamental facing.

Where a rose garden is constructed on sloping ground and terraced by cutting into the bank, low walls of these blocks, or of York stone, can be made to retain the soil. Arrange the plants in tiers, building up each bed with a retaining wall, so that the bloom is displayed in much the same way as on the show bench, almost at eye level.

A pleasing design for roses was noticed by the author in a small square town garden, combining the aesthetic charm of a rose garden with a useful playing space for children.

First, an outer circle was marked to the edges of the square, then an inner circle 6 ft less in diameter than the outer circle. Between the two circles four rose beds were made and filled with low-growing floribundas to give maximum colour, the spaces in the corners of the garden being filled with the old shrub

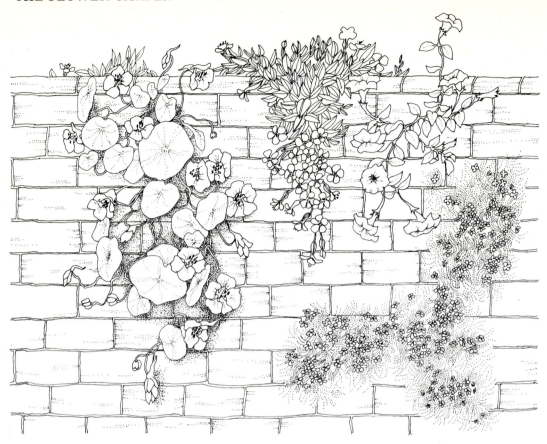

A dry-stone wall with plants growing both on top of it and in it

roses together with three pillar roses in each area. The centre of the garden was lawn where clock golf or croquet could be played or where children could play their own games. A terrace, with steps leading down to the garden and flanked by low walls filled with roses completed the picture, the garden being green throughout the year with its lawn, and colourful for many weeks with roses of every description. As an alternative to the shrub roses, ornamental trees and flowering shrubs could be planted in the corner spaces, some with colourful bark and berries to give colour during winter, spring and early summer before the roses come into bloom.

Roses for Small Beds and Low Walls

'All Gold'   The best yellow floribunda yet introduced, flowering profusely, the long elegant buds borne singly and in trusses.

'Kerry Gold'   An abundance of glossy foliage shows off the butter-yellow blooms to advantage.

'Marlena'   The glowing crimson flowers are produced right through summer in large compact trusses.

'Meteor'   Very low growing, the flowers are of deep blood-red and borne in large trusses.

'Orange Sensation'   The vermilion-red flowers are produced in long succession above bronzy-green foliage.

'Petite'   The shapely blooms are of hybrid tea form and are borne in large low trusses.

'**Susan**' The double blooms of cerise-red are borne in large trusses which are held just above the soil.

'**Tip Top**' A low-growing plant which throughout summer covers itself in glowing salmon-pink flowers.

THE QUALITIES OF ROSES

Before planting roses anywhere it is advisable to see them growing rather than simply displayed on the show bench, for one may then determine their habit of growth, their freedom of flowering and the quality of their foliage, which makes almost as great a contribution to the display as the flowers. One can also judge the capabilities of each variety growing under nursery or park conditions as to its flowering during wet sunless weather, whilst any long periods without bloom clearly mark those plants as needing time to recover from the first flush of bloom in early summer. Some roses, renowned for their prowess on the show bench often possess weak stems and sparse foliage, and to get them to bear just one or two blooms of exhibition quality will demand the care of an experienced grower. In comparison, the wonderful 'Wendy Cussons' with its long sturdy stems and healthy bronzy-green foliage is always a picture of vitality even in an exposed garden, whilst throughout summer it produces its exhibition-quality blooms

An informal paved garden with roses being grown on top of a dry-stone wall

in long succession. It is possibly the finest garden rose ever introduced—but how necessary it is to see all roses growing so that the garden qualities of each may be fully assessed.

It will be found that varieties with strong leathery leaves are less troubled by disease than those with sparse foliage. Healthy foliage usually means a healthy plant. Moreover, roses which form plenty of new growth through the season will soon cover any bare places about the beds and new wood ensures additional bloom later in the season. The bronzy-green foliage of certain varieties is particularly attractive and makes its contribution to the display. The following have this especially healthy looking foliage:

Hybrid Teas	*Floribundas*
'Alec's Red'	'Bonfire'
'Fragrant Cloud'	'Courvoisier'
'National Trust'	'Europeana'
'Oriana'	'Evelyn Fison'
'Prima Ballerina'	'Lili Marlene'
'Uncle Walter'	'Pineapple Poll'
'Wendy Cussons'	'Sweet Repose'

The above roses are also outstanding in their freedom of flowering, the hybrid teas bearing bloom of show quality.

Roses which have a compact habit, healthy foliage and which are continuous flowering, untroubled by adverse weather are listed here:

Hybrid Teas

Pink	*Crimson-red*
'Blessings'	'Alec's Red'
'Chicago Peace'	'Crimson Glory'
'Pink Favourite'	'Ernest Morse'
'Prima Ballerina'	'Fragrant Cloud'
'Shot Silk'	'National Trust'
'Wendy Cussons'	'Uncle Walter'

Planting a rose. Firm planting is essential. Full instructions are given in the text

Bi-colours	*Chrome*
'Croft Original'	'Beauté'
'Garvey'	'Diorama'
'Oriana'	'Doreen'
'Piccadilly'	'Whiskey Mac'

Yellow	*Vermilion*
'Grandpa Dickson'	'Alexander'
'King's Ransom'	'Duke of Windsor'
'Sunblest'	'Spode'
'Super Sun'	'Super Star'

Floribundas	*Yellow*
	'All Gold'
Pink	
'Elizabeth of Glamis'	*Chrome*
'Pink Parfait'	'Apricot Brandy'
'Sweet Repose'	'Courvoisier'

Crimson-red	Vermilion
'Aida'	'Ama'
'Europeana'	'Fred Loads'
'Evelyn Fison'	'Orange Silk'
'Lili Marlene'	'Princess Michiko'

Bi-colours	White
'Molly McGredy'	'Iceberg'
'Pineapple Poll'	'Pascali'
'Red Gold'	'White Cocade'

PREPARATION OF THE SOIL

Roses are happier in a heavy but well-drained soil than in a light sandy soil. A medium loam also suits them well, especially a marl soil, as instanced by the large number of roses raised in Nottinghamshire.

Roses in all soils should be given liberal dressings with humus, particularly well-decayed farmyard manure. When planting into a heavy clay soil it is advisable also to incorporate some grit or coarse sand to help with drainage. But farmyard manure must not be omitted from any soil, and where this is not readily obtained, wool shoddy, straw composted with an activator to which is also added pig or poultry manure, and even composted garden refuse are most valuable; peat and leaf-mould may also be incorporated. 'They luxuriate in rich manure—coarse fare', as Walter Wright put it in *Popular Garden Flowers* (1912), and indeed they do. Rank manure suits them admirably, the more the better. But though the rose delights in a heavy soil, this should be brought to as fine a tilth as possible by preparing the beds in November and allowing the soil to become weathered by winter frosts. Roses have a fibreless tap-root which is difficult to establish if the soil is excessively lumpy, and during a period of drought the plants may die back if the roots do not make full contact with the soil.

A chalky soil, often above gravel, or a light sandy soil will grow good roses, but to do so will require humus and rotted manure to be dug in each year, preferably in late autumn. All roses in any soil benefit from a liberal dressing of humus applied as a mulch around the plants in early summer. This keeps down annual weeds and conserves moisture in the soil, as well as feeding the plants. Where manure cannot be obtained in quantity, plants growing in light soil should be given 2 oz per sq yd of sulphate of potash as a dressing. This builds up a bloom able to withstand adverse weather conditions, and also improves the colour and quality.

PLANTING

In a friable loamy soil, roses may be planted at almost any time between November and early April, provided there is no frost in the soil and it is not too wet. Heavy clay loam will rarely be suitable for working between Christmas and early March; the same may be said of November planting, though frequently December is a dry month with few hard frosts, and is possibly the best time for the operation. But the ability of the rose to overcome almost all conditions was made plain when planting my own beds. Not having the land ready before early April, and not wishing to lose a season by delaying planting until the autumn, the trees were planted on 28 April, pruned rather more severely than usual, and given a heavy manure mulch. Several hundred trees came into bloom in early July with only 1 per cent loss.

It is most important to plant at the same level as the trees were previously planted. Too deep planting will cause trouble, being a cause of suckers forming. Again, the trees must be very firmly

Pruning a rose. The principles and purpose of pruning are explained in the text

trodden in, even in heavy soil. Loose planting will also cause suckers to form, and the plants may become badly damaged at the roots and above ground if there is excessive movement during windy weather. After planting, the beds are best given a mulch and then left undisturbed until the end of March, when pruning is done. It is not wise to prune roses for at least several weeks after planting. Heavy pruning on top of moving the plants can cause a check from which they make take considerable time to recover. Planting distances vary with almost every variety. The dwarf polyantha roses may be planted at 20 in apart, so that when they come into bloom in June there will be little or no soil to be seen —

nothing but a carpet of bloom. The weaker of the hybrid teas should be planted at about 2 ft apart, the more vigorous at almost 3 ft, though if planting polyanthas the distance may be greater.

PRUNING

With roses, above all other plants, this operation gives rise to the greatest controversy. Whether to prune hard or moderately has still to be decided definitely, and whereas one gardener suggests pruning hard to obtain few blooms of exhibition quality, others are equally enthusiastic about pruning hardly at all. The most satisfactory way to maintain a healthy vigorous plant would appear to rest somewhere between the two methods. Severe pruning not only deprives the plant of wood and foliage which is valuable in converting nutrition

from the atmosphere and therefore necessary in maintaining the health of the plant, but it also restricts the amount of bloom, which for a bedding plant is not desirable. More than anything, the modern rose is now a bedding plant and depriving the plants of foliage or bloom unnecessarily is to be censured.

The brilliant colours of the foliage of many of the modern roses are an added factor in their wide popularity for bedding, for even before they come into bloom many plants are already colourful. Those magnificent roses 'Peace' and 'Madame Guillot' bear foliage of a vivid glossy green, whilst 'Fragrant Cloud' and 'Piccadilly' have deep coppery-crimson leaves which are almost as gay from mid-May to mid-June, when the first bloom opens, as later when the plants are in full bloom. As carpeting plants are not

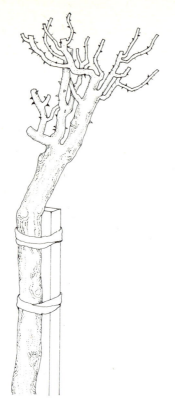

Exactly when to prune also gives rise to considerable discussion. Certain rose specialists advise pruning during the dormant or mid-winter period. But as all shoots should be cut back to a strong bud pointing away from the centre of the plant, this may be damaged by frost or cold winds if pruning is done during winter. To prune in early spring, about 1 April, when fear of severe frost has vanished, will make for a better plant. All dead wood should be removed, together with any damaged wood or dead blooms, towards the year end as soon as flowering has finished. Where pruning has been light, the plants will be helped in bearing bloom over an extended period if the first bloom is cut with as long a stem as possible, or a considerable length of stem is removed with the dead blooms. This

A rose pruned too close to a bud left, *too high above it* centre, *and correctly* right

A standard rose should be pruned hard in autumn and securely tied to its stake

generally used with roses, this question of early foliage should be given more consideration.

Against too hard pruning, unduly light pruning means a heavy first flush of bloom during July and August and then little more because little new wood has been made during summer. The blooms, too, will be of inferior quality. A system of pruning which falls somewhere between the two extremes will ensure continuity of bloom of top quality and at the same time promote the health of the plant. Much, however, depends upon individual varieties, some being exceedingly vigorous whilst others make little new wood and so require more careful pruning. To preserve the even appearance of the beds, those long shoots of the vigorous varieties should be cut back during August.

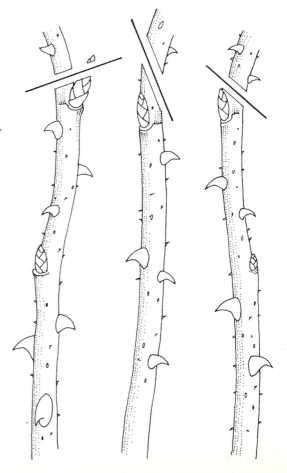

will stimulate new growth and act in the same way as if the pruning had been moderate.

With standard roses, initial pruning consists of cutting the head hard back in early spring after the trees have been planted so as not to put too much strain on the constitution of the plant until the rooting system has been built up. Afterwards, pruning should be moderate; consisting of the removal of decayed wood and those unwanted shoots which may tend to crowd the centre of the head. With weeping standards, which are so pleasing when used as a centrepiece for a bed, the twiggy growth should be thinned out if it becomes overcrowded, as often happens with weeping forms.

When pruning bush roses, the cut should be made about half an inch above the selected bud and should slope inwards.

HYBRID TEAS

(a selection of the best varieties)

(F = fragrant: † = free flowering in autumn: Cl = also climbers)

'Akebono' A Japanese rose of exquisite form and an exhibitor's favourite, the large blooms being chrome-yellow, flushed with rosy-pink at the petal edges.

'Alec's Red' It has taken over from 'Ena Harkness' as the most popular crimson rose with the real damask perfume. The blooms have a high spiral centre and are of glowing crimson-red.

'Alexander' Named in honour of that great soldier of World War II Field Marshal Earl Alexander of Tunis, it was introduced by Harkness & Co in 1973 after exhaustive trials had singled it out as the best vermilion since 'Super Star'. The blooms are of a slightly darker shade whilst the plant is of taller habit.

'Ballet' (F) Possibly the best pink bedding rose yet raised with plenty of healthy foliage and bearing enormous blooms of deep rose-pink from June until December.

'Bayadere'† Both for exhibition and garden display this is a magnificent rose. The blooms, of perfect shape, are enormous, salmon-pink in colour, flushed with coppery-orange and borne with great freedom.

'Bettina'† (F) A wonderful bloom for cutting and for garden display, the full medium-sized blooms being of a vivid orange colour, shaded pink and held on long stems. At its best in autumn.

'Blessings' The lovely blooms are of a unique shade of soft coral-pink with a touch of lilac which gives it a particular beauty under artificial light. Raised by Gregory, who also gave us 'Wendy Cussons'.

'Charles Gregory' (F) This has coppery foliage and bears a beautifully shaped bloom of vivid orange-scarlet, the outside of the petals being gold. In the bud form, it is perhaps the loveliest rose of the garden for both colour and shape, though it loses colour with age. The bloom is borne in profusion throughout summer.

'Chicago Peace' A 'sport' from 'Peace', it is a rose that should be in every collection for it blooms well in a dull, wet summer. The globular flowers are a delightful combination of peachy-pink, cream and gold.

'Croft Original' Named in honour of the famous sherry, it is a new bi-colour of merit, the large shapely blooms being of glowing cerise-red with a golden reverse.

'Diorama' One of the all-time great roses, the large handsome blooms being of deep yellow shaded and veined with rosy-red, and with outstanding perfume. Of ideal bedding habit.

'Duke of Windsor' Raised by Tantau who gave us 'Super Star', 'Oriana', 'Whiskey Mac' and 'Fragrant Cloud', and equally popular with sweetly scented blooms of glowing vermilion enhanced by dark leathery foliage.

'Elizabeth Harkness' As an exhibitor's rose it is without equal; the large blooms with their rolled petals are of unique colouring, being of creamy-buff, shaded amber at the centre and touched with pink and rose.

'Ena Harkness'† (F) Cl One of the most popular roses ever introduced. Of excellent habit, it is highly resistant to mildew whilst the blooms, of exhibition quality, are large, full, and of a bright crimson-scarlet colour. Free-flowering, it carries a good crop in autumn.

'Ernest H. Morse' May be considered to be an improved 'Ena Harkness', being of similar colouring but without the same rich perfume. It is, however, a rose of excellent bedding habit.

'Femina' A new rose of beauty, the blooms being of coppery-salmon-pink and held on long sturdy stems above handsome bronzy-green foliage.

'Fragrant Cloud' (F) Fairly tall growing, it has bronzy foliage, the largest foliage of all roses, which denotes its health and vigour. The blooms are of exhibition quality and produced singly and in trusses. The colour is deepest red and it has more fragrance than any other rose.

'Grandpa Dickson' An exhibitor's rose of immense beauty, the lemon-yellow blooms having a high spiral centre — similar in form to 'Peace' but more free flowering.

'King's Ransom' To date, the outstanding yellow rose though late to bloom. The beautifully formed flowers of pure mid-yellow are elegant in the bud stage and are held singly on long stems, making it ideal for cutting.

'Message'† (F) A superlatively good white rose. The long tapering buds open out to a bloom of classic shape, with a strong fragrance, the cool whiteness accentuated by pale green shading. Freedom of flowering and a compact bushy habit go to make this one of the best of all white roses for bedding.

'Mischief' No bedding rose has given a better account of itself since its introduction in 1961. The large shapely blooms of deep coral-salmon are borne with freedom whatever the weather.

'Miss Harp' (F) A deep yellow rose of outstanding beauty, with a high spiral centre and rolled petals, and carrying a rich perfume.

'National Trust' An exhibitor's rose of glowing red set amongst bronzy-green foliage, introduced in 1972. It is also an outstanding bedding variety, being most free flowering.

'Oriana' Raised by Tantau, this is a bi-colour of great beauty, being of crimson-red with a creamy-white reverse to the leathery petals. Repeat-flowering and an excellent bedding rose.

'Pascali' Possibly the best white rose since 'Frau Karl Druschki' of the 1920s. The blooms are of exquisite form, of purest white, and remain so in adverse weather.

'Piccadilly' The finest of all bedding roses during the cold, wet summer of 1963 when its enormous bi-coloured blooms of orange and gold, of perfect shape, were produced in long succession.

'Prima Ballerina' One of the outstanding pinks, with lots of healthy foliage and enormous deep pink flowers with a delicious perfume.

'Stella' The large handsome blooms, freely produced, are of exhibition quality and are creamy-white, 'painted' with cerise-red, making a most unusual colour combination.

Fuchsia *'Caroline', one of the new very large flowered but rather tender fuchsias*

'Sunblest' One of the best yellow roses. Its deep buttery-yellow colour does not fade and it stands up to adverse weather better than any yellow with the exception of 'King's Ransom'.

'Super Star' With 'Peace' and 'Fragrant Cloud', the most popular rose ever introduced. The clear vermilion flowers catch the eye of everyone, whilst it blooms and blooms whatever the weather. It is as popular with the exhibitor as in the garden.

'Wendy Cussons' (F) One of the finest garden and exhibition roses ever introduced, having masses of bronzy-green foliage almost as large as that of 'Fragrant Cloud' whilst its blooms of old rose-red possess as powerful a perfume.

'Whiskey Mac' With 'Alec's Red' and 'Fragrant Cloud' it was the most popular rose of 1973, its rich golden amber blooms having the same rich perfume.

FLORIBUNDAS

The crossing of the polyantha rose with the hybrid teas resulted in the introduction of the floribundas, those of compact habit being excellent plants for providing a long period of colour in the small garden. With floribundas there are few days during summer and autumn which are not colourful, for, unlike the hybrid teas, they do not bloom in flushes but continuously, requiring no rest periods.

The floribunda has been carried a stage further with the introduction of the grandiflora rose, which possesses the same freedom of flowering yet with a greater resistance to disease owing to the enormous vigour of the plants. The grandiflora also has more of the characteristics of the hybrid tea, so that whilst the blooms are borne in clusters they possess the true

One of the fancy-leaf pelargoniums and, right, a hardy hybrid agapanthus

hybrid-tea form, though they are not so large. For a small garden where the maximum amount of colour is desirable these plants should be given serious attention, for though they do not bear so refined a bloom as the hybrid teas, they possess greater value as a bedding plant. The plants are clothed in healthy foliage, possess a compact habit and bloom without interruption, no matter what the weather.

In comparison with the hybrid teas, the floribunda roses require little by way of pruning, for it is required of the plants that they bear a large amount of bloom rather than flowers of outstanding quality. So merely shorten any unduly long shoots after flowering, and cut out all dead and overcrowded wood in spring

Only those of compact bushy habit should be planted in the small garden, preference being given to varieties bearing plenty of healthy foliage.

Floribunda Varieties

'All Gold' Of compact bushy habit, this is a first-rate floribunda, and the most recent of the yellows. The blooms, of hybrid-tea form, are rich golden-yellow and produced with freedom above glossy, disease-free foliage.

'Ama' A magnificent rose bearing enormous trusses of deep crimson-red blooms which are fadeless whatever the weather.

'Anne Cocker' A plant of tall upright habit which throughout summer bears masses of small circular blooms of glowing vermilion.

'Bonfire' A striking orange and gold bi-colour, the hybrid tea-shaped blooms being produced singly and in trusses.

'Circus' A new rose of hybrid-tea or grandiflora form, the well-formed buds, borne in clusters and in profusion, opening as chrome-yellow and changing to orange and pink. Of vigorous but dwarf bushy habit, it is a fine bedding plant.

'Courvoisier' A new colour in floribundas, the hybrid tea-shaped blooms being of chrome-yellow, flushed and veined with apricot.

'Dickson's Flame' This is one of the outstanding bedding roses of all time. First to bloom, it bears its trusses of brilliant orange-scarlet from June until Christmas.

'Elizabeth of Glamis' (F) A 1964 introduction bearing blooms of salmon-pink and the only rose ever to win both the President's Trophy of the British Royal National Rose Society for the best of the year and the Clay Vase for a new rose with the most pronounced fragrance.

'Europeana' With purple-bronze foliage and the darkest crimson blooms of all roses, this forms a dense spreading bush.

'Evelyn Fison' A rose of ideal bedding form, with bronze foliage and bearing trusses of vivid scarlet-red through summer and autumn.

'Golden Fleece' This has the free-flowering hybrid tea rose 'Diamond Jubilee' for a parent, and shows the same freedom of flowering. It bears its straw-yellow blooms of hybrid-tea form in dense clusters and on erect stems.

'Iceberg' The best white floribunda, growing 3–4 ft tall and suitable for the shrub border. It has pale green glossy foliage and bears its white flowers in large trusses.

'Lili Marlene' Has 'Ama' for a parent, and many of its good qualities, bearing its bright crimson flowers in generous trusses.

'Masquerade' The early blooms open golden-yellow and change to orange and rose and finally to crimson as they age. Thus all colours appear on the plant together.

'Molly McGredy' A bi-colour with a difference, the elegant blooms being of ox-blood red with a white reverse to the petals.

'News' Raised by Le Grice, this heralds a new colour break, the blooms being of beetroot-purple whilst the habit is short and compact.

'Orange Silk' An outstanding variety, the orange-red blooms being borne in trusses above bronzy-green foliage.

'Paddy McGredy' A plant of compact habit with healthy dark foliage, it bears trusses of hybrid-tea-type blooms of rosy-red, and remains colourful from June until November.

'Pernille Poulsen' The colour is deep pink with a flush of orange, and the habit is ideal for bedding. The plant has plenty of healthy, glossy foliage.

'Pineapple Poll' Introduced by Cockers in 1970, this is an ideal bedding rose for it makes a short bushy plant and bears masses of golden-yellow and red flowers throughout summer.

'Pink Parfait' An all-American winner with dark leathery foliage and trusses of hybrid-tea-type blooms of contrasting shades of light and deep pink. Almost thornless.

'Princess Michiko' One of the most striking plants of the rose garden, the flowers being of brilliant scarlet-orange and of hybrid-tea shape. It remains in bloom, whatever the weather, throughout summer.

'Red Gold' Another all-American winner of ideal bedding habit. It bears large trusses of chrome-yellow flowers, the petals edged with red.

'Southampton' A floribunda unique in its colour, the beautifully tapering buds being of apricot-orange. Selected by the Mayor of Southampton and named in honour of the famous seaport.

'Sweep Repose' (F) Aptly named for

its white and pink flowers, among the sweetest of the garden and delicately scented.

'Violet Carson' A rose of excellent bedding habit which stands up to adverse weather. The blooms are of unique colouring, biscuit with a peach and gold reverse.

MAKING A MINIATURE ROSE GARDEN

Those who have a very small garden, possibly only a courtyard surrounded by a narrow raised border or perhaps nothing more than a trough or window box, may also enjoy their roses. Requiring little attention and remaining long in bloom, the quite inexpensive miniature roses are extremely hardy and long lasting and require nothing elaborate in their culture. The plants have so neat a habit that they may be used to make the tiniest rose garden imaginable. Small pieces of crazy paving stone may be used to divide the ground into sections of the required design, the stone being used as a pathway, though it should not be more than 6–8 in wide to keep it in correct scale with the miniature rose trees. Strips of grass, formed by laying turf or sowing seed, may be used as an alternative method of laying out the tiny garden, and kept neat by clipping with shears. There are now miniature standard roses which greatly add to the charm of the garden and, to obtain the best effect, tiny 'hedges' of evergreen box and dwarf conifers may be used. Most attractive is the dwarf juniper *Communis compressa* which forms a pencil-like tree only 6–8 in high, its feathery glaucous green foliage making a pleasing foil for the roses.

Where a miniature rose garden is being made, it is important to keep everything to scale. For a trough or window box and where space in the garden is at a premium use the most dwarf varieties. These grow

A sunken rose garden surrounded by compressed stone walls with grass and stone paths

only 8–9 in tall and separate varieties or colours may be planted to each bed. They are also most attractive planted in a small raised circular bed, surrounded by a path of crazy paving or by a tiny 'hedge' of dwarf box. These delightful little roses may also be used to edge a bed of the more compact of the hybrid teas and polyanthus where room permits the use of these more vigorous roses. They may also be planted about a rockery in groups of three or four together with the dwarf junipers. At all times they require a position of full sun but they do like a soil which does not allow their roots to dry out, and so the plants almost always flourish when planted on a rockery where pockets of soil between the stones are prepared by the addition of humus-forming materials.

Plants used in a trough or window box or to make up a small bed or garden in the open will require the same attention as to soil conditions, the addition of leaf-mould or peat augmented by some well-decayed manure (especially cow manure) being necessary to maintain summer moisture. Only dry conditions at their roots will harm the plants; neither frost nor cold winds cause them any trouble. An excess of manure, however, should not be given or the plants will form too much foliage at the expense of bloom. If decayed manure cannot be obtained, incorporate 2 oz bonemeal to each sq yd of ground and a similar amount where a trough garden is being made. If a little Kettering loam, yellow and fibrous, can be obtained, so much the better, but apart from these simple requirements the plants need nothing more except care to see that they do not suffer from lack of moisture during summer. An occasional application of weak manure water, obtainable in concentrated form in bottles from any sun-driesman will do much to enhance the bloom and prolong the display.

The miniatures seem to resent root disturbance more than other roses and so pot-grown plants should be used whenever possible. Plants from pots will become more quickly established and may be planted at any time except when the soil is frozen, though possibly October or March are the most suitable months to make a miniature rose garden. The plants should of course be removed from their pots or they will suffer from lack of moisture.

When planting, place the ball of compost holding the root just below soil level, for shoots which appear from below the ground will also bear bloom. These should be cut back half-way each autumn, likewise any unduly long or decayed shoots, to maintain the shape and health of the tree. Also, to prolong the display, in addition to occasional feeding, all dead bloom should be removed as it forms. This will also keep the plants compact and tidy. The plants should be allowed sufficient room to develop in, for though they will not grow tall they will spread out in bush-like fashion and grow as wide as they are tall, which will be about 9 in.

Propagation of Miniatures The plants may be readily increased by cuttings taken during early autumn and inserted in a sandy compost. The new season's shoots should be used, taking cuttings about 3 in in length and trimming to a leaf bud. They will root more readily if the base of each shoot is treated with hormone powder before inserting round the sides of pots or pans. They may also be planted in frames or under cloches. Plant firmly and keep the compost comfortably moist, shading the shoots should strong sunshine be experienced before rooting has taken place. As soon as the cuttings have formed roots, they should be potted separately into 3 in pots and grown on until ready to be planted out the following spring. Pinch out the growing point to encourage bushy growth. Clean, fibrous loam containing a little sand for drainage is all that is required for growing on the plants in pots. Remember that the roots must never be allowed to lack moisture.

Miniature roses may also be quite easily raised from seed and though not coming true to name, some lovely varieties may be raised in this way. A good strain of *Rosa polyantha nana*, the fairy rose, may be obtained in this way. Seed should be sown in boxes or pans containing the John Innes sowing compost, from mid-April to mid-May. Keep the compost moist and the seed shaded until germination takes place; this may be slow in comparison with most seeds. If growing outdoors, cover the box with a piece of glass until the seed has germinated.

The seedlings should be transplanted to small pots containing a good loamy soil in which a little leaf mould has been incorporated, and they should be kept comfortably moist. They will have formed plants suitable for setting out by the following spring or early summer.

Varieties of the Fairy Rose There are now many charming variations of the miniature or fairy rose, embracing almost every known colour so that there is something to suit every taste. New and quite unusual is 'Baby Faurax', which grows only 10 in tall and bears masses of tiny pale blue flowers of semi-double form. No other rose bears a bloom nearer to the true blue colouring.

One of the loveliest varieties is 'Josephine Wheatcroft', which bears a tapering bloom of true hybrid-tea form, about an inch across and of a lovely shade of rich buttercup-yellow, ideal for table decoration or as a buttonhole. As it grows to a height of about 15–16 in it should not be used for a trough or tiny garden, but is best planted in a small circular bed to itself.

Most other fairy roses bear a button-shaped bloom similar to those of the polyantha roses. The habit of the plant too, is similar and they may more accurately be described as miniature polyantha roses. Outstanding is 'Baby Masquerade', the pale yellow blooms being splashed with red, whilst equally lovely are the large deep pink blooms of 'Tinker Bell'. Most attractive when planted together are 'Maid Marion', with its double crimson button-like blooms, and the double white, pink-edged 'Cinderella', which grows to a height of 9 in. Equally free flowering is 'Humpty Dumpty', glistening pink; and 'Sweet Fairy', the blooms being of a pleasing shade of mauve-pink and fully petalled. Both varieties are very dwarf.

A lovely new introduction, making a plant about 9 in high, is 'Presumida', bearing circular fully double blooms of rich apricot edged with gold. 'Baby Gold Star', of similar height, with blooms of a deep buttercup-yellow, is also lovely; so is the true guinea gold, 'Rosina'. 'Perle de Montserrat' is of taller habit, its blooms being of a peach-pink colour. Extremely dwarf and dainty, and most suitable for a trough garden or the rockery are (in addition to 'Sweet Fairy'): 'Mon Petit', with its blooms of deep rose-pink; 'Pixie', pure white; and 'Twinkles', shell-pink.

Of similar habit to 'Josephine Wheatcroft' is the striking 'Perle d'Alcanada' with its tiny hybrid-tea blooms of deep carmine-red, whilst the lovely creamy-white 'Pour Toi' has similar glossy foliage and also grows to a height of 9 in. Two new varieties of polyantha form are 'Granada', blood-red, and 'Red Imp', crimson. They are extremely showy either as bushes or standards, in which form they reach a height of 16 in and look well planted at the centre of a small bed or trough. The stems should be supported with a neat cane.

Dwarf Floribundas and Polyanthas A new series of miniature roses of slightly larger habit are the first true dwarf floribundas which grow to a height of 14–16 in and form bushes almost as wide as they grow tall. These are the Walt Disney Compacta roses, the bloom being borne in trusses rather than singly. With their glossy green foliage they are well able to withstand the most adverse weather and are ideal plants for the top of a terrace or wall, or for planting in raised beds where their rich colouring may be appreciated to the full. They are also excellent for bordering a small path and for planting in almost any position about a very small garden.

Possibly the outstanding variety is 'Grumpy', which bears a large cup-shaped bloom of vivid scarlet, whilst of similar form is 'Sneezy', the bloom having a white centre. 'Bashful', geranium-red, is most striking, whilst 'Doc' and 'Sleepy' bear semi-double blooms of deep rose-pink. As yet there is no yellow-flowered variety, but a very compact floribunda bearing golden-yellow blooms is 'Goldilocks', which grows to a height of 18–20 in and is excellent for bedding in the very small garden. Of similar habit, the double yellow blooms having an attractive apricot tint, is 'Yellow Pinocchio'. Both may be planted at the centre of a bed and surrounded with 'Bashful' or 'Grumpy' for a display of great brilliance.

There are a number of floribunda and polyantha roses of very compact habit which makes them ideal for beds in a small garden, or they may be used, like the Compacta roses, along a terrace or wall. Among the floribundas are the new scarlet 'Concerto', the clear pink 'Fairy Princess', and 'Fashion' with its clusters of pure salmon-coloured flowers, all of compact habit and attractive deep glossy green foliage. Only slightly taller and of great brilliance of colour is 'De Ruiter's Herald', the flowers being pillar-box-red and the whole plant extremely disease resistant.

Of the polyantha roses, whose habit it is not possible to determine when the bloom is displayed on the show bench, many are very tall growing and suitable only for the largest of gardens, some are of medium height, whilst a few grow to a height of no more than 18–20 in and may be used with confidence in a very small garden. Outstanding among these is Wheatcroft's 'Golden Polyantha', the fully double blooms being of deepest

yellow and the best variety of this colour. Of those bearing a pink flower, 'Little Dorrit' with its masses of pale shell-pink button-like blooms, and 'Coral Cluster', of similar habit and bearing beautiful coral-pink blooms, are most charming. A magnificent variety is 'Cameo', of very dwarf habit, its coral-pink blooms flushed with orange. 'Ideal' bears a truss of deepest crimson, whilst the older 'Paul Crampel' bears a bloom of geranium-red. Of similar colouring is 'Pompone Beauty', whilst the dainty 'Posy' which grows only 16 in tall and bears clusters of rose-red flowers must not be forgotten.

THE SHRUB ROSES

The White Rose The Isle of Albion was so named, Pliny tells us, 'because of the white rose [*Rosa alba*] with which it abounds'. It was especially prevalent in East Yorkshire and was taken as their symbol by the Yorkist party in the Wars of the Roses. It is a plant of vigorous habit, growing as wide as it is tall and so must be planted 4–5 ft apart. The white roses require little pruning, merely the cutting-out of dead and straggling wood in spring. The flowers are followed by handsome hips.

R. alba maxima is the great double white, the Jacobite rose, and was used as an emblem by supporters of Bonnie Prince Charlie, the Young Pretender. It makes a bush 6 ft tall and almost as wide. Blooming in early June, it is one of the earliest of roses. *R. alba semi-plena* is the true white rose of York. The flowers are borne on graceful arching stems. Others are:

'Belle Amour' Grows to 5 ft and bears beautifully shaped blooms of clear pale pink with a clove-like fragrance.

'Félicité Parmentier' The most compact in this group, growing 3–4 ft tall, its creamy-white buds opening to rosette-

Rosa 'Belle Amour', a rose with unusually shaped flowers of subtle colouring

flowering like the modern hybrid teas and floribundas, and some consider them the most beautiful of all roses, the blooms being quartered and filled with overlapping petals.

Requiring little or no pruning, they were, during the nineteenth century, often planted in cottage gardens as a shrub or for a hedge or against a wall. All the pruning needed is to cut out any dead wood and to shorten unduly long shoots. Some of the best varieties are:

'Boule de Neige' This has dark green foliage and bears camellia-shaped blooms of snow-white. It does best against a wall which it will cover to a height of 7–8 ft.

'Constance Spry' A Bourbon hybrid, which forms long sturdy stems and may be used as a hedge, the shoots being trained along wires or planted against a trellis or wall.

'La Reine Victoria' With its compact habit it is suited to the smallest garden, and will fill it with the exquisite perfume of its large globular blooms of rosy-pink.

'Louise Odier' A lovely rose, growing 4–5 ft tall with dark leathery foliage and circular quartered flowers of rose-pink flushed with lilac.

'Mme Isaac Pereire' On a wall it attains a height of 10 ft and bears rosy-red flowers flushed with crimson.

'Mme Pierre Oger' A 'sport' from 'La Reine Victoria'; the cup-shaped blooms have almost transparent petals of creamy-pink and a pronounced scent.

'Prince Charles' A graceful arching shrub bearing throughout summer its clusters of deep crimson-purple flowers, circular and quartered.

'Zephirine Drouhin' The most valuable of all garden roses. It is thornless and bears from June until October clusters of dainty hybrid-tea-type flowers of clear cerise-pink with a silver sheen and penetrating scent.

shaped flowers of soft pink, with delicious perfume.

'Great Maiden's Blush' It was grown in mediaeval times and the late Lady Nicolson (V. Sackville-West) said that at her home, Sissinghurst Castle, it retained its blush-white petals longer than any other rose. A vigorous grower, it has handsome blue-green foliage.

The Bourbon Rose *Rosa bourboniana* is believed to be the result of a chance crossing between *R. chinensis*, the Chinese rose, with the autumn or repeat-flowering damask, *R. damascena autumnalis*, and this took place on the French island of Réunion, then known as Bourbon, about 1817. The Bourbon roses are unlike most other shrub roses in that they are repeat-

The Cabbage Rose   This is *R. centifolia*, the rose of a hundred petals, bearing the largest flowers of all roses, and depicted by the Dutch masters of the seventeenth century in their still-life paintings. *R. centifolia* grows 5 ft tall and bears flowers of soft china-pink on short lateral shoots during June and July. It requires the minimum of pruning: an occasional shortening of the shoots and the cutting-out of dead wood. Amongst the best are:

'Bullata'   Known as the lettuce-leaf rose, the large pale grey-green leaves being grooved like those of the cos lettuce. The large globular flowers are cherry-pink with a powerful fragrance.

'De Meaux'   Forms a neat bush 3 ft high covered in clusters of miniature flowers of a lovely shade of clear pink.

The common moss rose, an old-fashioned rose valued for its scent as well as blooms

'Gros Choux d'Hollande'   The old Dutch hundred-leaved rose, making a compact bush 3–4 ft tall, with small leaves and bearing tightly petalled flowers of an interesting shade of mushroom-pink.

'Tour de Malakoff'   Makes a dense broad bush with arching branches covered with large flowers of deep rosy-red, changing to purple and grey as they age.

The Moss Rose   A derivative of *R. centifolia*, being a mutation which took place about the year 1800 when moss-like hairs, usually crimson in colour, appeared on the stems, leaves and calyces. By 1860, William Paul, the famous Cheshunt grower and writer on the rose, said there were more than fifty named varieties, the rich purple and burgundy colouring of many providing a striking effect with the crimson moss.

The plants should be pruned harder than other shrub roses, cutting back the old wood to half-way each autumn, and the side shoots to the third bud. Some of the loveliest are:

'Blanche Moreau'   Bears pure white cup-shaped blooms whilst the plant is heavily covered with crimson moss.

'Captain Ingram'   A beautiful plant with purple moss, purple-tinted foliage and rosette-shaped blooms of rich velvety purple.

'Common Moss'   The chalice-shaped buds open to large cup-shaped blooms of clearest pink.

'Maréchal Davoust'   Grows to 4 ft and is covered in crimson moss whilst its cup-shaped blooms are of carmine-pink with a lilac edge.

The Damask Rose   *R. damascena* is known also as the holy rose and is always shown surrounding the Virgin as in representations of her appearing to St Bernadette at Lourdes. Prune early in spring, merely tipping back unduly long shoots and removing dead wood annually.

Amongst the best are:

'Blush Damask' Attaining a height of 6 ft, it makes an excellent hedge. The blooms begin in June, and are a lovely shade of clear pink with a deeper flush at the centre.

'Madame Hardy' Thought by many to be the loveliest rose in cultivation, the circular cup-shaped blooms are of ivory-white with a tight button centre of jade green.

'York and Lancaster' Or *R. damascena versicolor*. It grows 6 ft tall, its blooms being a mixture of rose-pink and white, splashed and in stripes.

The Red Rose *R. gallica* or the rose of Gaul, the oldest plant known to man which is still grown in gardens. It was used by Persian warriors to adorn their shields at the time of Alexander the Great and may have reached Britain with the Romans. It is also known as the apothecary's rose, for the petals retain their perfume long after the flowers are removed from the plant and were sold by apothecaries for all manner of uses. The gallica rose has survived because it is completely hardy and will grow well in any soil. They make neat little plants of 3–4 ft, ideal for a small garden. Prune in March, shortening the wood to half its length. The plants have no real thorns though are covered in stiff hairs. Some of the best are:

'Belle de Crecy' A rose of great beauty with dark green foliage and bearing flat honey-scented flowers of violet-pink flushed with grey.

'Camaieux' Grows only 2 ft tall and bears pretty cup-shaped flowers of crimson, striped with greyish-white.

Chamoisie Picotée' Makes a small upright plant and bears rosette-like flowers of light red, edged with crimson and spotted with brown.

'Rosa Mundi' Fair Rosamund's rose, the oldest of all named roses, so named for Henry II's mistress Rosamund Clifford who was buried in the nunnery at Godstow in Oxfordshire. It is the best of the striped roses, the white flowers being blotched and striped with purple, pink and red.

The Sweet Briar *R. rubiginosa* is a native rose, the refreshing fruity scent of its foliage claiming the attention of the poets through the ages. It is Shakespeare's eglantine and in addition to its deliciously scented foliage, its blooms of clearest pink are followed by scarlet hips of which the seventeenth-century herbalist Gerard wrote: 'The fruit, when ripe, maketh most pleasant, meats and banqueting dishes, as tarts and such-like . . .'

Sending out its long arching stems to 10 ft and more, it will make an impenetrable hedge if planted at 4 ft intervals. It grows to 6 ft and is armed with strong hooked thorns. Train the stems along wires and each year cut out any dead wood. Of several varieties, amongst the most choice are:

'Janet's Pride' Found in a Cheshire lane, the blooms are of brightest pink with a white centre.

'La Belle Distinguée' The double scarlet sweet briar, the crimson-red flowers being followed by fruit of similar colouring.

Crossing the sweet briar with several hybrid tea and Bourbon roses in 1890, Lord Penzance raised a number of fine hybrid varieties which became known as the Penzance briars. They have aromatic foliage and bear scented flowers. Amongst the best are:

'Amy Robsart' The large semi-double blooms are deep cerise-pink.

'Jeannie Deans' The blooms, which are semi-double are a startling shade of crimson-red.

'Lucy Ashton' An excellent hedge rose, it bears flowers of pure white with a distinctive pink edge to the petals.

The Musk Rose *R. moschata* is a native of the Himalayas and reached England early in the sixteenth century, being mentioned by Shakespeare. With its extreme vigour, it was used by the hybridizers, first the Reverend Pemberton in 1912 and later by Welhelm Kordes to raise a number of valuable shrub roses including:

'Moonlight' One of the best of the Pemberton musks, growing 10 ft tall with shining dark green foliage and bearing masses of small ivory-white flowers on graceful arching stems.

'Penelope' A seedling of 'Ophelia' and the musk rose, it is an excellent hedge rose with richly scented semi-double blush-pink flowers.

Of the *R. kordesii* hybrids, several of the best are:

'Ballerina' Introduced in 1937, a superb rose as a standard and as a shrub, bearing throughout summer masses of apple-blossom-pink flowers with a white centre.

'Bonn' Makes an upright bush 5 ft tall and bears semi-double blooms of deep scarlet-orange.

'Kassel' May be used as a climber or as a shrub and grows 12 ft high against a wall. It bears its deep crimson-red flowers in large clusters right through summer.

'Prestige' Introduced with Kassel in 1957, the last of the series and growing only half as tall as Kassel. The semi-double blooms of turkey-red have a striking golden centre.

The Burnet Rose *R. spinosissima* is also the Scottish rose, a thorny species which does well as a coastal windbreak on sandy soils and increases by underground runners. It is the first shrub rose to bloom before the end of May, the single creamy-white flowers being followed by jet-black fruits (hips). Several of the best are:

'Fruhlingsgold' Raised by Wilhelm Kordes in 1937, it grows to 7 ft, its arching stems being clothed in fragrant flowers of clearest golden-yellow. From this variety, crossed with 'McGredy's Wonder', came 'Marigold', bearing cup-shaped flowers of marigold-yellow.

'Golden Wings' Raised by Mr Roy Shepherd, it is of hybrid perpetual parentage which accounts for its continuous flowering. Grows 4 ft tall, has pale green foliage and bears bright yellow flowers enhanced by reddish stamens.

'Stanwell Perpetual' One of only two perpetual flowering burnet roses and a delightful variety in every way, being a chance seedling found in a London garden. Growing 6 ft high, it has graceful arching stems and small grey leaves; its blush-white flowers have a rich, sweet perfume. Believed to be a self-cross with the autumn-flowering damask.

The Ramanas Rose *R. rugosa* is also the Japanese rose, native to China and Japan and one of the hardiest of roses, being troubled neither by black spot nor mildew. It is continuous-flowering and makes a valuable hedge, its magenta-pink flowers being followed by hips of the highest Vitamin C content for syrup making. Some valuable hybrids are:

'Agnes' The result of a crossing with the yellow Persian rose, it grows to 6 ft and bears striking pompom-shaped flowers of tiger-yellow flushed amber.

'Blanc Double de Coubert' Grows 5 ft tall, and bears its double pure white flowers throughout summer.

'Conrad Meyer' Raised by crossing a seedling from 'Gloire de Dijon', that wonderful climbing rose with its buff-coloured quartered flowers, and *R. rugosa*. The result is a plant bearing hybrid-tea-type blooms of silvery-pink.

'Roserie de L'Hay' One of the best of shrub and wall roses, it has dark green foliage and bears hybrid-tea-type blooms of crimson-purple.

ROSE TROUBLES—
PREVENTION AND CONTROL

As roses are unfortunately troubled by pests and disease more than most garden plants, routine spraying of the bushes should be carried out—prevention always being better than cure.

Diseases

BLACK SPOT The disease appears during cold damp weather as black spots on the foliage, and later attacks the stems. The leaves fall, giving the plant a bare appearance. Orthocide Wettable, at a strength of $\frac{1}{2}$ lb dissolved in 20 gallons of water, applied immediately after pruning will prevent a serious outbreak. During summer Orthocide Dust should be applied at regular intervals.

GREY MOULD The same treatment as suggested for black spot will give adequate control.

MILDEW It appears as a white powdery mould covering the stems, foliage and petals, and causing the buds to decay when on the point of opening. The spores are able to winter on the buds from which the next season's shoots appear, so it is important to eliminate the disease at its first appearance. As a routine measure, the plants should be sprayed with lime sulphur (1 part in 10) as soon as they have lost their foliage. Lime sulphur, however, should not be used once the plants have come into leaf; instead, should the disease make an appearance, use karathane for dusting at fornightly intervals.

Pests

CHAFERS There are three forms of the chafers which attack roses. The larva lives in the soil and not only do the grubs attack the roots, but the beetles swarm on to the stems and make ugly holes in the buds. A severe attack on the roots may cause the plant to collapse, so before planting take the precaution of treating the soil with gammexane which, at the same time, will eradicate wireworm.

GREENFLY This, the rose aphis, is the most troublesome of all rose pests which puncture the leaves and feed on the juices of the plant, undermining its vitality. As routine during winter, wash the plants with Mortegg Tar Oil Wash at a strength of 1 part in 20 and during summer dust the plants at regular intervals with a non-poisonous derris extract.

TORTRIX MOTH CATERPILLAR This is Shakespeare's 'worm i' the bud', the maggot which attacks the leaves, causing them to curl up at the edges. The grubs may be killed by dusting with gamma BHC, which, unfortunately, kills the ladybird, the best friend of the rose grower, so perhaps a better method is to remove the grubs by hand.

Chapter 4

WINTER- AND SPRING- FLOWERING PLANTS

In addition to flowering trees and shrubs, and many of the miniature bulbs, there are a number of other plants which bloom during the winter and springtime to make the garden colourful and brighten the window box and tub until the summer-flowering plants take over in early June.

Polyanthuses and primroses may be used in a shady corner, likewise the forget-me-nots, the winter-flowering pansies and the violets, whilst the dainty double daisies and the Juliae primulas may be used to advantage in the trough garden, window box and tub. These are all plants of extreme hardiness, most of them as happy in an exposed northerly garden as in the most sheltered of situations. With their compact habit they are untroubled by strong winds, whilst periods of frost seem only to accentuate their freedom of flowering and the rich colouring of their bloom when it appears. They should be used about the garden as lavishly as possible to make their contribution in providing an all-year-round display of colour.

AURICULA

The lovely old border auriculas are ideal plants for the small garden for they have an even more compact habit than their close relatives the primroses and are tolerant of intense cold and town conditions. To edge a small path or a small shrubbery, for planting in tubs or ornamental vases, or given beds to themselves, they are amongst the most colourful of plants with their rich bloom and mealy grey-green foliage. They should be set out into a soil enriched with humus, and once planted should be disturbed as little as possible. The plants will, however, benefit greatly from a dressing of peat or leaf-mould given each year after flowering has ended in early June, for they tend to form their new roots almost at soil level. A mulch will also help to maintain moisture in the soil during summer.

The named varieties of *Primula auricula* are increased by root division, the plants being lifted every three or four years. They can also be raised inexpensively from seed sown under glass in April. A box covered with a sheet of clean glass will be satisfactory, the plants being transferred to small pots or boxes when large enough to handle, and then set out in their flowering quarters in October.

Of the named varieties 'Adam Lord' has a most compact habit, the navy-blue flowers with their white centres being held on sturdy 5 in stems. Of similar habit is 'Broadwell Gold', which bears a large golden-yellow bloom with a pleasing fragrance, the petals attractively waved and both blooms and foliage covered in 'meal'. Of extremely rich colouring is 'Craig Nordie', with large burgundy-red blooms and silvery foliage. 'Queen Alexandra' has a pale primrose-yellow bloom which is powerfully scented. The brilliantly coloured 'Southport', dainty in habit, has orange-scarlet blooms held on 4 in stems; and 'Linnet', equally compact, bears a bloom of green, brown and mustard colourings, the colours of the bird. The 'Old Dusty Miller' auriculas are suitable for the larger garden and have an old-world charm all their own.

DOUBLE DAISY

The most suitable varieties of *Bellis perennis* for a miniature garden or for planting as ground cover for bulbs are not the large-flowered types such as 'Snowball' and the red-quilled 'Etna', which tend to grow rather coarse, but the dainty 'Rob Roy', crimson; 'Dresden China', shell-pink; and 'The Pearl', white. These bear fully double button-like blooms on 3 in stems. They are most charming plants, never becoming coarse, and remaining long in bloom. They are propagated by root division, the offsets being planted into beds immediately after flowering. They should be set out in their flowering quarters in autumn, 4–5 in apart. They are delightful planted about a rockery in groups of three or four, or around a tub. They may also be used in a trough garden, in a window box and as an edging to a small bed. Charming in this way is 'The Pearl' when used to edge a bed of 'Betty Green' primroses with their brilliant scarlet blooms. Or plant a circular bed of the compact primrose 'Snow Cushion' with 'Rob Roy' daisy to achieve an attractive combination of crimson and white.

ERYSIMUM

For winter and spring colour in small beds, or in window boxes, at the front of a shrubbery, or on a rockery, *Erysimum achroleucum* 'Golden Gem' will be perpetually in bloom from October until May. It is closely related to the wallflowers (*Cheiranthus*) and is known as the alpine wallflower, being like a miniature cheiranthus in habit and in the shape and colour of its bloom. It makes a compact, tufty plant well able to withstand severe winter weather. Plant 6 in apart and in a soil which is well drained, or in a slightly raised bed. Seed should be sown in early April in drills in the open and if the seedlings are thinned early then transplanting may not be necessary, the plants being set out in October.

HELLEBORUS

In almost full shade and where the soil is heavy and cold, in fact where few other plants will survive, the beautiful Christmas and Lenten roses will be long-lived. They may be planted in any odd corner or in the herbaceous border or shrubbery. In heavy soils work in some grit or old mortar, for the plants grow well in calcareous conditions, and to increase the humus content dig in some well-decayed manure such as old mushroom-bed compost or used hops. A deeply dug soil is necessary for the long life of the plants and they will benefit from a yearly mulch of decayed manure and leaf-mould given early in summer when they have finished flowering.

Plant in autumn, about 20 in apart, setting the crowns 2 in below the surface. Plant firmly, and set the Lenten roses (*Helleborus corsicus* and *H. orientalis*), which grow to almost 2 ft, where they will not be blown about by winter winds. The Christmas rose *H. niger* grows to only 6–8 in and if it is in a corner where the winter sunshine can reach it and is covered with a cloche, it will bear its flat circular white flowers, protected from splashing soil, before the end of December. Unprotected plants will begin to bloom in mid-January and continue until the Lenten roses come into flower. And remember that the richer the soil, the better they will bloom.

The true Christmas rose is known as 'Bath Variety', for in that fair city it used to be a fashionable flower with the ladies for evening wear and in Georgian times was grown by nurserymen in huge quantities. But possibly the finest form is 'St Brigid', an Irish variety which bears

Pansies. Seed should be sown in July or August to flower the following spring

large refined flowers of ivory-white. The Lenten roses bloom in March or even earlier, *H. orientalis* bearing its flowers on a 20 in stem above glossy evergreen foliage. Several nodding white flowers, shaded pink or purple on the back, are borne on each stem. The white form, 'Alba', is even finer, for the blooms are shaded with green. *H. atrorubens* bears crimson flowers with creamy-white anthers, on naked stems of similar height and is usually the first of all to flower. *H. corsicus* is taller and has handsome greyish-green foliage. An established plant will grow to nearly 3 ft across and will bear a profusion of apple-green flowers in large branching sprays from late in March until the end of May. By planting one root of each of these hellebores there will be a succession of flowers from the new year until well into summer.

MYOSOTIS

Forget-me-nots are indispensable for a shady bed, for planting with bulbs to form ground cover, or for massing in beds with yellow wallflowers. In the large garden the tall-flowering varieties may be used and these are allowed to seed themselves, for it is rarely necessary to keep them within bounds. The hybridist has, however, raised a number of new varieties most suitable for the small garden or window box. They make charming little plants or bushes 6 in tall and of similar width and remain covered in bloom for weeks on end. One of the best is 'Monarch Blue Ball', which bears a large bloom of deepest indigo. Excellent, too, is Carter's 'Azure Beauty', a lovely shade of pale smoky-blue; 'Star of Love' bears a bloom of mid-blue.

Seed should be sown in a shaded bed outdoors during the early weeks of June. If the seed is thinly sown transplanting may not be necessary, for myosotis is of easy culture and makes a bushy, fibrous-rooted plant without much help. Plant out in October 6 in apart, a little closer in a window box.

PANSY

All pansies and violas raised from seed sown the previous July or August come into bloom the following spring though some bloom earlier than others, whilst the winter-flowering strain and the new 'Clear Crystals' will bloom throughout a mild winter and be a mass of bloom from early April onwards. If a second sowing is made in gentle heat or under a frame early in March, the plants should be in all their glory during the latter weeks of summer and throughout autumn, when the earlier-flowering varieties are coming to an end.

Though pansies and violas raised from seed may be left to bloom a second year, their culture is so easy and the seed so inexpensive that, to enable the beds to be cleaned and to enjoy greater freedom of blooming, they are best treated either as annual or biennial plants, a first sowing being made in July and another in early March. No plants are more useful about a garden than these. In the small garden go for compact habit, with small neat bloom. Pansies and violas are happy in partial shade and just as satisfactory in a town garden as in the country. If they have a preference it is for the cooler regions. In a position of full sun they should be given a soil well enriched with humus in the form of a little decayed manure, leaf-mould, used hops or peat. Where the plants do not lack summer moisture they may continue to bloom over a very long period, almost for twelve months.

Seed is sown either in a frame or in the open ground towards the end of July or early August. Where growing only a few plants, seed should be sown in boxes or pans containing John Innes sowing compost, just covering the seed. It should be kept moist or germination will be delayed. As soon as the seedlings are large enough to handle they should be transplanted either to boxes or to a small open-ground bed and grown on until October when they are transferred to their flowering quarters and set out at 6 in apart.

Where space and labour are at a premium, inter-planting is to be recommended. With the 'Clear Crystals' strain the plants may be set out between bulbs or dwarf polyanthuses and primroses. If the bed is planted in late October, the plants will come into bloom during the first warm days of spring and remain colourful until the end of autumn. Small pots of bulbs such as *Crocus imperati* can be inserted in the bed, with the pot rim just covered, to come into bloom early in the new year; and if the hardy polyanthus 'Barrowby Gem' with its yellowish-green almond-scented blooms is also used there will be rich colour throughout the latter part of winter, through spring and into early summer when the pansies come into their full beauty. Where the true winter-flowering pansies are grown, they will come into bloom early in winter from a July sowing and continue through periods of inclement weather from that time until the latter weeks of summer.

To prolong the display, all dead bloom should be removed as it forms so that the plant does not use its energies in setting seed. A little peat, pressed around the crown of the plants during early summer will do much to retain moisture in the soil and keep the roots cool.

Of the winter-flowering pansies, the dark velvet-blue 'March Beauty' and the golden 'Helios' are attractive planted together; also the pure white 'Snowstorm' planted with 'Wine Red'. Others of beauty are 'Blue Boy' with its blooms of silvery-lilac; 'Winter Sun', yellow with a dark eye; and 'Orion', bearing a large golden bloom.

Others of compact habit are the Felix pansies, their immensely rich blooms in shades of bronze, fawn, purple and crimson having pronounced black 'whiskers'. Excellent too, is the 'Peter Pan' strain in mixed colours and particularly attractive are the pure china-blue flowers of the first named variety, 'Porcelain Blue'. The glorious 'Swiss Giants' and strains such as 'Engelmann's Giant' are better for the larger bed, but of more compact habit is 'Harrison's Syston' strain, the small blooms having the familiar pansy blotch and a remarkably fine colour range. The blooms of the 'Clear Crystals' strain consist of the most beautiful self-colours and are without any blotch or markings, giving them a brightness equalled by few other pansies.

PRIMROSE AND POLYANTHUS

Almost all the *Primula* species and varieties may be classed as having a compact habit, but some are more suitable than others for a very small garden. Indeed, whereas the lovely new primrose variety 'Perle von Bottrop', which bears a vivid royal purple bloom, makes a quite substantial plant with foliage of upright habit, a number of the Juliae primroses are of almost prostrate habit and bear their bloom on short 2 in stems above the foliage. Such varieties are ideal for troughs, for edging tiny beds of miniature bulbs, and for planting in shaded beds entirely to themselves. They are also excellent carpeting plants for bulbs. Extremely hardy and tolerant of the town garden conditions, these dwarf primroses will quickly form a clump as large as a dinner plate. Propagation is by dividing the roots after flowering or in autumn. The smallest pieces will make a good-sized plant within twelve months.

Unnamed varieties may be raised, and will provide rich colour for at least ten weeks, from seed sown in spring in glass-covered boxes in the open or in a cold frame. They will have formed good-sized plants by October and will bloom in spring. The plants may be left untouched in their flowering quarters for at least a second season, after which they should be lifted and divided.

All members of the primrose family appreciate partial shade and so may be planted around the roots of orchard or ornamental trees. The plants will also prove colourful in beds or corners to which the sun does not penetrate and where few other plants would flourish. Late autumn is the best time for planting and a soil enriched with humus to retain summer moisture will be necessary. A plant which has not sufficient moisture at the roots will not only make little new growth but will have only a short life. Humus should be provided in the form of hop manure, seaweed, decayed farmyard manure, peat or leaf-mould.

To give colour during the earliest days of spring, the polyanthus-primrose 'Barrowby Gem', which carries a delightful perfume, should be grown. Its yellowish-green flowers are held on sturdy 6 in stems and it will bloom from the early new year until early June. Another of similar type and in bloom over the same period is the new 'Hunter's Moon', its bloom being best described as luminous apricot and possessing as powerful a fragrance as the 'Ena Harkness' rose. But of those of particularly compact habit the

Above Portulaca is among the most colourful of annuals.
Below A colourful bedding scheme

dainty 'Keith', bearing lemon-yellow blooms on 4 in stems like a miniature polyanthus, is most attractive for a very small garden. Others include 'E. R. Janes', with its blooms of salmon-orange; 'Snow Cushion', its clear white blooms held above the most dainty foliage on 1 in stems; 'F. Ashby', tiny crimson blooms and attractive crimson stems and foliage; 'Bridget', clear mauve-pink blooms appearing late; 'Garryarde Victory', paeony-purple blooms and bronzy-green foliage; and 'Dinah', its velvet-crimson blooms having an attractive olive-green centre. Two others of extremely neat habit and producing dainty blooms on stems shorter than 2 in are 'Pam', with its crimson-purple blooms, and 'Tiny Tim', a cherry-red counterpart with vivid green leaves.

Most of the lovely double primroses are of neat habit, possibly more so than the single Juliae primroses but are rather less robust. Enchanting is 'Red Paddy', with dainty button-like blooms of orange-red laced with silver. Equally neat is 'Bon Accord Lilac', the lilac-pink blooms having an attractive orange centre. Another for the tiny bed is 'Chevithorne Pink', its dainty rounded blooms of lovely orchid-pink being held in polyanthus fashion on 3 in stems. Others are 'Our Pat', amethyst-blue with bronzy foliage; 'Cloth of Gold', pale yellow; 'Arthur du Moulin', deep violet-purple; and 'Quaker's Bonnet', known to Elizabethan gardeners, of delicate clear mauve. 'Marie Crousse', its royal purple blooms having a delicious scent, should also be in every collection.

Of the hose-in-hose primroses, one bloom growing inside another, there is a tiny form of 'Pam', whilst 'Lady Mollie'

Top left Dahlia '*Devil du Roi Albert*'.
Right summer bedding.
Below Encryphia milligannii

bears a bloom of bright rosy-mauve. Most charming too is 'Lady Lettice', the cream and apricot flowers held on 4 in stems, dancing in the spring breezes.

The polyanthus hybrids require exactly the same culture, and are all suitable for the small garden; for the very small garden there are miniatures. There are several lovely named varieties, and a new strain which comes true to type from seed and was evolved by the Barnhaven Gardens of Oregon, USA—extremely dainty blooms held on 4 in stems. Of the named varieties, 'Lady Greer' with its neat, rounded foliage and blooms of pale moonlight-yellow borne on 5-6 in stems is a charming plant, ideal for edging or for planting on a rockery or in a window box. Similar in habit is 'McWatt's Claret', the bloom being a pure shade of claret-purple.

Auriculas are easily raised from seed, but good forms can be increased by division

The gold-laced polyanthus is of neat habit, the crimson blooms, some almost black, being beautifully edged with gold. Of the ordinary bedding strains, one of the most compact is 'Sutton's Superb', embracing a wide colour range. Blackmore & Langdon's Pink and also their Blue strain are of compact habit, ideal for window boxes and small beds. They are delightful edged with the double daisy 'Dresden China'.

STOCKS

James Thomson in his poem 'The Seasons' wrote of 'the lavish stock, that scents the garden round', and Henry Phillips, friend of John Constable and tutor to his children, said: 'Though less graceful than the rose and not so superb as the lily, its splendour is more durable, its fragrance of longer continuance.'

There are spring-, summer-, autumn- and winter-flowering stocks. The spring-flowering are the Brompton stocks, *Matthiola incana*, developed in the nineteenth century at the Brompton Road Nursery of Messrs London & Wise (who laid out the present gardens at Blenheim Palace). The plants are biennial and are sown early in July. Use the John Innes compost for sowing and water in the seed with Cheshunt Compound to prevent black-leg disease which is fatal to stocks. Remove the dark green seedlings as these will give only single flowers. Keep the rest on the dry side and transplant to boxes or pots in August. They may be wintered either in a frame and planted out in March or, in districts with a favourable winter climate, they may be planted out in beds or in the border early in September. They will bloom during April and May. Two outstanding varieties are Lavender Lady and the crimson-flowered Queen Astrid.

The ten-week or summer stocks are so named because they bloom ten weeks after sowing the seed towards the end of March. 'Hansen's 100% Double' is the strain recommended; these plants are branched and grow only 9 in tall. They are obtainable in all the usual stock shades including apple-blossom-pink, sky-blue and sulphur-yellow.

The autumn-flowering stocks are also known as the Intermediate or East Lothian stocks for it was in a Scottish garden in East Lothian that they were first seen growing. They also are sown in March for they take longer to reach maturity, being at their best in early autumn and remaining in bloom until the late November frosts. The Kelvedon strain, in all the rich stock colours, is outstanding.

Winter-flowering stocks, grown under glass in a temperature of 50°F (10°C) are the finest of all, growing up to 2 ft and making bushy plants of branching habit. They produce their dense flowering spikes throughout winter from a sowing made in early July. The best strain is Winter Beauty or Beauty of Nice.

VIOLET

Unlike the primrose, the violet is never happy in the polluted atmosphere of a town garden. Clean air is essential to healthy plant life and only in seaside or country gardens does the violet flourish. Though widely grown in the south-west for its early bloom, this does not imply that it is in any way tender. Indeed, the violet is amongst the hardiest of plants and is to be found on the hills of Lanarkshire as well as about the hedgerows of Sussex. Like all members of the *Viola* family, the violet makes a sturdier plant when growing under cool conditions, where it bears a bloom of much finer quality. It is quite happy in shade, and dappled shade suits it best of all. Like all its relatives it does well in a soil which retains summer moisture, so incorporate as much humus as possible.

As the plants reproduce themselves from runners, they are best planted in a bed to themselves where their runners do not interfere with other plants. Violets may also be increased by division of the crowns, early May being the most suitable time. Rooted runners may be detached as they form. As the 'strings' which join the rosettes will also form roots, a small piece should be severed with the rosette. This will ensure the plants getting away to a good start in their new bed. Plant 6 in apart and remove any runners or bloom which may form throughout the summer so that the plants can concentrate their entire energy on the production of bloom in the following spring. Through-out summer too, the plants should never be allowed to lack moisture. To enjoy very early bloom one or two plants may be covered with a cloche, but a sunny position should be selected for plants expected to bloom early.

After the plants have finished flowering and the runners have been removed, the old crowns should be dressed with either peat or decayed manure so that they will bloom well the following year, after which they should be divided and replanted into a new bed.

There are some very beautifully coloured violets quite apart from those of typical violet colouring, and a few plants of each should find a place in the smallest garden. One of the best of all is 'Admiral Avellan', an extremely hardy variety bearing bloom of bright reddish-purple and possessing a strong perfume. Equally hardy though not having so strong a fragrance is the new 'Bourne-mouth Gem', the blooms being of a deep purple-blue colour. A variety strangely neglected is 'Coeur d'Alsace', which

bears its sweetly perfumed rose-pink blooms on long stems. Owing to its resistance to pest and disease, the scentless 'Governor Herrick', which flowers well in a shallow soil, has become popular. Its blooms are a bright purple colour. One of the loveliest is the little known 'John Raddenbury', bright china-blue and sweetly perfumed. Most attractive, too, is the creamy-buff 'Irish Elegance', and another beauty is 'Countess of Shaftes-bury', its lavender-blue flowers having a centre ring of petals of rose-pink and green stamens. The double-flowering varieties are less hardy than the singles and suitable only for southern gardens.

Wallflowers are now available in a wider range of colours than ever before

WALLFLOWER

Everybody's favourite on account of its richly coloured and fragrant blooms, and nowhere is *Cheiranthus cheiri* more appreciated than planted close to a doorway or window, where their rich perfume drifts into the house during the calmer days of spring. In the unduly exposed garden, wallflowers may suffer from frosts and cold winds, unless so well grown that they have attained bush-like proportions at planting time. (The primrose and polyanthus are untroubled by such conditions and should be grown where extreme hardiness is desired.)

To grow wallflowers really well they should be given a long season, and the end of April is not too early to sow the seed. Use seed saved the previous summer so that it is fresh and will germinate quickly. Sow thinly in drills 6 in apart, or broadcast in a small seed bed thoroughly cleaned of weeds with some peat added to the soil. Rake in the seed lightly, and keep moist. To prevent any woody taproot from forming, the old gardeners would transplant three or four times during summer over a slate bed, but equally good wallflowers may be grown if the young plants are moved to a bed of prepared ground as soon as large enough to handle, spacing them 4 ft apart. All too often the plants are allowed to remain in their seed bed far too long, until they have become 'drawn' and weakly, from which condition they may never recover. Where ground is at a premium, seed may be sown in deep boxes and the plants moved to boxes containing 6–8 in of soil. Set out the plants into beds towards the end of October, giving them a deeply dug, fairly rich soil and firm planting.

The most suitable for small beds and for tubs and window boxes is Messrs Sutton's special Dwarf Bedding strain, growing to no more than 8 in and including all shades of yellow, brown, rose and crimson. Also suitable are the varieties Orange, Primrose, Scarlet and Golden Bedder, each growing to a height of only 9 in. Planted 6–7 in apart, in strips or circles of individual colours, the effect will be extremely rich from April until early June.

Of the taller-growing varieties, 'Fire King' grows to 15 in and for contrast plant with it 'Cloth of Gold' or 'Primrose Monarch'. The older 'Vulcan', velvet crimson-brown, is also lovely.

Chapter 5
HALF-HARDY PLANTS FOR SUMMER BEDDING

Where there is a small greenhouse or frame available with sufficient heat to exclude frost, a number of the most beautiful half-hardy summer-flowering plants may be grown. Indeed, some may be wintered in the home in the sunny window of a room, provided there is sufficient warmth to keep out frost, and it may be possible to grow enough in this way to provide a colourful display for a small bed. These could be augmented by the tuberous multiflora begonias, it being possible to bring into growth as many as fifty tubers in a single box, to be planted directly into open-ground beds when hardened.

In districts with a warm spring climate, most of the half-hardy plants may be grown outdoors throughout the winter with only the minimum of protection, but they will not tolerate cold, damp conditions and for this reason, where the plants are to be grown in a greenhouse or in the home, sufficient warmth will be necessary to maintain a buoyant atmosphere. The use of electric heating controlled by thermostat will prove both labour-saving and reasonably inexpensive, but where there is no supply available one of the modern paraffin-oil heaters of the hot-water radiator type will be found quite efficient. They are fumeless and inexpensive to maintain.

Though each of the less hardy plants described here is of perennial habit, and may be used again and again, they do tend to become woody and somewhat straggling, and fresh stock should be brought on each year to maintain the vigour of the plants. Those of tuberous habit will, of course, die back, the tubers being brought into new growth each year after a rest period.

BEGONIA

Though the large-flowered begonias may be used for summer bedding, it is the multiflora type with its less formal habit and continuous flowering whatever the weather that is most suitable for bedding. Though widely used in our corporation parks, these remain comparatively unknown yet are amongst the most valuable of all summer bedding plants and of the easiest culture. The small rosette-like blooms are held in sprays of a dozen or more above the foliage and possess those rich bright colours unknown in plants other than the begonia. The blooms are accentuated by the dark green leaves which are of true begonia shape and, being native of the humid tropical parts of South America, no amount of rain will trouble them. Making neat, bushy plants 8–9 in tall, the multiflora begonias are ideal plants for a small garden, for no plant bears more bloom in comparison to its size, nor over so long a period.

The tubers should be started into growth about the last day of March. They will grow in a cold house or frame, though but slowly, and it will be July before they come into bloom. With gentle heat they will be ready for planting out in early June, and will come into bloom by the middle of the month. The compost for starting the tubers into growth should consist of fibrous turf loam to which has been added some peat and coarse sand, in the ratio of 2 parts of turf to 1 part each of peat and sand. Begonias like some lime added to the soil, so to each bushel of compost add $1\frac{1}{2}$ oz superphosphate and $\frac{3}{4}$ oz lime. The tubers may be started in boxes, being merely pressed into the top of the compost, and for the first weeks before they commence to make growth will require little water. When they are making growth they will prove to be copious drinkers.

This same demand for moisture will continue through summer, and if the plants are to be set out in a light sandy soil, it must be fortified with farmyard manure, peat, spent hops, or any similar form of humus. A heavy soil, which is preferable provided it is well drained, should be opened up by adding some grit and some peat. But, above all, some lime is again essential, for begonias are never happy in the acid soils of our cities. A dressing of bonemeal at 2 oz per sq yd will provide food over the entire summer.

The plants should be set out in early June, when all fear of frost has gone. Plant 9–10 in apart, placing the tubers 3 in below the soil surface and taking care not to break the brittle stem. From the time the plants are set out they must be watered copiously, and should be given a mulch of peat in late July to conserve soil moisture through the summer. All dead blooms should be removed as they form so that they do not set seed, but this is not necessary with the multifloras. At their best in a season of damp, humid days when the zonal pelargoniums ('geraniums') and calceolarias look anything but happy, begonias are particularly suited to the English climate in spite of their South American origin.

Lifting and storing begonias calls for care. The plants should be lifted with only their blooms removed, the foliage and stems being intact so that they can be placed in a frost-proof room which is

Dividing a corm or tuber. Each section must have an 'eye' or growing point

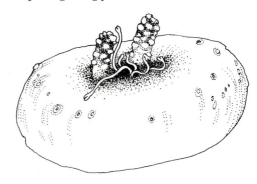

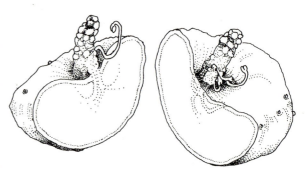

dry and well ventilated, and there be left to die down gradually. Care must be taken with lifting as in planting, so that the stems are not broken. If the plants are lifted at the beginning of October, the stems and leaves will come away from the tubers naturally by the month end. The tubers should then be placed in boxes of dry peat, where they will remain through winter.

As the tubers become older they increase in size and, if not divided, will tend to die back. The best method is to divide large tubers when they have commenced growth in spring, for it is necessary for each piece to contain a shoot. The cut portions should be dusted with sulphur or charcoal to help the cut to heal. Alternatively the stock may be increased by taking cuttings as the young shoots appear in spring, generally a single shoot from an overcrowded tuber being removed. Side shoots may also be removed when 3–4 in long as they appear on the main stems. Take care not to damage the 'eye' which will be seen at the base of each shoot and which must be removed with it.

As with pelargoniums, the shoots are placed around the sides of a 60-size pot containing a mixture of sand and peat and, if kept moist, they will root in from three to four weeks. The best time to take cuttings is during June and July; if taken later they may not root too readily. The rooted plants should be potted into small pots containing a compost of loam and decayed manure, together with a little peat and some grit.

Of the multifloras, 'Red Thousand Beauties', each plant of which covers itself in masses of vivid red blossoms, 'Flamboyant' (cherry-red), 'Madame Richard Galle' (orange), and 'Madame Helen Harms' (double yellow), are reliable bedding varieties.

CALCEOLARIA

As William Robinson rightly points out in *The English Flower Garden*, published in the 1880s, the shrubby calceolaria used to be seen in thousands in both park and private garden, especially the rich-brown-coloured 'Kentish Hero'; now it seems to be neglected, probably on account of its being rather subject to pest attack and because it has to be wintered in heat. Modern insecticides, however, prevent any trouble with pests, and with its rich colouring the calceolaria should once again come into favour, 'Bronze Beauty' and 'Golden Gem' being the two most popular modern varieties.

The best time to take cuttings is in September, and only those shoots which have not borne a flower should be removed. Firm side shoots should be selected and inserted into boxes containing a mixture of peat and sand, and, if kept in a temperature of 60 °F (16 °C), will root in several weeks. They take longer to root than most plants for the shoots are hard and woody. Early in spring, when well rooted, the plants should be transferred to 3 in pots containing the same materials as for salvias (see page 79) and from then onwards are given the same treatment. As the cuttings show a tendency to damp off they should be kept dusted with sulphur whilst rooting, and powdered charcoal should be scattered over the compost. Alternatively, Bordeaux mixture may be used.

A colourful combination is to use yellow calceolarias immediately behind blue lobelia, backed by scarlet zonal pelargoniums ('geraniums') or antirrhinums. Such a display has often been called blatant and too formal, but for colour it is difficult to beat and will remain in bloom from mid-June until the autumn, requiring the minimum attention.

FUCHSIA

A charming plant when used for bedding along with marguerites and blue lobelia, the fuchsia is today finding increased popularity, especially in the milder districts. They may be used in a most attractive way as standards, several to a bed, contrasting colours being used for standards and for bedding. Or the plants may be grown with the maritime cineraria whose silvery-grey foliage blends most pleasingly with the subdued colourings of the fuchsias.

Fuchsias are in no way difficult, but demand attention to detail if they are to be grown to perfection. Cuttings are taken from stock plants reserved for the purpose, which are grown on in large pots outdoors from June until early September, and from September until early April in a warm greenhouse. The cuttings, taken when about 12 in long, root readily in a compost of peat and coarse sand, and, if sprayed daily to prevent wilting, will be rooted in about three weeks. As the rooting compost will be sterile, the cuttings should be removed to individual pots as soon as well rooted, into a compost of fibrous loam and decayed manure, together with a small quantity of peat and grit. Fuchsias, unlike begonias, are not lime-lovers.

The plants are grown on in a temperature of $55-60\,°F$ $(13-16\,°C)$, as they must not be allowed to grow 'hard', which will cause them to bloom prematurely. Regular syringeing and adequate ventilation are necessary, and if the spring sun is unduly warm, some shading should be given to prevent leaf scorch. Plants 'struck' before Christmas will require a second move to larger pots in early March to keep them growing, and when 8–9 in high must have their shoots pinched back to encourage bushy growth. From early April the plants should be fed with liquid manure water, and should be moved to frames for hardening in mid-May. They are bedded out in early June, planted firmly, and spaced 12 in apart.

To build up a strong standard, the terminal shoot is allowed to grow on unchecked, but the side shoots are removed as soon as they are large enough to handle. When the terminal shoot, supported by a cane, has reached a height of 3 ft, it is allowed to grow on until a number of side shoots form, and it is then stopped, the side shoots, which make the head, also being stopped when 6–7 in long.

There are many outstanding varieties, but for planting together try 'Ballet Girl', with its red sepals and double white corolla, and the free-flowering 'Scarcity' with its red sepals and mauve corolla. The all-pink-coloured 'Fascination', also a double, and the rose and purple 'Profusion' look well together. All of these varieties are easy to grow, are tolerant of wet weather, and are free-flowering.

GERANIUM: see Pelargonium

HELIOTROPE

This old favourite, which children call cherry pie, is a delightful plant for bedding with fuchsias or with the maritime cineraria. With pink or salmon-coloured pelargoniums it is also most pleasing, and provides a foil to the more formal pelargonium. Those who possess a heated greenhouse should try it again. It is a plant which requires much the same winter conditions as the pelargonium and calceolaria, and could be grown with them. The plants require a dry soil whilst dormant, and should be watered only when coming into growth again in spring.

Cuttings are taken from stock plants in late spring, when the plants have formed vigorous young shoots. Owing to their long rooting period, which in these days of mass production has tended to go against the heliotrope, the plants are not used for bedding until the following summer. Rooted in pure sand to which has been added a sprinkling of peat to retain moisture, the cuttings may take eight to ten weeks to form roots, but this will be speeded up if they are dipped in hormone powder. The cuttings are moved to small pots as soon as rooted, and transferred to 60-size pots during summer. The plants are kept almost dry throughout winter, and in spring are brought on for bedding out early in June, after being hardened in the usual way.

Heliotrope may also be raised from seed sown in a warm greenhouse during August. The seedlings are pricked out into small pots when large enough to handle and are grown on through winter as dry as possible. Started into growth again in spring, they may be large enough for outside bedding by early summer, or could be repotted into 60s, placed in a frame over summer, and used for bedding the following year. The new Regal hybrids bear large trusses of fragrant blooms in shades of purple and mauve; they are suitable both for bedding and as pot plants.

MARGUERITE

Because of their rather informal habit, marguerites were at one time planted with pelargoniums and calceolarias; their whiteness, long-lasting qualities, and their ability to flourish under all conditions, made them a perfect foil to the brilliant colours and stiff habit of their neighbours. The plant may be classed as almost hardy, yet for propagation the cuttings should be struck in gentle heat. October is the best time to remove the shoots from the leaf joints, when the plants are being removed from the beds. They are inserted in a compost of loam, peat and sand, and kept in a temperature of 55 °F (13 °C), spraying them occasionally to prevent flagging. As soon as rooted, the plants should be potted into 3 in pots in a compost containing some decayed manure and some grit. Like the pelargonium, the plants should be given very little water until the sun's rays stimulate growth towards the end of March. During April, as with all these half-hardy plants, heat is only necessary at night; and from 1 May not at all. Early in May the plants should be moved to cold frames and hardened off in the normal way.

PELARGONUM (Geranium)

So popular during Victorian times, the bedding pelargoniums, *P. × hortorum*, still popularly but erroneously known as geraniums, lost ground during the years between the two World Wars, giving way to bedding plants of less formal habit. Today, however, the plant has recaptured all its former glory, and for a prolonged display, both in the garden and later as a pot plant in the living-room, no plant is more labour-saving or more colourful. But for all those who grow the large-flowered zonal pelargoniums, few know of the charms of the fancy-leaf varieties which bear a long profusion of dainty flowers hovering above the plants like butterflies. A small bed planted with the attractive 'Lass O'Gowrie', which has tricolour leaves and bears dainty scarlet flowers on short wiry stems, will command attention from all who see it. With the blatant 'Paul Crampel' plant the silver-leafed 'Caroline Schmidt', which also bears red flowers, to accentuate the beauty of the bed with silver-edged foliage. The bed may be edged with the almost black-leafed 'Black Vesuvius', to give a display of outstanding beauty. It is only when a bed contains nothing but 'geraniums'—the garish scarlet ones—that these plants are seen to the best advantage.

Propagation Pelargoniums are propagated from cuttings which can be taken at any time of the year except during the mid-winter months. However, to make substantial plants for bedding out in May and June, cuttings are best taken in August, when they will root in about fifteen days, without fear of damping off. The cutting should be short-jointed and as near as 3 in in length as possible, the lower leaves being removed so that the shoot has not to support too much foliage whilst at the same time forming roots. It will be found that cuttings root more quickly and with almost 100 per cent regularity if placed round the sides of 48-size pots (ie pots with 48 to a 'cast') filled with a compost of sand and loam. If unsterilized soil is used they may be troubled with black rot before they are rooted. They can be put in a cold frame or greenhouse at this time of the year, shading to give protection from the summer sun. Nurserymen who may have rooted cuttings in this way in mid-summer will find that the tops of the plants, where wintered in gentle heat to keep out the frost, may be removed in early April to encourage bushy plants; these shoots also may be rooted in gentle heat—the greenhouse can play an important part in pelargonium culture—but it must be said that only just enough heat is needed to exclude frost; pelargoniums are never happy in a warm, stuffy atmosphere.

The cuttings will root more readily if left away from the rays of the sun for an hour before inserting in the pots. This will remove some excess moisture, which pelargonium cuttings find detrimental

Cuttings of pelargoniums being raised in a greenhouse for summer bedding

to easy rooting. The shaded frame or greenhouse will ensure that the cuttings retain all the moisture necessary while rooting, for at no stage in its life does the pelargonium enjoy excessively moist conditions. As soon as rooted, the cuttings are moved to individual 3 in pots containing a mixture of equal parts of well-rotted manure (mushroom-bed compost is ideal), turf loam and coarse sand, with a sprinkling of bonemeal. Though pelargoniums, being natives of South Africa, enjoy dry conditions, they thrive in a reasonably rich compost. If this is provided from the beginning it enhances the quality of the bloom and size of the plant, but an excess of nitrogenous manure in the flowering beds causes the plants to make too much leaf at the expense of the blooms.

If the plants are potted in September, they may remain undisturbed through winter, being given only the very minimum of moisture, of which the fibrous roots are able to take in only the very smallest quantities during the winter period. By mid-April the plants should be removed to a cold frame to harden off gradually, so that they will be ready for outdoor beds and window boxes by the end of May. If the plants are not to be used until mid-June—and in a northerly district a late display of tulips may not warrant their lifting before that time—they should be moved to larger pots containing a mixture of fibrous loam and rooted manure, otherwise they may become starved, pot-bound and drawn. At all times it is desirable to build up a sturdy, short-jointed plant.

Planting When planting out in the beds, choose a damp, calm day if possible, so that the plants get away to a good start. If dry conditions prevail, see that they are kept moist at the roots until they become established, when they will take care of themselves, thus showing their worth as bedding plants in those dry borders beneath the walls of house or terrace. Their need for so little attention also makes them ideal plants for parks and large gardens, where labour is required elsewhere. Space the plants 12–14 in apart and plant firmly; they are never happy in a loose soil. If sending pelargoniums away, the nurseryman should, after removing them from the pots, wrap each plant separately in paper and stand them upright in deep boxes. In this way, with the top of the box left open, the plants are put on rail, and should reach their destination free from harm.

The bed to accommodate the plants should receive some preparation, for, though pelargoniums will flower well in the impoverished dry soil frequently found in town gardens, they bloom so much better in a soil enriched with well-rotted manure. Particularly does the pelargonium, in its numerous forms, enjoy decayed manure, more than any other material and much more than either peat or leaf-mould. Peat is used only in small amounts for rooting cuttings, and even here well-decayed manure or used mushroom compost may be conveniently substituted. The manure should be well forked in a full week before the plants are to be set out, so that the soil has time to settle down. Lime is of the greatest importance to pelargoniums; they may, in fact, be classed as real lime-lovers, and town soils especially should be given a liberal dressing with lime whilst the beds are being made up. Equally essential is potash. This will build up a 'hard' plant, able to withstand excessive rains, and will correct any tendency for the plant to make too much soft leaf. At the same time, potash in the soil will bring out richness of colouring in the blooms, and increase their size. A dressing of 2 oz per sq yd is sufficient, supplied in the form of sulphate of potash.

After planting, pelargoniums require little attention other than the removal of the dead blooms, but they appreciate a weekly application of dilute manure water from the end of July, given if possible on a wet day.

The pelargonium is so accommodating that it may be planted in almost any position in the garden. Though happiest in full sun, especially in the dry soil of a border beneath a wall, it will bloom abundantly in partial shade. One of the loveliest beds that it has been my privilege to see was oval in shape, situated in the corner of a garden, and almost surrounded by tall evergreens, judiciously planted so that the rays of the sun from the south could reach the bed unhindered. The bed, filled with nothing but the glowing pink 'Queen of Denmark', was one of great beauty, and showed that the zonal pelargonium could be incorporated with success into a natural setting.

Lifting After the bedding season is ended, the plants should be lifted before the frosts arrive. In my own garden overlooking the North Sea I have allowed the plants to continue to bear the odd bloom or two until the end of November, for early frosts are rarely experienced close to the sea. In inland gardens it is advisable to lift at the end of October, and in any case the beds may be required for a spring display of tulips, wallflowers or forget-me-nots, which should be in the ground by November.

One of the great difficulties when using pelargoniums for bedding is in retaining the plants for flowering another season. Owners of a heated greenhouse will have no trouble, and already cuttings may have been removed, and will by late October have become rooted. Plants from the beds should be lifted and placed in dry, sandy soil, either in pots or boxes. In a frost-proof house the plants will winter without any trouble, and may be potted up to provide more cuttings in April. They may be utilized for bedding for another season, being repotted in April after the cuttings have been removed. Where there is not a heated greenhouse available, then a frost-proof room may help the plants to survive the winter. Here the plants should be cleaned of all soil and stripped of most of their leaves. The stems should be tied together in small numbers, and the plants should then be suspended from a beam or large nail. But the room must be quite *dry* and frost-proof. Alternatively the plants, with most of the foliage removed, may be kept in boxes of dry soil.

Plants may also be lifted and potted, and, after shortening any unduly long shoots, may be grown on in a warm room where they will continue to bloom throughout the winter, to be planted out again in May.

Zonal Pelargoniums for Bedding

'Audrey' Fully double and one of the loveliest of all geraniums, the flowers being of a most attractive shade of pure phlox-pink.

'Banbury Cross' A new variety, the bloom a red-brick colour, of large proportions, and most striking with its pronounced white eye.

'Beatrix Little' A valuable variety owing to its dwarf, compact habit, making it an ideal bedder for a small garden or for a window box. The colour is scarlet.

'Colonel Drabbe' Most striking with its large well-formed bloom, fully double and of a deep shade of crimson with a white centre.

'Doris Moore' Of good bedding habit with large blooms of a lovely shade of cherry-red.

'**Double Henry Jacoby**' An old favourite of dwarf habit, bearing fully double flowers of rich turkey-red.

'**Elizabeth Angus**' A 1966 introduction bearing huge single flowers of orange-red with a cream eye.

'**Elizabeth Cartwright**' Quite outstanding with its large flowers of carmine-red shading to signal-red at the centre.

'**Gustav Emich**' The Buckingham Palace 'geranium'; the semi-double blooms being of a striking orange-scarlet.

'**John Cross**' A new variety, the salmon-pink flowers possessing a bright silvery sheen.

'**King of Denmark**' The ever-popular semi-double in a delicate shade of shell-pink.

'**Lady Ellendon**' A new introduction, vigorous and free-flowering, the rose-coloured blooms retaining their colour through sunshine and rain.

'**Lady Wilson**' Of dwarf, compact habit and most free-flowering. The white blooms are strikingly edged and veined with turkey-red.

'**Lord Curzon**' A really remarkable variety, the rich purple blooms having a clear white eye.

'**Mauretainia**' A most beautiful variety to plant with 'Audrey'. The large blush-white blooms are ringed at the centre with rose-pink.

'**Mrs E. Hill**' Its lovely shade of salmon-pink has made it a most popular bedding plant of recent years.

'**Muriel Parsons**' A variety of outstanding beauty, the solid semi-double blooms being of a unique shade of dusky lavender-pink.

'**Orange Sonne**' From Switzerland, it makes a compact plant and bears double blooms of clearest orange.

Bedding plants are usually most effective against a background of permanent shrubs

'Paul Crampel' Of excellent bedding habit, its single scarlet blooms have given us the colour known as 'geranium-red'.

'Pierre Courtoise' A magnificent variety, the huge blooms are of a rich shade of velvet-crimson.

'Pink Bouquet' A variety of exquisite charm, bearing double blooms of soft salmon-pink.

'Queen of the Whites' Free-flowering and compact, the pure glistening-white flowers act as a pleasing contrast to those of richer colouring.

'Willingdon Gem' A very lovely pelargonium, the large blooms being of purest tangerine with a striking white eye.

Ornamental Leaf Pelargoniums These interesting plants are grown almost entirely for the rich colouring of their foliage—for their blooms, in most cases, are insignificant. They are valuable not only for providing a contrast to other bedding plants, but should be used where soil is unduly poor, and the garden shaded. Apart from the removal of any yellowing leaves, they will require little or no attention throughout summer. There are many lovely varieties, all retaining their foliage in the home throughout winter. Some of the most striking are:

'A Happy Thought' What a lovely name for a plant, and a good name too, for the soft green foliage, each leaf having a pale yellow 'butterfly' in the centre, makes a plant of the utmost charm.

'Caroline Schmidt' Bearing a silver-green leaf edged with palest gold and the largest bloom of all the ornamental-leaf geraniums, this is a variety which should be more widely grown. The blooms are fully double and of deep blood-red.

'Lass Gowrie' A striking variety, rich cream-coloured leaves being marked with crimson. The plant has a dainty, compact habit, its single brick-red flowers hovering above the foliage.

'Maréchal McMahon' A fine plant for grouping in a shrub border or for providing a contrast to a bed of carpeting plants. The almost symmetrical leaves of 'Maréchal McMahon' are of a rich golden colour, heavily zoned with bronze and edged with palest yellow.

'Masterpiece' Striking in that its almost black leaves are edged with gold.

'Mrs Burdett-Coutts' Extremely rare and only for the connoisseur; the leaves are marked with zones of cream, pale green, crimson and bronze.

'Mrs Henry Cox' One of the best in this section and a real exhibitor's tricolour, the exotic leaves being zoned with gold, silver and red.

'Mrs Pollock' Very inexpensive, in that it is of vigorous habit and propagates readily. Even so, it is a most arresting plant, the green leaves being zoned yellow, bronze and orange.

'Verona' An old variety, still valuable for the marked contrast its pure golden-yellow leaves provide to the darker-foliaged pelargoniums.

Miniature Pelargoniums These delightful little plants grow no more than 6 in tall, and with their small richly coloured leaves and dainty flowers are ideal for edging or for use in small beds.

'Black Vesuvius' Makes a tiny shrub-like plant with dark bronze leaves and bears large vermilion flowers.

'Golden Harry Hieover' This old, dwarf variety has leaves of an almost pure gold colour, and tiny vermilion flowers.

'Kleine Liebling' An old variety from Germany, having brilliant green leaves and tiny flowers of deepest pink.

'Madame Fournier' Makes a plant of compact habit, having dark-zoned leaves and bearing bright scarlet single flowers.

'Mephistopheles' One of the oldest of the miniatures, raised in France, and having almost black leaves; its vivid orange-scarlet flowers are in striking contrast.

SALVIA

No plant gives a more brilliant patch of colour in the garden than the scarlet *Salvia splendens*, the short flower spikes of brilliant red being in marked contrast to the bright pale green foliage. The plants grow only 6–9 in tall and are of shrubby habit, coming into bloom early in June and continuing until early November, when they may be lifted and planted in small pots to continue the display under glass or in the living room for several more weeks. A circular bed containing a dozen plants and surrounded with white alyssum or dwarf golden tagetes will, for weeks on end, provide the most brilliant corner of the garden. With their upright flower spikes the plants occupy little space, the new 'Scarlet Pigmy' growing only to 6 in, whilst the crimson-flowered 'Blaze of Fire' is only slightly more robust.

The plants are readily raised from cuttings taken in autumn. These should be about 4 in in length and are inserted around the side of a pot in exactly the same way as for pelargoniums. Or plants may be lifted from the beds late in October, transferred to pots or boxes, and, if kept in gentle heat, will continue to bear cuttings during winter. These may be removed and rooted in batches as they form. They should be kept in a temperature of 55 °F (13 °C), syringeing them frequently to guard against red spider mite, and as soon as rooted should be transferred to 3 in pots. The salvia is a gross feeder and must be given a compost containing a stiff fibrous loam, decayed manure, a little grit to keep the compost 'open', and a small quantity of bonemeal. To keep the habit compact, the plants should be firmly potted. They should be transferred to cold frames for hardening about mid-May, and given copious amounts of water. Bed out in early June, setting them 9–10 in apart into a soil well enriched with rotted manure.

Chapter 6

AUTUMN COLOUR IN THE GARDEN

In autumn the new brilliantly coloured dahlias and the enormously improved michaelmas daisies combine with the still-flowering modern hybrid tea roses and the late annuals and bedding plants to make this the most colourful time of the year. Usually September and October are the driest and sunniest months of the year, and with less work to do on the cutting of grass, clipping of hedges, watering and weeding, the many lovely plants may be enjoyed to the full.

CARDINAL FLOWER

Surprisingly, this is *Lobelia cardinalis* though in habit as much unlike the blue bedding lobelia as imaginable. It is native of the southern states of the USA, but in 1629 according to Parkinson it was already to be found in English gardens, where today, though not entirely hardy in colder parts, it makes a brilliant autumn contribution either in the border or in a small bed of its own.

It requires a rich, deeply worked soil but one which is well drained in winter if this plant is to be long living. Ashes or a mixture of peat and sand should be heaped over it when it dies down in November, to protect it from frost. Like the michaelmas daisy, also a plant of the New World and in bloom at the same time, it will give a good account of itself in semi-shade.

The cardinal-red lobelia-like flowers, accentuated by the bronzy-red foliage, are borne in long spikes on 3 ft stems and they remain in bloom all autumn. So handsome is the foliage that the plant was at one time widely used to lend height and additional colour to Victorian bedding schemes.

Propagation is by root division in spring, but in cold gardens it is advisable to lift the roots in November and to winter in a frame or warm greenhouse, replanting in May. The soil should be enriched with some decayed manure together with peat or leaf-mould.

CHRYSANTHEMUMS (SPRAY)

The large-flowering outdoor chrysanthemum is rarely satisfactory as a garden plant since it requires specialized culture in staking, disbudding, and the removal of those side shoots which present a difficult problem where growing in a thickly planted border. The new spray-flowered chrysanthemums, however, are ideal border plants, having a long flowering season and, apart from the minimum of staking, demand no more attention than any other border plant. They may also be treated as semi-permanent, propagating in exactly the same way as other border plants, whereas to maintain the quality of bloom of the large-flowering varieties annual propagation must take place from rooted offsets or cuttings.

The spray chrysanthemums suitable for border colours may be divided into three classes: (a) the Koreans, (b) the Pompons, and (c) *Chrysanthemum rubellum*, which may be considered a cross between the first two. They require exactly the same culture and are extremely hardy, flowering until the end of November. It should be said, however, that the very late-flowering varieties such as the new 'Crimson Bride' which comes into bloom late in October should be confined to southern gardens in Britain, for adverse weather experienced in the north from that time onwards may mean that the buds do not open at all, and in any case, deposits of soot and fog will greatly harm the blooms. All those varieties which come into bloom after the first few days of October should be avoided where growing in the less favourable districts. The late September-flowering varieties will, in any case, continue to bloom until well into November, when the border is cleared. Nowhere do they look more attractive than when planted near michaelmas daisies, their blue and purple colourings providing a pleasing contrast to the autumnal colourings of the Koreans, and in no way do they clash. The bright green serrated foliage of the spray chrysanthemum greatly contributes to its charm, whilst the strong sage-like aroma of the foliage should ensure their inclusion in a border of fragrant plants. The plants require a sunny, open situation. Chrysanthemums grow best in a rich, well-

manured soil; of all flowering plants these are possibly the greatest feeders, though it should be said that the soil need not be so rich for the sprays as for the large-flowering varieties, for size of bloom is not so important a consideration. In poor soil, however, the blooms will be much smaller than where growing in soil of good 'heart', and will also lack colour, and especially that pyrethrum-like sheen which makes them so impressive when cut and in water.

The young plants should be obtained towards the end of April and planted 20 in apart, either in beds or in the border. Where growing in the border, put them near plants which bloom early and will give early spring protection. They will then have finished blooming and have begun to die back before the chrysanthemums make their bushy growth. Firm planting is essential and, as the plants will be small when set out, mark their position with a stick. It is essential that the young plants do not suffer from lack of moisture during their early days in the open ground, and during July and August weekly applications of manure water will enhance the size and colour of the blooms.

After flowering, the plants should be given a mulch of peat or decayed manure, which is placed around the roots, but not over them; by November next year's flowering shoots will have begun to appear, a second batch appearing in May when the soil begins to warm.

For two or three years the plants may remain undisturbed, after which time they should be lifted and divided in the usual way by using two forks. The old woody centre should be discarded. They may be lifted early in November each year following, or in alternate years, when propagation may be carried out in several ways. Gardeners who do not possess a greenhouse, or who do not

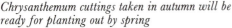
Chrysanthemum cuttings taken in autumn will be ready for planting out by spring

intend to propagate on a commercial scale, may remove the green shoots with a portion of root attached and plant these 4 in apart in a frame, over which is placed a glass light or a piece of windo-lite. There the young plants remain throughout winter, and will be ready for planting out again in April. The plants should be given almost no water during winter and, to prevent mildew, should be treated once a month with flowers of sulphur. Just before the plants are set out they should have the growing point removed to encourage them to build up a bushy plant. This is better done a week before they are moved, so as not to cause them any undue check. Plants obtained through the post and not already 'stopped', should not have the growing

point removed until they have become firmly settled in the ground.

Where it is not possible to use a frame, the plants should be left undisturbed throughout winter. In April, when the new shoots have appeared, they may then be lifted and the rooted offsets 'teased' away from the old root and replanted at once.

Koreans Varieties growing to about 2 ft are suitable for the small garden; those of taller habit should be confined to the larger garden or to the market garden. The following will provide autumn colour in the small garden:

'Caliph' A superb variety, bearing double blooms of deep blood-red. Early September.

'Carlene' A magnificent new variety, bearing huge double blooms of bright pure orange. Early August.

'Coral Mist' A new variety, coming into bloom early in August, and bearing a large single bloom of coral-pink.

'Dawn Pink' The large single blooms are of a pure shell-pink colour with a lovely silver sheen. Mid-September.

'Derby Day' The single blooms are of a rich shade of burnt orange. Early September.

'Eugene Wonder' Raised in America, the fully double blooms are a bright golden-yellow, flushed with orange. Mid-September.

'Honey Pot' For the front of the border. Makes a mound covered with small honey-coloured blooms. Mid-September.

'Margery Daw' The large single blooms are of a rich cerise-red, like the 'Harold Robinson' pyrethrum.

'Moonlight' The semi-double blooms are of a pale primrose-yellow. Early September.

'Polly Peachum' A new variety, bearing a large double bloom of deep peach-pink. Late August.

'Spindle Berry' The single blooms are of a rich shade of salmon-pink. Early September.

'Startler' Outstanding, the double blooms being of a deep shade of claret-pink. Early September.

'Sunny Day' One of the very best varieties, the double bloom canary-yellow, with a rich perfume. Mid-August.

'Tapestry Red' The fully double blooms are of deep crimson, with an attractive green centre. Early September.

'Tapestry Rose' The double flowers are of a soft rose-cerise colour, with an attractive green centre. Early October.

Pompons The habit of the Pompons is more compact than that of the Koreans, the button-like blooms being small, but produced in great freedom over a period of eight to ten weeks. The plants produce all their blooms at the same time, the latest opening by early October. They grow to a height of about 2 ft, and are ideal for an exposed garden.

'Andy Pandy' The stems are almost devoid of foliage and are covered with tiny ball-like blossoms of brilliant yellow.

'Babs' Dwarf, neat, and covered with interesting, flat, shell-pink blooms over a long period.

'Bob' Of compact habit, the plants cover themselves with tiny buttons of brilliant scarlet.

'Cream Bouquet' The small button-like blooms are of a rich cream colour and are borne in profusion.

'Denise' The habit is very compact, the plant coming into bloom towards the end of August, when it covers itself with rich golden-yellow blooms.

Fairie' The tight button-like blooms are of a most attractive shade of strawberry-pink.

'**Jante Wells**' Growing to a height of 2½ ft and bearing masses of golden-yellow buttons, this is an excellent cut-flower variety.

'**Kim**' It makes a plant of densely branched habit and bears masses of bronzy-scarlet blooms.

'**Lemon Bouquet**' One of the famous Bouquet series, which are excellent for cutting or for border decoration. The ball-shaped blooms are of a soft shade of lemon-yellow.

'**Lilac Daisy**' The large button-like blooms are of an attractive shade of dusky lilac-pink.

'**Little Dorrit**' Neat, button-like blooms of a deep shell-pink colour are produced in profusion.

'**Lustre**' Of most compact habit, it bears tiny flowers of the unusual shade of antique lustre ware.

A deep pink dahlia being grown specially for picking in a reserve garden

'**Masquerade**' A recent novelty, the flat button-like blooms are silvery-rose, with a dark pinky-brown centre.

'**Morcar Gem**' Of very dwarf habit, making a plant as wide as it grows tall, and bearing masses of rosy-apricot flowers.

'**Orange Lad**' The button-shaped blooms are of brilliant orange flushed with red at the centre.

'**Pat**' One of the most beautiful Pompons, the blooms being in the form of a double Michaelmas daisy; the petals are of a rich deep-pink colour.

'**Titania**' A new variety, bearing large ball-like blooms of rich amber-bronze.

'**Tommy Trout**' One of the most striking varieties, with flowers of rich coppery-amber.

'**White Bouquet**' The first pure white pom, being of similar habit to 'Jante Wells' and just as free-flowering.

DAHLIAS

No garden plant has been more greatly improved during recent years than the dahlia; to provide colour from July until the appearance of the first hard frost blackens the foliage, there are a number of varieties of dwarf compact habit which for quality of bloom rival those of more pretentious form. Dahlias growing up to 3 ft and bearing flowers of small decorative and cactus form produce quite as rich a display as the taller-growing varieties, and require only the minimum of support and protection from strong winds.

A pleasing use of the dwarf dahlias may be made by growing them in small circular beds, using varieties of contrasting colours, with those of slightly taller habit planted towards the centre. Or a small border of dahlias may be made, planting those which are taller-growing to the back, with those of more dwarf habit to the front.

Varieties of Merit for a Small Garden

'Anadonis' Grows to 30 in and bears flowers of Jersey cream colouring with attractively fimbrated petals.

'Apex' A miniature decorative of top class, bearing perfectly formed blooms of crimson-red.

'Brandaris' A small cactus growing 3 ft tall and bearing rich scarlet flowers with a gold centre.

'Broadacre' Grows about 30 in tall, its blunt-tipped flowers being of rich orange and borne on long stems.

'Cha-cha' A small cactus of unusual charm, the flowers being white, tipped with bright carmine-red.

'Cheerio' Growing to 3 ft, it bears its cherry-red flowers, tipped with white, on wiry stems.

'Chinese Lantern' A small decorative, 30 in tall, bearing vivid orange-scarlet blooms with a gold reverse.

'Dalhousie Peach' 2 ft tall and bears, in long succession, double blooms of small decorative type and of an attractive shade of peach-pink.

'Dedham' A small decorative and an exhibitor's favourite, the blooms being lilac, shading to white at the base.

'Delicious' Early flowering and growing to 3 ft, it bears multitudes of bright pink flowers of small cactus form. Excellent for cutting.

'Dr Grainger' A superb dahlia, bearing large ball-shaped flowers of rich clear orange.

'Downham' This variety is now firmly established as a bedding dahlia of excellence. It grows 18 in tall, bearing large semi-cactus blooms of brilliant pure yellow in endless profusion. It comes quickly into bloom, and its flowers have long stems which make them useful for indoor decoration.

'Dunshelt Flame' Grows just over 30 in tall and bears a profusion of bright scarlet blooms.

'Eclipse' A lovely variety, less than 30 in, and coming early into bloom. The small decorative blooms are orange overlaid with a unique shade of rosy-vermilion.

'Flame' One of the earliest to bloom. It grows 3 ft tall, and bears on long wiry stems blooms of bright apricot shaded with tangerine.

'Freeman' A truly magnificent variety, growing to about 30 in, its deep carmine-red flowers tipped with gold.

'Goya's Venus' A small cactus growing 3 ft in height, its deep orange flowers overlaid with salmon-pink.

'Hamari Fiesta' A small decorative and one of the most colourful of all dahlias, the canary-yellow flowers being shaded vermilion.

'Jill Edwards' A small cactus, the pale lemon blooms overlaid with pale pink.

'Langstem' A new variety growing 3 ft tall and bearing globular flowers which are of a delightful combination of apricot and gold colouring. It is one of the longest in bloom, and one of the most free-flowering of all dahlias.

'Lemon Hart' For best effect plant it with 'Market King', for it grows to a similar height and bears bright lemon-yellow flowers which have attractively quilled petals.

'Margaret Harris' It grows just over 30 in tall, bearing flowers of small cactus form, cream at the centre, the petals being tipped and edged with lilac-pink.

'Market King' Though growing to about 30 in it makes a compact bushy plant, and bears a bloom of the colour of a ripe tomato, the petals being veined with gold.

'Mary Broom' It grows 3 ft tall and is one of the most spectacular varieties ever raised. The blooms are almost globular, the small but wide pillar-box-red petals being tipped with white.

'Meiro' A small decorative of clearest mauve, the flowers being produced with freedom.

'Peach Bedder' Makes a bushy plant almost 2 ft tall, and bears masses of star-like blooms which are a bright apricot-orange rather than peach in colouring.

'Procyon' The small decorative blooms are a brilliant combination of scarlet and gold.

'Rival' Grows to a similar height as 'Market King', and bears a profusion of semi-cactus blooms of bright rose-cerise on long wiry stems.

'Rothesay Castle' Grows to only 18 in, comes early into bloom, and is most free-flowering. The flowers are a combination of cream overlaid with rose-pink.

'Stonyhurst' An excellent dahlia for the small garden, growing little more than 2 ft high and bearing masses of exhibition-quality blooms of uniform cherry-red.

'Sweet Auburn' A recent introduction, growing to only 20 in and bearing auburn and gold blooms of cactus form, which often measure 4 in across.

'Vigor' A small decorative, bearing masses of sulphur-yellow flowers on long wiry stems.

'White Rays' This is a pure white small cactus of great merit, bearing its blooms with freedom until well into November, unless terminated earlier by frost.

Sprouting and Planting A heated greenhouse is not essential to grow dahlias; indeed a greenhouse is not necessary at all. The tubers may be started into growth in a cold frame, or even in deep boxes placed in a sunny position outdoors and covered with a sheet of glass. Additional protection may be provided by heaping soil, sand or straw around the boxes. Where the tubers are to be started

Dahlias can be grown from tip cuttings to flower the following year

without artificial warmth they will be later in coming into growth, though if spring brings more than average sunshine, the tubers will have made sufficient growth when planted out early in June and will soon come into bloom.

The tubers should not be planted before 1 April for until that time there will not be sufficient heat from the sun to stimulate them into growth. Also, as they should not be planted out until the frosts have gone, which will be during the first days of June, it is not advisable for the tubers to make excessive growth before that time. If the shoots are about 12 in high when they are planted out they will withstand the moving without any undue 'flagging', provided they are not allowed to lack moisture.

The tubers should be quite plump and clean when planted and, if they have to be stored for any length of time, they should be placed in boxes of sand in a frost-free room away from a fire or any form of central heating which will cause them to shrivel. They should be planted on a layer of peat placed either in the boxes or on the floor of a frame. The tubers may be packed quite close together, a mixture of peat and sterilized loam being pressed about them so that there will be no air spaces, and just covered with compost. Give them a thorough soaking, place the glass in position, and all that is necessary during the next two months is to keep them comfortably moist and to ventilate by day as the sun gathers strength.

When all fear of frost has vanished, the tubers should be planted out, and they must be moved with care so that the shoots are not damaged. The holes, sufficiently large to accommodate the tubers, must be made before the dahlias are removed from the pots, so that they may be set out in their flowering quarters with the least possible delay and disturbance. Do not bury the tubers too deeply. They should have about $\frac{1}{2}$ in of soil over the top after being placed on a layer of peat. To prevent damage from strong winds, the shoots are given some support by means of stout twigs, and never must the tubers be allowed to lack moisture. Dahlias are copious drinkers and heavy feeders, so incorporate decayed manure or bonemeal into the soil before planting, in addition to giving a liberal dressing of peat. The plants will also benefit from a top dressing of peat given during the last days of July.

Set out the tubers about 2 ft apart or, better than planting all varieties at the

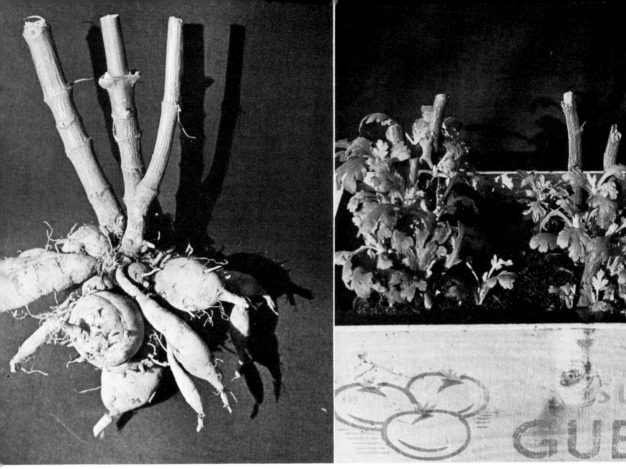

Dahlia tubers lifted, washed, trimmed clean and dried ready for winter storage

same distance apart, allow the same amount of space between the plants as their eventual height.

During an average autumn the plants will continue to bloom until the end of October, or even well into the middle of November, when the tubers should be lifted with care and cleaned of all surplus soil. After drying in a cool, airy room, they are placed into boxes of sand or ashes to remain there until required for starting into growth again in April. To prevent mildew, it is advisable to dust the tubers with flowers of sulphur before storing.

MICHAELMAS DAISIES

The culture of *Aster novi-belgii* presents few difficulties. It is a moisture-loving plant and, like the phlox, is always at its best in a heavy, humus-laden soil; where growing in a light soil the plant blooms at its best only during a wet season. Because the plant puts up a brave display in all soils, in a position of semi-shade or full sun, its real requirements for the highest quality of bloom have been overlooked. In this respect it has suffered in the same way as the montbretia and flag iris. Grown in a soil retentive of moisture, the size of the bloom and the depth of colour of the modern varieties will surprise those who have seen this plant growing only under adverse conditions. Where the soil is a heavy clay, work in some grit and a quantity of peat to assist winter drainage. This is one of the few plants to succeed in a heavy clay soil provided it is reasonably well drained in winter. An ordinary soil will require almost no attention. No rank manure

fibre. Place it around the plants, and when the border is cleaned in late autumn the material may be worked in to provide much-appreciated additional humus.

Planting may be done at any time from the end of October until the end of March, but as the plants must not lack moisture during their first weeks in the border, November planting is greatly to be preferred where the soil is light. A dry spring could prevent the plants from getting away to a good start, which would mean that they would provide little colour in their first year. Set the plants 2 ft apart where planting at the back of the border and 18 in apart where planting towards the front, spreading out the roots. Plant deeply so as to prevent the roots drying out by strong winds, or from being lifted from the ground by early frosts before they have taken a firm hold.

For the small garden, only varieties of compact habit should be grown. Plant those growing to about 3 ft at the back of the border, with the dwarf hybrids to the front. The mid-border plants will require only the minimum of staking, just sufficient to prevent the plants from 'spreading' when in full bloom, when their rich colourings would not show to the best advantage. A strong stake should be placed at the back of the plant so that it remains unseen. Around the plant green twine is loosely tied. The stems should in no way be bunched together. The more compact front-of-the-border varieties should not require support.

The plants should be divided every three years, and nothing could be more simple. It is quite possible to divide without having to lift the whole root. Merely remove the sections with an efficient trowel. When planting in groups of three, one plant may be lifted and

should be given, for this would encourage mildew, harming both foliage and bloom, a trouble to which many varieties are unfortunately susceptible where the soil is too rich. A light, sandy soil should have as much humus as possible incorporated, and this may take the form of material from the compost heap, or used hops, peat or leaf-mould. Where the soil is not retentive of summer moisture, growth will be stunted and the blooms small. Old mushroom-bed compost suits the plants well, but it is necessary to supply unlimited moisture rather than an excess of nitrogenous manures. The plants, however, are deep rooting, and impoverished soil will quickly bring about a deterioration in vigour, the foliage turning brown instead of being an attractive glossy green. The plants also appreciate a mulch given during mid-summer. This may be of peat, old mushroom compost, or bark divided in November after two years, another after three years, and the third the following year, so that at no time will there be any shortage of bloom in the border, nor will there be any plants which have lost vigour. When dividing older plants, it is the outside parts of the plant which are the most vigorous; the woody centre should not be retained.

Older plants may be divided by the usual method of using two forks, but this is necessary only where there is a large amount of old wood at the centre. Plants which are lifted and divided frequently may readily be split up into small offsets. These may be grown on in a bed for twelve months before replanting in the border. When required for immediate replanting, the roots should be divided into only three or four pieces, each containing several new shoots.

A well-grown pale yellow dahlia. Note that the supporting strings are out of sight

Where it is considered necessary to increase a new variety quickly, cuttings 3 in long may be taken early in May and inserted into a frame containing a compost of peat and sand. The same root, which may be an expensive new variety, will then produce further offsets which may be removed in autumn with their roots attached.

Selected Varieties (to 3 ft) To assist gardeners who are making a new border, perhaps with the idea that it should be devoted entirely to michaelmas daisies, the following list contains a selection of the finest of the new varieties growing no more than 3 ft tall. Prolong the display by including in any collection some of the earlies, such as 'Fontaine' and 'Tapestry', some mid-season, and some that come later into bloom and remain colourful until the end of November. Two very late varieties are 'Charmwood' and 'Royal Velvet'.

'Alpenglow' Forms a plant of stiff pyramidal habit and covers itself with bright rosy-red flowers. Early. 2 ft.

'Beechwood Challenger' The crimson-red blooms are small, but have attractively quilled petals. Mid-season. $2\frac{1}{4}$ ft.

'Blue Radiance' A recent introduction forming a compact bushy plant covered in masses of star-like flowers of brightest blue. Mid-season. $2\frac{1}{2}$ ft.

'Carnival' The fully double blooms are of clear crimson-red and borne in profusion. Flowers mid-season and grows to about $2\frac{1}{2}$ ft.

'Charmwood' One of a new trio of a similar habit to 'Winston Churchill', being excellent for cutting. The blooms are of a vivid rose-pink colour. Late. 3 ft.

'Chartwell' The richly coloured blooms are rich violet-purple, flushed with crimson. Late. 3 ft.

'Chequers' Of similar habit to 'Winston Churchill', the flowers are a rich violet-purple. Early. 2½ ft.

'Eventide' An outstanding variety, bearing large flowers of a deep purple-blue. Early. 3 ft.

'Fellowship' A glorious variety bearing masses of fully double blooms of a lovely shade of deep shell-pink. Mid-season. 3½ ft.

'F. M. Simpson' The largest-flowered variety, the semi-double blooms being of glowing purple. Early. 3 ft.

'Fontaine' Similar in habit to 'Tapestry' and just as beautiful. The large shaggy blooms are of a lovely shade of tawny-pink with an orange eye. Very early. 2¾ ft.

'Gayborder Royal' Best described as doge-purple, the blooms are of exquisite form. Mid-season. 2½ ft.

'Jean Gyte' The blooms measure 2 in across and are fully double. They are deep carmine-red with quilled petals. Mid-season. 3 ft.

'Jezebel' For the front of the border where in early autumn it will be a mass of glowing red. Early. 2 ft.

'John Shearer' A new variety, bearing a bloom of deep wine-blue. Early. 3 ft.

'Lassie' The semi-double blooms with their conspicuous yellow centre are a pure shade of apple-blossom pink. Early. 3 ft.

'Malvern Queen' The semi-double blooms are of a rich deep-pink colouring, the habit of the plant being ideal. Late. 2¾ ft.

'Melbourne Early Red' A link between the dwarf hybrids and those of taller habit. The garnet-red flowers are produced with freedom. Early-flowering and grow up to about 2 ft.

'Percy Thrower' An outstanding new variety, the deep amethyst-blue flowers having a silver reverse to the petals. Mid-season. 3 ft.

Pinching out the growing tip of a dahlia to make the plant more bushy

'Red Sunset' Of more compact habit than the earlier Beechwood varieties; the petunia-crimson blooms are borne in great profusion. Early. 2½ ft.

'Royal Velvet' Very new and, with its bright violet blooms, freedom of flowering and resistance to mildew, it is certain to become a favourite. Late. 3 ft.

'Rufus' A beautiful variety, bearing double blooms of a rich shade of reddish-plum. Early. 2 ft.

'Schoolgirl' One of the finest pink varieties, the blooms being large and fully double and of a unique shade of glowing cyclamen pink. Late. 3 ft.

'Sputnik' Released in 1960 and a beautiful variety, bearing arching sprays of double blooms of a most attractive shade of soft shell-pink. Early. 2½ ft.

'Tapestry' Ernest Ballard's favourite, and he raised more good varieties than anyone. The habit is ideal, requiring no staking; the huge shaggy blooms are of a glorious shade of pastel-pink. Very early. $2\frac{1}{2}$ ft.

'Violet Lady' Of bushy habit. The blooms are borne in profusion and are a deep violet-blue. Early. 2 ft.

'Winston Churchill' The blooms are not large but borne in profusion and are a vivid shade of beetroot-red. Mid-season. $2\frac{1}{2}$ ft.

Early

'Alpenglow'
'Chequers'
'Eventide'
'F. M. Simpson'
'Fontaine'
'Jezebel'
'John Shearer'
'Lassie'
'Red Sunset'
'Rufus'
'Sputnik'
'Tapestry'
'Violet Lady'

Mid-season

'Blue Radiance'
'Carnival'
'Fellowship'
'Gayborder Royal'
'Jean Gyte'
'Percy Thrower'
'Winston Churchill'

Late

'Charmwood'
'Chartwell'
'Malvern Queen'
'Royal Velvet'
'Schoolgirl'

Dwarf Hybrids For planting at the front of a border, or as an edging to a path, in small beds, or about a rock garden to provide autumnal colour, the dwarf asters are most charming. Most bloom over a long period, from early September until the beginning of November.

'Alice Haslam' This new variety is the best 'red' dwarf yet raised. It makes a tiny bushy plant, covering itself with bright cerise-red flowers. 8 in.

'Audrey' The large blooms, which completely smother the plant, are a delicate shade of pastel-blue. 15 in.

'Autumn Princess' A new variety, the semi-double blooms being a brilliant lavender-blue. 15 in.

'Court Herald' A new introduction, forming a compact mound of soft rosy-lilac flowers. 10 in.

'Dandy' The medium-sized blooms are bright rosy-red and produced over a long period. 12 in.

'Hebe' Not nearly so well known as it should be; the bloom is a rich shade of strawberry-pink. 10 in.

'Lady in Blue' A new variety of compact habit, bearing masses of semi-double mid-blue flowers. 9 in.

'Little Blue Baby' A perfect miniature, the tiny rounded plants being smothered in sky-blue flowers. 6 in.

'Little Red Boy' Until there is a real crimson variety, this plant with its rose-pink blooms is a good substitute. 12 in.

'Niobe' The single pure white blooms are borne in profusion. 9 in.

'Pink Lace' A new variety likely to become a favourite, the double blooms being of a lovely shade of clear pink. 15 in.

Chapter 7

COLOURFUL ANNUALS

An annual is a plant that completes its life within a single year, though a number of those classed as annuals may, if hardy, be treated as biennials and be sown the year previous to that in which they will bloom. In this way they grow sturdier and come earlier into bloom. Both annuals and biennials are grown from seed and it is correct to say that they will bloom within twelve months of sowing the seed.

Annuals may be classed as (a) hardy and (b) half-hardy. Hardy annuals will usually withstand the winter unprotected if sown the previous autumn (and treated as biennials), or they may be sown in spring, where they are to bloom, possibly under cloches if early bloom is required. Half-hardy annuals are generally raised under glass by sowing the seed early in the year, possibly in gentle heat, and planting out early in summer when fear of frost has vanished; or they may be planted out after hardening, in late spring, and given cloche protection until the frosts and cold winds have departed.

Annuals may be used for bedding or grown for cut flowers for home decoration or the market; they can be sown or planted in small groups about the herbaceous border or shrubbery to fill in any gaps caused by winter losses amongst perennial plants or shrubs. Their other virtues are that they are inexpensive, come quickly into bloom, are of easy culture, and are labour-saving if sown where they are to bloom. Many flower for four or five months for an outlay of only a few pence. By using modern strains for bedding, staking is eliminated, whilst freedom of flowering leaves little to be desired.

For rapidity in coming into bloom and for providing a continuation of the spring display, annuals are difficult to better. Early in July, almost as soon as the later-flowering tulips and the polyanthus have finished flowering, the annuals are ready to take over if they have been set out between the plants of the spring display. This should be done early in May if the annuals are hardy or at the end of the month if only half-hardy; or seed may be sown in the open ground where the plants are to bloom. There will thus be a continuation of bloom from the same beds from early April until early November and, moreover, the ground may be cleared entirely of plants and weeds at the end of the season, ready and perfectly clean to commence again the following summer, or to plant at once with bulbs or spring-flowering biennials. The ground is thus kept free from weeds which are difficult to eradicate from a herbaceous border, whilst the soil does not become sour or ridden with pests or disease. Beginning each season with clean ground makes for very little weeding through the summer when there are so many other jobs about the garden to demand attention.

Annuals also fit well into rotational cropping, especially with tulips and spring-flowering biennials which finish flowering during June; the beds may be cleared completely, thoroughly cleaned and replanted the same day with summer annuals.

When using window boxes, suitable annuals may be planted amongst the dying foliage of spring-flowering bulbs such as crocus and dwarf tulips, hyacinths or primroses, and they will be ready to take over the flowering soon after the spring display has ended. For window boxes there is a wide range of annuals with a dwarf, neat habit, whilst for tubs about the garden or round a courtyard, those with a trailing habit are charming when draped around the outside of the tubs with taller subjects in the centre. Here again the plants may be set out as soon as the bulb display has ended, without any disturbance to the soil or bulbs. By this means one can achieve a succession of flowers with little trouble.

Remember to select a position of full sun for the annual display; they are never happy too near tall trees, or where adjoining property casts its shadows to shut out almost all the summer sunshine. But even in these conditions certain plants will put up a brave show. With annuals there is something for every garden.

PLANTING FOR MAXIMUM EFFECT

Annuals, then, may be used in various ways: for edging, for carpeting, for spring and summer bedding, or planted about the border or shrubbery, and in rows or beds for cutting. The range of plants is so extensive that a garden may be a thing of great beauty by the use of annuals alone. But in whatever manner they are used, they will only reveal their full glory when planted in mass. The odd plant dotted here and there about the garden will appear insignificant, lost amidst the foliage of the garden, but plant the same plants in beds or in clumps of a dozen or so and the effect will be one of great brilliance. This does not mean that the plants should be crowded together in such a way as to give them little room in which to develop in their natural form. This would be a waste of plants and would not enable them to give of their best; but to plant in groups, correctly spaced, will be to ensure that the plants reveal their maximum brilliance. In this respect the annual has moved far from its reputation of a century ago, when Robert Thompson, then in charge of the Royal Horticultural Society's gardens at Chiswick, wrote, 'a large proportion have a weedy appearance and are but ill-suited for the decoration of the flower garden'. Perhaps this really was the case when Thompson wrote his *Gardener's Assistant*, but since that time the annual has been developed out of all recognition.

PROPAGATION OF ANNUALS— GENERAL

Perennial plants are propagated either by division of the rootstock or from cuttings, for only in this way will a true stock be obtained. Annuals, however, are almost entirely propagated by sowing seed, the modern strains being most reliable in producing a plant which will bear a bloom differing in no respect from the parent variety whilst the F_1 hybrids assure greater vigour and freedom of flowering.

Raising plants from seed is both inexpensive and satisfying; it is in fact the easiest method of plant propagation. One does not have to be gifted with so-called 'green fingers' to be able to manage the sowing and raising of most annuals. A child can do it—indeed most gardeners will recollect their first tiny gardens where they sowed Virginian stock and marigolds from vividly coloured packets, and their joy at the successful germination and flowering. There is still the same enjoyment to be had from the sowing of annuals, but there is far more to it than sprinkling a packet of seed about the garden in spring.

For sowing purposes, annuals may be divided into five distinct groups:

(1) Those plants that have so hardy a constitution as to permit them to be sown in autumn, and wintered unprotected in the open. The same plants may also be sown in early spring as soon as the frost has left the ground, but are better given biennial treatment. They may be called 'extremely hardy' rather than just 'hardy'.

(2) Then there are those which are quite hardy and may be wintered under a cold frame or under cloches in the north of England, though in the more favoured areas of the south-west they would come to no harm if unprotected. The same plants may be sown in gentle heat in a greenhouse early in the new year and planted out late in spring after hardening.

(3) Another group, which may be classed as only partially hardy, or half-hardy, may either be raised in a heated greenhouse early in the year, or sowing may be delayed until the coldest weather

has passed, the seed then being sown in a frame or greenhouse or even under cloches in early April. In any case these plants cannot be set out until all fear of frost has departed.

(4) There is yet another group which by their nature and habit possess a shorter flowering season than other annuals and which respond best to sowing directly into the position in which they are to bloom. Whereas the calendula is in bloom from May until October from an autumn sowing, the viscaria and Virginian stock flower only for a short season during July and August, and however early the seed may be sown the season cannot be prolonged. There is thus no reason for sowing in any other way than directly where the plants are to bloom.

In this group may also be placed all those plants which resent transplanting and which are better sown where they are to bloom. Many of these also give a display of richness only over a relatively short period, and even if they were tolerant of transplanting there would be little point in it. These plants are generally used for sowing about a border or shrubbery or in those odd corners about the garden which are devoid of colour. They may also be used on a rockery or for making an annual border. They are indispensable members of the race of annual plants and are possibly used in greater numbers than any of the others.

(5) Into this last group fall those plants which, though not correctly annuals, are allowed to bloom for a single season and so are treated as such. These include the biennials (bi-annuals), and certain plants really of perennial habit. After all, the antirrhinum is a true perennial, but it has become so much a part, possibly the chief part, of the summer display of annuals that it cannot be treated separately from them.

In the first group, sowing and care of the plants present no difficulties. Into this group come many of the annuals used for cut-flower purposes: larkspur, calendulas, annual gypsophila, nigella (love-in-a-mist), cornflowers and Shirley pop-pies, all of which may be sown in a prepared bed in the open ground.

It is important to select a sunny position, and one sheltered from the prevailing winds. Especially is this vital where cold winds blow off the sea or across low-lying land and cause 'burning', or browning, of the foliage. The seed may be sown where the plants are to bloom, as for larkspur and nigella which seem to resent transplanting, or the plants are moved in spring to the beds where they are to bloom, as in the case of calendulas. Plants which are to be moved may be sown in dappled shade, such as is provided by an orchard, but those sown where they are to bloom must receive ample sunshine. These remarks apply also to plants in group 5, which, though they are sown at a different time, are given similar treatment to group 1 annuals.

AUTUMN SOWING IN OPEN GROUND

Annuals sown in autumn should have made sufficient growth to be able to withstand a hard winter, yet the plants themselves must be grown 'hard'. A soft plant making excessive foliage will be 'burnt' by cold winds, so guard against too much manure. Soil containing a little old mushroom-bed manure, some spent hops, or peat, will prove ideal provided it is well drained and friable. Soil from which winter moisture cannot drain away will be quite unsuitable for the autumn sowing of annuals.

The seed should be sown early in September so that the plants will be just the correct size by November. In the north it is advisable to sow the seed towards the end of August, for the plants will make little growth after the end of September. But first bring the soil to a friable tilth containing few stones. Where the plants are to remain in the sowing quarters to flower, it is advisable to work in a small quantity, say 2 oz per sq yd, of bonemeal, which will release its food value at a time when the plants are making growth late in spring. To help the plants through winter, the soil should be given a dressing of 1 oz sulphate of potash per sq yd. This will build up a 'hard' plant and the potash will also increase the quality and richness of colouring of the blooms. It is important to sow in a soil which is not short of lime, and this should have been applied the previous winter or well before the seed is to be sown. Allow the soil to settle down and consolidate before sowing—in a loose seed bed the tiny seedlings may collapse owing to their roots not being in full contact with the soil. Some gardeners go so far as to roll the ground before sowing, but this should only be done where the soil is light and sandy. It must be remembered that where plants are to bloom where they are sown they will occupy the land for almost twelve months, so the ground should be well prepared and must be well drained.

The seed is sown in drills about 15 in apart to allow ample room for development. Always sow thinly and thin out the seedlings as soon as large enough to handle if they appear overcrowded.

The drills are made $1\frac{1}{2}$ in deep, with the back of a rake. Too deep sowing is not advisable and in a heavy soil 1 in is quite enough. The seed should not be sown when the soil is too wet.

The common sunflower, Helianthus annuus, *among the most spectacular of all annuals*

Always use seed from a reliable seed house and choose modern varieties which have proved their worth. Seed of inferior quality is never worth the time taken in sowing. And sow fresh seed, for if it is a year or two old it may not be reliable and will not give quick germination. It is always better to obtain exactly the right amount each year so that none is left over.

Never at any time must the seed or the young plants be allowed to suffer from lack of moisture. A soil containing some humus will retain moisture to a greater degree than one without, but all the same check that the soil is comfortably moist. The sun will have lost much of its strength by the time the seed is sown in early autumn.

Apart from thinning any overcrowded plants, the seedlings will require almost no attention other than the placing of twiggy branches about the rows to provide slight protection from cold winds. Weeding will not be necessary if the seed was sown in clean ground, but the hoe may be taken between the rows and the soil slightly drawn up on either side of the plants as a protection against cold winds.

These extremely hardy annuals may also be sown in prepared seed beds in early spring, early in March in the south, at the end of the month in the north; but the plants will be a month later than autumn-sown plants in coming into bloom. A spring sowing, as well as an autumn one, is often made of plants that have a fairly short flowering season, so as to extend the flowering period right through summer. Also, if gardening in a cold, exposed position and in a heavy clay soil, there may, in a severe winter, be considerable losses from an autumn sowing.

Top left   Dicentra spectabilis.
Right   Dahlia 'Enterprise'.
Below   pond and paving

SOWING WITH WINTER PROTECTION

The second group of annuals were those requiring glass protection through winter —they include antirrhinums, sweet peas and Brompton stocks. Here again it must be realized that these plants will produce an earlier and more vigorous display from autumn-sown seed than if sown in heat in the new year, which is an alternative method.

Value of a Cold Frame   There are several ways of providing protection, by using a cold greenhouse, frames or cloches, but of these frames are the most satisfactory.

For those who wish to raise their own annuals both for garden display and for cutting, a frame will be indispensable not only for wintering certain annuals but for hardening off those plants raised in heat. The ideal is to have two frames available, their size depending upon the size of the garden and the number of plants needed to stock it. In one frame are placed the boxes of plants sown in autumn, and when these are removed early in April for planting out, seed may be sown of the half-hardy annuals; the other frame may be kept for hardening, or if half-hardy plants are grown in heat as they frequently are, then the one frame would be sufficient.

A cold frame may be quite cheaply constructed from old railway sleepers which have been creosoted and are therefore free from disease; or any stout boards may be used. As an alternative, bricks or breeze blocks are equally suitable. They are durable and should remain free from pest or disease.

It is advisable to use a strong new frame light rather than chance a second-hand one which may in any case be very difficult to clean thoroughly. Any form of glass used to accommodate plants must be kept really clean otherwise the plants will become drawn and weakly through lack of sunlight. This is of particular importance where plants are being grown under glass in an industrial town.

The size of light should be 5×4 ft, certainly no larger, otherwise it will prove too heavy for the women of the household to move and it is they who so often must attend to midday watering, shading and ventilation during spring.

No particular care need be given the soil in the frame unless plants are to be transplanted, or seed sown, directly in it rather than into boxes accommodated there. In this case the frame soil must be well drained, friable and porous, yet containing some moisture-holding humus. Incorporate some peat or leaf mould together with some coarse sand, then immediately before planting or sowing gently press down this compost. Set out the plants 3 in apart, planting them firmly.

Raising the Plants The seed of these less hardy plants will have been sown late in August or early September either in boxes or pots of prepared compost, or directly into the compost of the frame. Always sow thinly, either in drills 4 in apart or broadcast. The seed of sweet peas and zinnias is often sown singly in Jiffy pots, the plants giving a better display if they have no root disturbance.

The compost for the seed sown in pots or boxes, whether this is to go under frames or in a heated greenhouse, should be of the John Innes formula:

2 parts loam
1 part coarse sand
1 part peat   per bushel
$1\frac{1}{2}$ oz superphosphate
$\frac{3}{4}$ oz ground limestone

This compost is suitable for the raising of all annuals from seed.

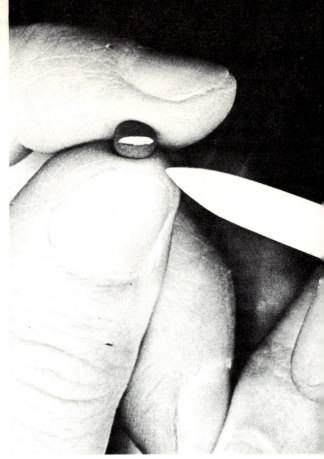

'Nicking' the seeds of sweet peas. Take care not to damage the fleshy seed inside

Use kipper boxes or special seed boxes which are made in easily handled sizes and about 2 in deep. Earthenware seed pans are also suitable. Make certain that the containers are quite clean. They should be scrubbed before being filled with compost. The compost must be stored in a dry place and away from frost if being used during winter.

The thinly sown seed is just covered with compost and kept comfortably moist though not in any way saturated. The boxes or pans may be stood in a partially shaded position in the open, each box being covered with a sheet of clean glass; or they may be placed in the frames to germinate. When large enough to handle, the seedlings are pricked out into boxes of four dozen plants each, or directly into frames, where they remain throughout the winter, being watered only on rare occasions and given ventilation whenever the sun is warm. Excessive watering between November and early March, whilst the plants are more or less dormant, will cause them to damp off. Ventilation is important, for the plants must be grown as 'hard' as possible; they require no coddling, being quite hardy even though winter protection is desirable in some parts.

SOWING IN HEAT

Plants which may be classed as being only half-hardy, those of group 3, are sown either over a mild hot-bed in early March or in a warm greenhouse early in the new year. It is quite possible to sow seed in a cold frame in April or even in the open ground at the month end, but whilst some degree of success may be obtained the plants will come very much later into bloom. This means that though they provide colour in the garden during late summer and autumn they may be cut off by frost long before they have finished flowering.

Plants sown in heat or over a hot-bed will be ready for hardening off by mid-April and may be planted out towards the end of May, depending upon climatic conditions. They will come into bloom before the end of June, a month before those sown in cold frames and six weeks earlier than those sown in the open ground.

Seed sown in the warmth of a greenhouse will require more attention than that sown under cool conditions. It needs to be watered more often and greater care must be given to ventilation. When watering seedlings, give the box a thorough soaking so that the moisture penetrates to the roots. Failure frequently occurs through too light watering, the roots

Sowing sweet pea seeds. These should be lightly pressed on to the soil

tending to grow to the surface in search of moisture.

High temperatures are not required, between 45 °F and 50 °F (7–10 °C) being ideal; if too hot, the plants will grow soft and lanky and collapse with the first cool wind when planted in the open. Neither should the greenhouse be too humid. A close, stuffy atmosphere will encourage disease and contribute to a weakly plant, so ventilate on all suitable occasions. To prevent risk of frost damage, all plants should be watered during winter before midday so that any surplus moisture will be dried off before nightfall.

Where growing in heat the plants should be kept as close to the light as possible. If the greenhouse bench is not of a suitable height, shelves should be placed close to the glass and the boxes placed on these.

It is important to prick off the seedlings as soon as they are large enough to handle, otherwise they become drawn. Remove by means of a dibber, holding the seedlings carefully but firmly and making them quite firm in their new boxes. After transplanting, see that the boxes are thoroughly watered.

BUYING FROM GROWERS

It is realized that not all annual plants, biennials included, which are to be used for spring and summer display will be raised by those who are to plant them. Some gardeners may not be able to find the time to prick out young seedlings and to rear them to planting size, with all the business of specially prepared composts and attention to watering and ventilation. Where half-hardy annuals are being used for bedding, lobelia, alyssum, phlox drummondii, etc, the gardener may not have facilities at his disposal for their correct cultivation. A need for only a few such plants, in the case of a small garden, would not warrant the use of a heated greenhouse, or even of a hot-bed, supposing it possible to use either.

There are specialist growers who supply annuals for every purpose of garden display and for cutting. Many advertise their plants through the gardening and daily press, and in most cases can be relied upon to send through the post a well-grown plant, well-packed, and likely to give satisfaction if planted into a soil which has received average treatment. It must, however, be emphasized once more that certain plants will succeed only under certain conditions. In a heavy soil and in a garden troubled by cold winds, the zinnia will have but little chance of success however well grown the plants may be.

What Constitutes Good and Bad Plants Not all nurserymen who advertise annuals in spring and summer send out a plant worthy of their calling. So often they are 'drawn' and of a pale yellow colour, denoting that they have been raised in considerable heat, often sown late as a second batch, under almost forcing conditions. They are hurriedly hardened off and sent out, far from being sufficiently hardened for colder regions. As soon as planted out they wilt under the first puff of wind, and it will take several weeks for them to revive, if indeed they ever do so.

Or the plants may have been sown too soon and been left in the boxes far too long awaiting transplanting, or even for long after having been transplanted. Some plants may have been moved to a none-too-suitable compost early in spring and hardened off in the normal way, only to be left in the boxes until well into June, by which time they have become woody, the boxes being root bound and the individual plants lacking moisture and food. Here again these plants will have their work cut out to give satisfaction.

They will be helped during a wet summer, or by a moist period immediately after planting when they may take in the much-needed moisture, but if dry conditions prevail after planting out they will never make suitable growth. They will come quickly into bloom and finish just as quickly.

The art of growing good annuals, whether for bedding or for planting for cut bloom, is in correct timing, as in growing outdoor tomatoes. The well-grown annual plant should be a rich medium-green; if it is too yellow in colour this signifies the use of too much heat and indicates that the plant has not been correctly hardened. Such a plant should be rejected.

A good plant should also be short jointed, sturdy and compact. Again, those long lanky plants which flop over should be avoided. If they cannot be replaced, they may be made to give a reasonable display by pinching out the main shoot to an inch or so of ground level after planting, to encourage more compact, bushy growth. The modern strains of bedding annuals are now noted for their compact habit but there is little use in the hybridist giving us plants with such valuable assets if the grower cancels out their good qualities by poor cultural methods. The same remarks apply to raising plants at home. Whether grown or bought, the result should be the same in the end, ie a healthy vigorous plant by the time it is required for planting out.

HARDENING THE PLANTS

Hardening the more tender annuals is of the utmost importance, for no matter how carefully the plants have been raised, all the good work will be nullified if the plants are not properly hardened before planting out. It should be said that those hardy annuals given the winter protection of a cold frame or cloches require almost no hardening apart from the removal of the glass by day from mid-March until early April, with its replacement each evening. Plants grown in heat take three weeks for hardening, ie for the plants to become gradually accustomed to outdoor conditions. The process of hardening must be gradual and it is of no use being able to raise the tender annuals in heat if there are not proper facilities available for their hardening.

Plants will be ready for setting out according to site and situation and upon the varying degree of hardiness enjoyed by the plants. For instance, the antirrhinum or marigold, raised in gentle heat, can be planted out three weeks or so before plants of a less hardy nature. Likewise, gardeners living in the south and south midland areas of Britain may commence hardening a fortnight earlier than northern gardeners; and those in the south-west even a fortnight earlier still. Again, much depends upon the season. In the spring of 1955 in Britain there was severely cold weather lasting almost until the end of May, so that hardening of the tender annuals was delayed as long as possible and in the north did not commence until the beginning of May.

There is always the desire to hurry on the hardening operations in the natural desire to have the plants into bloom at the earliest possible moment, but it is disappointing to see plants which have been given so much care and attention during the first three or four months of the year suffer a severe set-back simply because of one's impatience.

Hardening operations can be started even whilst the plants are growing in heat by the simple procedures of reducing the temperature and providing more and more ventilation as the heat of the sun gathers strength. Open up the roof ventilators of the greenhouse, but guard against draughts caused by a half-opened door, and always open the ventilator windows away from the prevailing winds. Cold winds of March can play havoc with a batch of healthy-looking seedlings. And take care to see that the ventilators are closed and the temperature increased by nightfall, for a frost, even if only light, may also put an end to all the previous good work.

It will be about mid-April when the plants are taken from the greenhouse to commence the real process of hardening, a little later in cold districts, though much depends upon the prevailing weather. Never fall into the trap of hastening the hardening process because a mild April is experienced. More often than not the following month will be severely troubled by frosts and cold winds. No matter how mild the late spring weather, it is not safe to give plants their freedom until all fear of frost has departed, which is seldom before 1 June, though all but the most tender can be planted out during the latter days of May. In colder areas, however, the spring bedding display of biennials and bulbs will frequently, due to a late spring, occupy the ground until mid-June and the summer bedding plants must wait their turn. This is why it is important not to have the plants too long in the boxes in case they become root bound before mid-June. This is where inter-planting proves its worth, for where polyanthus and violas and various bulbs are used for the spring display, the summer-flowering annuals may be set out between the spring-flowering plants at the correct time and even slightly earlier —say by mid-May—for they will receive protection from the already established spring plants. This will get them away to a really good start.

There is no better way of hardening the plants than by the use of a cold frame, however roughly it is put together. Should it be necessary to move the boxes to the frame whilst the weather is still very cold, additional warmth may be provided if soil or, better still, hot-bed manure is heaped around the sides of the frame and the light is covered at night with sacking. If the heated greenhouse is required for an early crop of tomatoes it may be necessary to move annuals out by 1 April, but normally they should go into the hardening frame towards the middle of the month, the lights being placed over the plants, ventilation at first being given during daytime only. In case of frost it is advisable to cover with sacking in the evening for the first week or ten days.

This stage of hardening off should again be gradual, and towards the end of April ventilation may be given at night. Then during early May the lights may be removed half-way, and finally altogether, the material of the frame being sufficient to keep frost and cold winds from the plants until they are ready to go out towards the month end.

Where no garden frames are available, boxes of half-hardy annuals may still be satisfactorily hardened by using barn-type cloches wide enough to take a standard-size box. The cloches may be covered with sacking or hessian canvas for the first nights and gradually more air may be admitted, on the pattern outlined above, using the cloches as if they were miniature frames, until finally the top glass is removed. Or the cloches may be placed on their sides against the prevailing wind for the final hardening off.

PLANTING OUT

When the plants have been hardened and kept growing on by careful attention to watering, so that the soil is sufficiently moist to prevent the formation of a hard woody plant, they should be planted out at the first opportunity. If cold winds persist, it is better to wait a few days.

To complete the hardening, the plants should be removed to the beds where they are to be planted several days before they are set out. This will give them the opportunity to sample the conditions where they are to bloom, yet they will still have the protection of each other. Water them well, thoroughly soaking the compost in the box so that it will adhere to the roots when the plants are removed from the boxes. Plants grown in one's own garden or purchased from a local nurseryman in the boxes may thus be planted out with a large ball of soil on the roots. This gets them away to a better start than plants purchased through the post, which will be almost devoid of soil upon arrival. However well grown the plants, there is sure to be a check if the roots are so disturbed. Plants whose roots are disturbed as little as possible will come into bloom considerably earlier than where root disturbance has occurred.

Planting should not be done until the soil is free from stickiness. This may prove troublesome when planting the hardy annuals in early spring, but rarely when planting out the tender plants towards the end of May or early in June. Then the weather is most likely to be dry and the soil lacking moisture, so whenever possible await a shower of rain before planting out. If dry conditions persist then give the plants a thorough watering as soon as set out, otherwise they will tend to flag and may take several days to recover.

If the spring display is not ended by the time the summer bedding plants are ready to be planted out, move these to a shady position where they can be kept comfortably moist and away from the sun's rays. Moist peat should be pressed around the plants and if the boxes can be stood on a bed of moist peat this will keep the roots cool. Then plant out at the first occasion. This is yet another point in favour of home-grown plants: they can be set out just at the right time.

Always plant firmly and, whilst all annuals look at their best when massed or planted in groups, too close planting should not be done, or the plants will tend to grow up rather than make that bushy-like growth which is the hall-mark of a well-grown plant.

Plant with a trowel, removing the plants from the box and replanting into the beds with one action, so that the roots are not subjected to the drying rays of the sun a moment longer than necessary. On average set them out about 9 in apart, using alternate spacing to allow

Pinching out the growing tip of a sweet pea seedling to encourage branching

them the maximum of room to develop.

Too formal a planting of annuals is not desirable; they are essentially informal plants and should not be set out in straight rows by means of a garden line, as are pelargoniums for example, but at the same time they must be given plenty of room.

The natural habit of the modern annual is short-jointed and bushy. However, many annuals will become even more neat and bushy if the leading shoot is pinched out when the plant is about 4 in high. Remove the growing point with 1 in of stem (if less is removed it will perhaps grow again) and the plant will then commence to make fresh growth towards the base of the stem.

There has always been considerable discussion as to the best time to 'stop' the plants, as this removal of the growing point is called. It depends much on individual growth and no definite rule can be given. But one thing is certain — it is not wise to 'stop' the plants at the time when they are being planted out. Plants obtained through the post and not already stopped should first be planted and allowed to become acclimatized to the soil for a full week before removing the growing points. Again this is where plants raised at home or obtained from a local nurseryman give the best results, for they may be stopped a week or two before planting. They will then have recovered from the shock before they are set out. A plant that is almost devoid of soil at the roots and then is pinched back heavily upon planting will suffer so great a shock as to need possibly the whole summer to recover.

After planting keep the plants growing on by watering whenever necessary. Ensuring that the ground is free from weeds and the soil constantly stirred up to permit air and moisture to penetrate to the roots will make for a most rewarding display.

When the plants have become thoroughly established, and as they are about to come into bloom, occasional applications of dilute manure water will greatly enhance the colour and quality of the bloom and help to prolong the flowering period.

ANNUALS FOR BEDDING

Where the maximum of colour is required over the longest possible period, no plants are more valuable than the numerous annuals which possess a neat compact habit and come into bloom early in summer.

No plant makes a more colourful display than the calendula, the pot marigold of olden times. From early Victorian times the antirrhinum has held pride of place with the pelargoniums and calceolaria for the main summer display, and alyssum and lobelia have never lost their popularity as edgings. But until recently there were few other suitable plants for bedding, generally because of the absence of a compact habit, whilst the colour range available was not nearly so wide as it is today. For example, the dwarf French marigolds not so long ago used to be simply either yellow or orange, flowering on 10 in stems, and whether they turned out single or double was in the lap of the gods. Today, the dwarf French marigold may be obtained in more than a dozen varieties of both single and double forms, of various heights, and the blooms possessing all manner of unusual markings. With their long flowering season these dwarf marigolds have become one of the very best plants for summer bedding.

The same may be said of the antirrhinum, which today may be obtained for cutting, for border colour, for large and small beds and for the rockery, in a wide range of glorious shades and varying in height from 2–3 in to more than 3 ft. There are now also a number of rust-resistant varieties.

Those fortunate gardeners who possess a heated greenhouse or are able to make use of a mild hot-bed and a frame can not only raise a wider variety of annuals but also obtain considerable interest from trying out new plants of a half-hardy nature not so commonly used for bedding. For the less fortunate there is still a wide variety of annuals available for bedding and much room for enterprise. Indeed, there is a great need for a little more originality. For instance, a welcome change from the all too common white alyssum and lobelia edgings would be the dainty powdery-blue ageratum, the new lilac alyssum and the Tom Thumb antirrhinum. These plants are not yet easily obtainable, but if you tell your local nurseryman of your summer requirements well before the new year, when he makes his first sowings, he will be only too pleased to raise plants of your choice.

Making the Beds Provided the soil is in good heart, little in the way of manures will be required when getting a flower bed ready for annuals. A good friable loam will ensure a display of brilliance from most annuals, but a bonemeal dressing of 2 oz per sq yd forked in just before planting will help to maintain a vigorous display of bloom right into autumn. If the soil is of a sandy nature, work in some peat or leaf-mould to retain summer moisture.

When making a new bed on a lawn or alongside a path, some care should be taken to show the bloom to the best advantage. For a circular bed first determine the size and position and mark the centre with a stake. Then place a stake firmly in the centre and, taking a strong piece of garden twine, tie a cane to it at the radius required. The circle can then be drawn in the turf simply by walking round, pressing the tip of the cane into the ground and keeping the twine taut. The turf should be removed in sections and used elsewhere in the garden. The soil is turned over, humus materials and bonemeal being incorporated at the same time, then dressed with lime and if possible allowed to weather through winter. Finally rake the soil towards the centre to make the bed higher here than at the circumference, so that the plants display their bloom to the best advantage.

Annuals Suitable for Bedding

(H) = hardy
(HH) = half-hardy
(P) = perennial treated as annual or biennial

Amaranthus, a great favourite with flower arrangers and a joy in the garden

Ageratum (HH) There are three forms of this annual. 'Tall Blue' which should be grown for cutting or planted in the herbaceous or annual border; 'Imperial Dwarf Blue', growing to a height of 10 in and suitable for a main bedding display; and 'Little Blue Star', growing only to 3 in and valuable for edging or carpeting. Seed should be sown in heat, the plants being set out early in June, 6 in apart.

Alyssum (HH) This is the sweet alyssum *A. maritimum* at its best when used for edging a bed of scarlet pelargoniums ('geraniums') or petunias. The plant, with its spreading habit, is even more useful for carpeting and could be used more often with these two plants. The best forms are 'Snow Cloth', and the rich violet 'Royal Carpet'. Both are sown in gentle heat. They should be allowed 9 in in the beds when planted out.

Amaranthus (HH) 'Love-lies-bleeding' is its more popular name. It bears dark amaranth-red tassel-like flowers on 2–3 ft stems and makes a striking centrepiece for a large circular bed. In bloom from mid-July until late in October. Seed is sown in gentle heat early in March or in a cold frame about the same time.

A. caudatus atropurpureus is the best form. There is also a form bearing palest green tassels and the two make an eye-catching contrast when planted together.

Anchusa (A) The annual form (*A. capensis*) of the more commonly known perennial is in every way an impressive plant for bedding. Sutton's strain of the variety 'Bedding Blue' makes a compact plant bearing masses of sky-blue flowers through July and August, like large forget-me-nots. 'Blue Angel' is equally fine. Seed should be sown in a frame as the plants may not survive a severe winter in an exposed garden. Sow seed in March or April.

Antirrhinum (HP) This most popular of all bedding plants is truly perennial but is best treated as a biennial, the seed being sown in a cold frame late in August, the seedlings pricked into boxes and wintered under a frame. In this way they may be planted out early in May and will come into bloom towards the end of June. The growing point should be removed to encourage a bushy plant. Another method is to sow seed in heat in January, or over a hot-bed in March, but the plants will be a month later in blooming and will not be so robust.

For bedding, the intermediate varieties are most popular, growing to a height of 15 in. Outstanding are 'Malmaison', silvery-pink; 'Guardsman', orange-scarlet with yellow lips; 'Eclipse', deep crimson; and 'Golden Queen'. There is also a strain of more dwarf habit for bedding, the plants growing to a height of 9 in. Amongst the best are 'Pink Exquisite', 'Yellow Prince' and 'Cherry', but the colour range is considerable.

For gardens troubled by rust disease there is a new range of rust-resistant varieties, which grow to a height of 12 in. 'Pink Freedom', with its almond blossom flowers, 'Golden Fleece', yellow and apricot, and 'Victory', buff and orange, are outstanding.

For edging or carpeting, the 'Tom Thumb' and 'Magic Carpet' hybrids are delightful, having a large colour range and an almost prostrate habit, whilst the 'Little Darling' strain bears bushy plants only 9 in tall.

Aster (HH) *Callistephus* spp: the value of this plant and the range for bedding and for cutting is enormous, there being something to suit every taste. The seed may be sown either in gentle heat or in a cold frame in March. Germination and plant growth is rapid and the plants will be ready to go out at the end of May after the usual transplanting and hardening. A sowing may also be made under cloches early in April or in the open ground at the month end. The aster is a late summer flowering plant and so has plenty of time to make growth through the early summer before coming into bloom towards the end of July. As the plants are of bushy habit allow 9 in spacing. They also like a soil containing plenty of humus.

One of the best asters for bedding is the new Dwarf Queen strain, wilt-resistant, and making a short bushy plant obtainable in rose, crimson, white, blue and mauve. This is the first aster to come into bloom.

With their tiny, button-like flowers obtainable in the usual aster colour range, the Lilliput asters, growing to a height of 15 in and with a branching habit, are excellent for bedding and valuable as pot plants. Of similar form are the new Remo asters with their very rich colours, whilst the dwarf Waldersee strain which flowers over a long period at a height of 9 in is most attractive. The Pepito asters with their mounds of star-like flowers are lovely, and most striking of these is 'Gusford Supreme', the red poms having a white centre. These button asters look most delightful when edged with the silvery-grey leaves of maritime cineraria.

Also suitable for bedding are the Ostrich Plume asters, their long, twisted petals providing a shaggy appearance. The blooms are large and produced with great freedom.

Like stocks, asters are prone to black-leg disease, which causes the stems to turn black near the base and the plants to collapse and die. Watering with Cheshunt Compound from the time germination has taken place will prevent an outbreak of the trouble. But as with stocks, grow the plants as dry as possible and

transplant before the seedlings become overcrowded.

Balsam (HH) *Impatieus balsamina*: this is amongst the most tender of the half-hardy annuals and though classed in the same half-hardy group as the aster and the African marigold, it is not nearly so hardy. It must be raised in heat and should not be hardened until mid-May, being planted out early in June and then given a sheltered sunny position.

For bedding, the Rose-flowered and Dwarf Bush strains are the best, the plants having a compact habit, not making excessive leaf, whilst the flowers show some of the most charming colours to be seen among annuals, being of various shades of pink, salmon and cream, and at their best during August and September. A bed is most effective when edged with delicate pastel-blue ageratum.

Convolvulus (H) The new range of dwarf bedding plants are a welcome addition to the range of hardy bedding annuals, far removed in their habit from that obnoxious weed with the lovely white tubular flowers. The new varieties of *C. tricolor*, 'Royal Ensign', with its bright ultramarine-blue trumpets, and the almost prostrate 'Lavender Rosette', a lovely carpeting plant with lavender flowers and grey foliage, should be more widely grown.

The plants may be raised in a cold frame from an early March sowing or may be sown where they are to bloom, thinned out and transplanted.

Cornflower (H) *Centaurea cyanus* has long been popular for cutting, but there are now dwarf forms ideal for bedding, making bushy plants and growing to a height of only 10 in. Seed may be sown in gentle heat in early February, or in a cold frame in late summer to come early into bloom the following year. Or sow in a frame or under cloches in early

March. Plant 9–10 in apart, setting out the plants in April.

The first of the dwarfs was 'Jubilee Gem', with its rich cornflower-blue flowers; then followed the lovely 'Lilac Lady', and now 'Rose Gem'. They all look most charming planted together.

Lobelia (HHP) Though, like the antirrhinum strictly a perennial, *L. erinus* is always given annual treatment. The seed is sown in heat in February, covered only lightly with sand and a sheet of clean glass put over the box to hasten germination. Whilst being hardened, it is advisable to pinch back straggly shoots to encourage bushy growth. The plants should be set out at the end of May or early in June when the spring bedding display has finished, being used entirely for edging and spaced 5–6 in apart.

Though the navy-blue 'Mrs Clibran' with its striking white eye is the most popular of all lobelias, the paler 'Blue Stone' is far more attractive when planted with pink-flowering plants. The dark sea-blue 'Crystal Palace', the white 'Snowball', and the uncommon crimson-red 'Prima Donna' are all worth using by way of originality. Lobelias are most effective when groups of three or five are planted together.

Marigold (HH) This is not the calendula, but the *Tagetes* species, the French and African marigolds (*Tagetes patula* and *T. erecta*)—which actually both come from Mexico—and which have now become so popular for bedding. They have been improved more than any annual plant during recent years. Both may be raised in gentle heat from an early March sowing or seed may be sown mid-March either in a cold greenhouse or frame. The plants may be classed as being almost hardy and require no detailed care in any way. Both the African and French varieties are ideal plants for

a northern garden, being planted out towards the end of May and remaining in bloom until November. The French varieties are ideal for small beds and especially for planting between polyanthus. Their vivid orange and yellow colourings are unsurpassed for a vivid and prolonged display.

Most of the African marigolds are tall growing, reaching a height of 2 ft and more and so are more suitable for cutting or for planting in the herbaceous border or in large beds where they are not troubled by wind. Their sturdy habit makes staking unnecessary. The blooms are globular, almost as large as a cricket ball and freely produced. Two of the most compact varieties are 'Orange Queen', which does not exceed a height of 20 in, and the golden-yellow 'Crown of Gold' with its reflexed underpetals. There is also a very dwarf form called 'Cupid', which bears equally large blooms on 6 in stems.

The French marigolds may now be obtained with the most arresting markings of mahogany and gold, quite unique amongst flowers. Outstanding in the double-flowered section are: 'Gold Laced', the golden flowers having an attractive edging of carmine-red; 'Harmony', rich orange, with outer petals of deep mahogany; and 'Rusty Red', its crimson petals edged with orange. These rarely exceed a height of 12 in. In the single-flowered section, 'Naughty Marietta', a tiny compact plant with golden blooms blotched and striped maroon, is most unusual.

Mesembryanthemum (HH) These dwarf-growing succulent plants, natives of South Africa, should be given a sunny position in a dry, sandy soil. They will survive almost desert-like conditions and are ideal for bedding in the sandy soils of sea-coast gardens where they remain in bloom throughout summer and autumn, the daisy-shaped flowers opening only when the sun shines on them. *M. criniflorum*, known as the Livingstone daisy, has the most brilliant colour range of all annuals with its blooms of crimson, pink, apricot and yellow and numerous art shades.

For early flowering the seed is sown under glass, either in heat, or under a frame or cloches in early March, the plants being set out towards the end of May. Seed may be sown early in May where the plants are to bloom, though by this method flowering will be delayed several weeks.

Nemesia (HH) Like the French and African marigolds, the modern nemesia has been improved out of all recognition during recent years; it is now more compact of habit, more free flowering and remains longer in bloom. Though classed as half-hardy it is almost hardy, and like the marigolds is ideal for a northern garden. In sheltered gardens the plants may be set out, after hardening, at the end of April, and a second planting made early in June to carry the flowering period right through summer. For an early planting, seed is sown in gentle heat in early February, a month later for any early June planting; or seed may be sown in a cold frame early in March.

Both 'Blue Gem' and 'Dwarf Orange' may be used for edging, and are delightful as an edging to a path for they grow only 8 in tall. The large-flowered or Suttonii strain is used for the main bedding display. Their freedom of flowering and richness of colour are difficult to equal, and like the dwarf marigolds they are not troubled by wet weather. To make a bushy plant the growing point should be pinched out whilst the plants are hardening.

Nicotiana (HH) This plant used to be confined to the mixed border, for as it

Tobacco plants open their flowers fully and give off most scent in early evening

grew to a height of 4 ft and opened its blooms only at night it was planted solely for its perfume. The new hybrid nicotianas not only make a dwarf compact plant but are extremely free flowering and, what is more important, the flowers remain open right through the daytime, a compensation for their having lost some of their perfume.

All the tobacco plants are given the usual half-hardy treatment and may be planted out from mid-May, spacing the plants 12 in apart and planting firmly. The varieties 'Crimson Bedder' and 'White Bedder' make compact bushy growth and are seen at their best when planted together and edged with dwarf antirrhinums.

Perilla (HH) This plant is used for its

rich purple foliage, making an attractive centrepiece for a large circular bed. *P. nankinsensis* makes a compact plant 18 in tall. It is raised from seed sown in heat in early February, for it is slow to germinate. Plant out in early June, allowing 15 in between the plants.

Petunia (HH) Though really perennial, the bedding petunia is always given half-hardy annual culture. It is one of the more tender bedding plants requiring to be raised in heat and being planted out in early June. With their ruffled trumpets of the most intense colouring, great freedom of flowering and compact habit, petunias make a really exotic display and over a long period.

For outdoor planting the more compact dwarf bedding strains should be used, the more robust varieties being given greenhouse culture. Outstanding for bedding are the American variety 'Comanche', with trumpets of fiery scarlet, the American Alldouble strain, with fringed petals, and, most striking, the double red and white Empress strain. Two others of merit are the bright rose-coloured 'Rose of Heaven', and 'Silvery Lilac', also well described.

The seed is sown in heat in early February, or, for a later display, towards the end of March in a cold frame, the plants being set out 9 in apart early in June.

Phlox *drummondii* (HH) Quite the best strain for bedding is Sutton's Beauty, obtainable in every colour imaginable and of almost a prostrate habit. To obtain a bed of these plants at their best, the shoots should be pegged down over all the bare soil patches as they make growth. In this way the bed will soon become a veritable sea of bloom in the most glorious art colours.

Though the plants must be given a warm sunny position, they do like a soil containing some moisture-holding humus, particularly a little well-decayed manure. They are given the usual half-hardy treatment and in favourable districts should be planted out in early May; early in June in the north. They come into bloom in mid-July and continue until mid-October.

Salpiglossis (HH) No annual is more exotic with its large, tubular, velvety-textured flowers of the richest colours, veined in the manner of orchids. They grow to a height of 2 ft and though when massed in a bed they hold each other up and require no staking, a bed should only be made up where there is shelter from strong winds. The plants are raised in heat and planted out in early June, or seed may be sown in a border early in May and the plants thinned to 8 in

The sweet pea takes skill in cultivation to produce blooms as good as these

apart. This is a late-summer flowerer, the best strain being the Mixed Large-flowered.

Stocks (HH) This is everybody's favourite on account of its freedom of flowering and its clove perfume, there being no better sight than a bed massed with these plants in one of those delicate colours, chamois, rose, mauve or pale blue, for which the stock is famous. The plants are not too easily raised for they suffer from black-leg disease at almost any age and to ensure immunity it is necessary to use a sterilized soil. Water only when absolutely essential and then with Cheshunt Compound. The plants should be given fresh soil in alternate years when planted outdoors. Apart from this give the usual half-hardy treatment.

The best strain is Hansen's 100% Double, which originated in Denmark. When the seedlings are ready for transplanting, having been raised in gentle heat, the boxes are placed in a temperature of just under 45°F (about 7°C) for 48 hours, and it will be found that a small number of seedlings have turned a dark green colour. These should be removed and destroyed for they would produce only single blooms. The others are returned to the greenhouse, transplanted and grown on in a temperature of about 50°F (10°C), and the result will be 100 per cent doubles.

The plants should not be set out until towards the end of May, being planted 8 in apart in the beds. At all times keep the young plants as dry as possible.

Sweet Pea (H) The recent introduction of the 'Little Sweetheart' variety of this ever-popular plant, making compact rounded bushes 6–8 in high and the same distance wide, has brought about its use for bedding. The plants may be sown in early autumn, in a cold frame in March, or in gentle heat and planted out in early May. The plants should be set out 9 in apart and will require no staking. They cover themselves in large waved flowers and are deliciously fragrant.

Tagetes (H) This is one of those annuals which may be classed as hardy in certain districts, but in less favourable areas should be given half-hardy treatment. Of the same group as the French and African marigold, it is *T. signata pumila*, a tiny compact plant popularly called the tagetes. The two outstanding varieties are 'Golden Ring', which is brilliant orange, and 'Lulu', lemon-yellow. Though of branching habit they need not be planted more than 6 in apart.

Vendium (HH) Natives of South Africa and liking a light, sandy soil and a position of full sun. At their best in a dry soil where their large daisy-like blooms with impressive black centres remain constantly in bloom through the latter part of summer and early autumn. For a small bed, the Dwarf Hybrids should be planted for they grow to a height of only 12 in. They may be obtained in a wide variety of colours: ivory, straw, yellow, orange, and intermediate shades.

Taller growing, reaching a height of 2 ft, is *V. fastuosum*, the large orange flowers held above the interesting silky-grey foliage.

The plants are raised in heat in March, hardened in the usual way and should be set out from the end of May, a week later in the north.

Verbena (HHP) This delightful bedding plant is yet another of those tender perennials which is usually given half-hardy treatment. As with *Phlox drummondii*, the shoots may be pegged down to fill the bed with colour. Their flat heads in red, pink, purple and white are composed of numerous tiny flowers each with a striking white eye, and are most attractive, especially when used to under-plant a bed of gladioli. Verbena enjoys a position of full sun, but likes a soil containing some moisture.

Zinnia (HH) This glorious annual, a native of Mexico, is one of the more tender plants. It likes a sunny position, a light sandy soil, and an absence of rain. In the north it is happy only in a summer where the weather is above average and then to see it at its best it should be given a seaside or country garden where the air is in no way polluted. Where it flourishes, the modern zinnia, with its vivid colourings and the rubbery texture of the bloom, far surpasses all other summer-flowering plants in the brilliance of its display.

Though growing to a height of 2 ft, the flower stems are so sturdy and erect that staking is not necessary. As the zinnia resents transplanting, seed is germinated in a heated greenhouse in March and as soon as they are large enough to handle, the seedlings are transplanted into $2\frac{1}{2}$ in pots and kept growing. Later they are moved to 3 in pots and hardened off during May. Alternatively sow one seed to a $1\frac{1}{2}$ in Jiffy pot. As for stocks and asters it is advisable to water only sparingly and then with Cheshunt Compound made by dissolving 1 oz of Compound to 2 gallons of water. The Compound is made by crushing together 11 parts of ammonium car-bonate and 2 parts of copper sulphate.

The plants should not be set out until early June, being planted from the pots with their ball of moist soil. Plant 12 in apart. They will come into bloom mid-July.

For bedding a good choice is the Giant Double strain with its beautifully rounded blooms obtainable in rose, white, yellow, orange and scarlet and always looking their best when mixed. With larger blooms and more globular in form are the Giant Dahlia-flowered zinnias, whilst the blooms of the Chrysanthemum-flowered strain have long shaggy petals. For a miniature bed or for edging, the tiny Pompon strain, growing only 8 in high, is very pleasant.

ANNUALS FOR CUTTING

For providing cut blooms, annuals are most valuable plants, free flowering, hardy and most inexpensive to raise. Nor are they particular as to soil, being happy in any well-drained loam and not requiring copious amounts of manure as do chrysanthemums and many other perennial plants. There are annuals suit-able only for cut-flower purposes, which would on account of their tall habit be out of place if used for bedding, though many are suitable for the annual border. But there are also a number of dual-purpose plants, perfectly happy as bed-ders as well as providing cut bloom. In this category come the zinnia and aster.

A pleasant idea is to grow the annuals for cutting where they will divide the kitchen garden from the flower garden, or even to divide the various vegetable crops. In this way they help to give each other protection from cold winds. For instance if a bed of larkspur or nigella is sown alongside a bed of mature Brussels sprout plants which will remain in the ground until the early spring, these will provide excellent shelter. Cut-flower annuals also fit readily into rotational cropping in the vegetable garden for they are at their best when sown in soil which has been manured for a previous crop. They could follow a crop of lettuce after potatoes, the seed of the most hardy varieties being sown towards the end of

Top Coreopsis verticillata.
Below left Phlox paniculata.
Below right pinks

August, or early September in the south, and would make sturdy growth before the severe weather. If they are planted amongst vegetables then annuals require no additional protection, otherwise twigs should be stuck into the soil about the plants. They should, of course, never be sown where they are exposed to cold winds, especially those cold winds of early spring which cause the foliage to 'burn' just as new growth is commencing. These winds can cause more harm than frosts.

But, important as the provision of some protection is, all the cut-flower annuals require a sunny position. To grow them in shade, possibly too close to a hedge, will result in plants that are spindly and weak, and liable to winter damage.

Where cloches can be used then this is the ideal method, for it is then possible to make autumn sowings of all the hardy annuals including those which are not quite so hardy as others. Not only are the plants given valuable winter protection, but they will come into bloom several weeks before the unprotected plants.

It is essential to sow the seed thinly, for seed obtained from a reputable house will give an almost 100 per cent germination and overcrowding will produce a spindly plant which will never recover to produce the maximum bloom. Even where the seed has been thinly sown, it may be necessary to thin out the seedlings as soon as they are large enough to be handled. Especially is this necessary where the plants are sown in their flowering quarters; any undue bunching together will again make for a disappointing display. Larkspur, nigella and cornflowers are the plants which resent disturbance

Top left the Madonna lily Lilium candidum.
Right Lilium szovitsianum.
Below Colchicum autumnale

and are always allowed to bloom where they are sown, being covered with cloches in the more exposed districts during winter. Where winter weather is generally severe, sowing should be delayed until early spring, but then, even though cloches are used, flowering will be a month later than from autumn-sown plants.

Those plants which bloom better when transplanted are either pricked out into prepared beds at an early stage so that they become established before winter or else left in the drills until early spring. Sowing will determine this for seed sown late and taking rather longer to germinate than expected would be better left undisturbed in the drill except for thinning. Much depends upon the situation and prevailing weather.

From the moment the seed is sown, the soil should never be allowed to suffer from drought. If the weather is dry, then artificial watering should be carried out whenever necessary. Dry conditions at the roots will cause young seedlings to die back, and even if this is only partial it will mean that they will take several weeks to recover, with inevitable delay in flowering time. For this reason, it is necessary to incorporate a considerable amount of humus into the soil; soil which quickly dries out will not produce a really good plant.

The plants need little attention after being thinned out in autumn, but as they make considerable growth in spring the taller-growing plants will require staking. This is done by passing strong twine along the rows at both sides of the plants, holding it in position by stout stakes driven in at intervals.

Before the plants make new growth in spring the hoe should be taken between the rows to break up the soil which may have become packed by winter rain.

After the plants have finished blooming, they should be cut away at soil level either with the shears or with a spade and then be chopped up and left on top of the soil for a day or two. They should then be dug well into the soil rather than burnt, or they may be moved to the compost heap. Most annuals are an excellent source of green manure, and especially where the soil is impoverished they should be dug in during autumn and allowed to decay over winter.

SELECTED CUT-FLOWER ANNUALS

Acroclinium (H)   This is a hardy annual which deserves to be better known. The seed is sown either in early September in favourable districts, or under frames or cloches in March. It is an everlasting flower growing to a height of 15 in and bearing delicate rose-pink flowers which are exceedingly long lasting when cut and dried early in autumn. There is also a double form, *A. flore-pleno*, now correctly *Helipterum flore-pleno*, and a white counterpart. When fully opened the bloom is cut with as long a stem as possible, almost at ground level. It is made up into bunches and left suspended for a fortnight in an airy room, not a greenhouse, before being used for home decoration.

Agrostemma (H)   This is a hardy plant which blooms best from a sowing made in autumn or early spring where it is to bloom. The novelty 'Milas', bearing large flowers of a pleasing shade of soft lilac on 3 ft stems, is the plant to grow for cutting. Sow the seed thinly and space to 6 in apart. The bloom should not be picked until fully open, when it will remain fresh in water for several days.

Aster (HH)   This is the China, or large-flowered aster **Callistephus chinensis**), which is so valuable for cutting. Seed is sown in gentle heat in March, or under cloches or in a cold frame in April, to get the plants in bloom as quickly as possible. Where no glass is available, sow the seed in the open in early May.

Annual asters are great lime-lovers, so work into the soil liberal quantities a month or so before the plants are set out at the end of May. They also like a firm soil, so allow several weeks for it to settle down in before planting.

The beds should be made 5 ft wide, for ease of picking, and as the plants are of branching habit, give them 12 in in the rows. Staking is not necessary.

For cutting, the Californian Giants with their double blooms and shaggy petals, flowering on 2 ft stems, are lovely, especially the shell-pink Los Angeles. The Crego asters with their interlaced petals are also valuable and come in glorious shades of purple and salmon-pink. But none are longer lasting in water than the single Marguerite asters, nor are any more prolific. They bloom profusely right through autumn.

Calendula (H)   The pot marigold, one of the easiest and most popular of all annuals. It is generally sown in mid-September in cold frames or under cloches, the plants being pricked off in March into beds 5 ft wide, with the plants 8 in apart. They then come into bloom in early June, and like the cornflower prove profitable well into August. Or seed may be sown in frames or under cloches in early March, when the plants will commence to bloom in mid-July. Both methods are satisfactory, though as with all hardy annuals the early bloom catches the most profitable markets. A sowing may also be made in May or early June and the plants transferred to frames or cloches in August (a time when frames are not much in use) to come into bloom late in autumn when they will be in great demand. In favourable districts the plants continue to bloom at least until the year end. Whilst it is not desirable to give the calendula too much nitrogenous manure lest the plants make too much foliage at the expense of bloom, it does appreciate some humus by way of peat or hops. This plant is never happy in a dry soil.

Calliopsis (H) There is an excellent bedding variety, Golden Sovereign, which bears masses of bloom on 9 in stems, whilst for cutting *C. atrosanguinea*, growing to a height of 3 ft, and the maroon-edged yellow 'Dazzler', flowering on 18 in stems, are useful. Seed is sown in late August or early March under cloches, the plants being thinned to 8 in apart. They come into bloom in early July and continue until the frosts.

Carnations are easily increased by layering. Cut the stem as shown in the drawing

Carnation (H) No annual is more pleasing for use as cut bloom about the home than the Chabaud carnation of Raoul Martin of France. The blooms are fully double, having long stems, and carry a delicious fragrance. Flowering begins late in June and goes on continuously until autumn.

This carnation should be treated as a biennial for best results, the seed being sown in a frame, preferably in boxes covered with glass, in July. The seedlings are pricked out in September, left in the frames over winter, and planted out into beds in early April. Or the seed may be sown in gentle heat in boxes or seed pans in February and after the plants have been hardened they are planted out in early May. The best method is definitely to sow in mid-summer for then the plants come early into bloom the following season. For a sowing compost use one of loam, sand, a little peat and a small quantity of lime rubble. Where the plants are to be kept in frames through winter they should be dusted with sulphur once every month to prevent mildew.

Set out the plants 9 in apart in a position where they receive full sunlight. They like a soil as light as possible containing plenty of lime and enriched with a small amount of cow manure.

There are at least thirty varieties, and among the most outstanding are: Légion d'honneur', geranium-red; 'Rose Pale', salmon-pink; 'Dame Pointe', burgundy-red; 'Marie Chabaud', primrose-yellow; 'Mikado', slate-lavender; and 'Éntince-lente', scarlet.

Chrysanthemum (H) Bearing a great similarity to the calendula, the annual chrysanthemum, coming into bloom in mid-summer and flowering until early autumn, might be more popular than is the case. They have a longer flowering season than most plants, last well in

Zinnias are among the most colourful annuals. Colours come in every shade

water and do not drop their petals. True, the plants do not winter well unless under glass, but this cannot be the reason for their lack of popularity with the public. Probably the new varieties of *C. carinatum* (formerly called *C. tricolor*), will help to bring this flower into favour again.

The seed is sown under glass in September, preferably broadcast in a frame, and there the plants remain through winter for planting out 9–10 in apart in beds early in April. No staking is required. The bloom is cut when almost open.

Excellent for cutting is the variety 'Golden Crown' (*C. coronarium* species). This is a bright buttercup-yellow, the bloom being full, the petals frilled, and held on 2 ft stems. Noteworthy in the *C. tricolor* section are: 'The Sultan',

coppery-scarlet; 'John Bright', pure golden-yellow; and 'Northern Star', pure white with a zone of pale yellow.

Clarkia (H) The clarkia is a most dainty flower when bunched, and popular for the small vase in the small modern room. It does not like transplanting and for this reason should be sown in early April where it is to bloom. Neither does it winter too well except in the mildest districts, or in a walled garden where it may be sown in mid-September. If sown in spring, it should be cloche covered for it naturally blooms early. Plants from an autumn sowing will come into bloom towards the end of May, a most welcome time for there are then few flowers in the shops.

Seed is sown in drills 12 in apart and the young plants should be thinned to 3 in apart. Under good cultivation the plants will attain a height of almost 3 ft and should be supported by twine on either side of the rows. Liberal-sized bunches should be made up. Amongst the best varieties are: 'Chieftain', delicate mauve; 'Enchantress', satin-pink; 'Crimson Queen'; and 'Illumination', rose, suffused with orange.

Cornflower (H) *Centaurea cyanus* is always in demand, especially the pink shade which has now superseded the blue in popularity. The seed should be sown in early October in favourable districts and a month earlier elsewhere, possibly at the end of August in the most exposed gardens. Sow 2 ft apart and thin out the seedlings to 12 in apart in March, for the cornflower makes a tall, bushy plant. In early gardens the first bloom may be picked about 1 June from an autumn sowing; in less favourable areas, late June will see the first bloom. The best varieties for cut bloom are those of the Monarch Ball strains, long stemmed, fully double, and very early flowering.

Valuable among these are: 'Pink Ball', shell-pink; 'Red Ball', rosy-red; and 'Blue Ball', devoid of the usual purple colouring —a very true blue.

Cosmos (HH)   Also known as cosmea, this is an elegant flower for cutting, at its best through late summer and autumn. It is late flowering for it does not readily transplant and must be sown early in May either under cloches or in the open. Sow thinly and thin out to 9 in apart for the plants grow to 3 ft or more and require some support. The best strain for cutting is the new Early-flowering Crimson and the rose-pink Gloria.

Gaillardia (H)   The annual form, *G. pulchella picta*, of the familiar perennial gaillardia is not so well known for cut-flower use as it should be. Like the annual scabious, it is rather overshadowed by its perennial sister. Bearing similar flowers to the perennial form, on 18 in stems, and of yellow shades often combined with mahogany and bronze colourings, this annual should be more widely planted. As it readily transplants, sow under glass in early March and plant out in early May 12 in apart.

Gypsophila (H)   This is *G. elegans*, the annual form of gypsophila. It likes a limestone soil, so where this is not available work in quantities of lime rubble before planting. A small sowing of this plant should be made in every garden, in any corner which receives the sun, for it is invaluable for mixing with other annuals, especially carnations and sweet peas. Seed is best sown in early September, and the seedlings thinned to 12 in in early spring. The plants produce a large quantity of bloom from mid-June until late in September, and should be supported by twine fastened round the clumps. The Monarch White strain is excellent; plant with it *G.* 'Crimson' and 'Rosea', both very lovely.

Helianthus annuus *'Sutton's Red', the striking new 'red' sunflower*

Helichrysum (H)   *H. bracteatum* readily transplants and is best sown either in gentle heat or in a cold frame in March, planting out in early May 12 in apart. Few annuals possess a wider colour range, the fully double blooms being obtainable in all shades of rose and crimson, as well as gold, white and orange, all enhanced by an attractive silvery sheen.

Larkspur   This is one of the most popular of all annuals today for it is a delightful plant for mixing with blue scabious and with other mid-summer flowers on account of its dainty, feathery habit. It is extremely hardy, but because it does not like disturbance the seed is sown early in September, in drills 2 ft apart, where it is to bloom. As larkspur grows to 4 ft it should be given a sheltered position though it enjoys ample sunshine. The plants require staking against strong winds but otherwise no additional attention. The bloom must be cut as soon as it shows colour, whilst many buds are still green, for not only is the bloom enhanced by the green tint, but larkspur quickly drops its petals when fully open. The Giant Imperial and Double Stock-flowered strains (*Delphinium consolida*) are the most popular. Worthy of special mention are 'Los Angeles', with salmon, rose-tinted blooms; 'Rosamond', pure bright pink; 'Dazzler', rosy-scarlet; 'Blue Bell', bright mid-blue; and 'Sweet Lavender'.

Nigella (H)   Love-in-a-mist is its more popular name on account of its misty green and blue appearance produced by its green ruff. Because the plants from an early September sowing are in bloom by mid-June it is always popular, for apart from pyrethrums and Dutch iris there is little else available at that time. The seed is sown in drills 18 in apart and very thinly so that further thinning is not necessary. Dappled shade suits this plant well and it likes a soil containing some humus, where it grows to a height of 2 ft. As flowering finishes in about three weeks it is best to sow again in late March to prolong the season and give mid-summer bloom, not quite so profitable commercially, but still worth while. The bloom is cut just as it shows colour. It is better marketed locally rather than transported long distances.

Saponaria (H)   It is the species *S. vaccaria* and the variety 'Pink Beauty' which is so useful as a cut flower. It grows to a height of 2 ft or more and bears its long sprays of deep pink flowers through late spring and early summer, when cut flowers are always in demand.

The seed is sown thinly in drills 12–15 in apart in August; further thinning

should be unnecessary, neither should the plants be moved. In favourable districts they winter unprotected but it is advisable to cover plants with cloches.

The bloom is cut just as it is opening, rather like gypsophila, taking a handful of stems and cutting off just above ground level.

Scabious (H)   The annual form of the scabious, *S. atropurpurea*, has for some reason never become as popular as the perennial, yet it possesses all the qualities of a top-class cut flower, lasting well in water with blooms of richer colouring than most flowers, produced on 3 ft stems. It is best sown where it is to bloom, late in August in drills 12 in apart, the seedlings being thinned out to 6 in apart in early spring. Any well-drained soil is suitable provided it is not lacking in lime. The plants appreciate some lime rubble worked in before sowing.

Lovely for cutting is 'Blue Moon', of a glorious shade of sky-blue. The petals are large and give the appearance of *Primula denticulata*. Equally attractive is 'Cherry Red', well named; and 'Rosette', rose-pink shaded with salmon, has a bloom similar in shape to the 'Esther Read' chrysanthemum.

Statice (HH)   Though more correctly of biennial habit, the well-known *Limonium sinuatum*, so popular for drying for winter decoration, should, like the helichrysum, be treated as a half-hardy annual. The seed is sown in gentle heat in early March, the young plants being moved to the open ground in mid-May. Like all everlasting flowers they prefer a light, sandy soil. The plants grow to a height of 18 in and should be planted that distance apart.

The bloom is cut at ground level as soon as the bloom is nicely showing colour. The best varieties are 'Market Rose', 'Market Grower's Blue' and 'Lavender Queen'.

Sweet Pea See following section.

Sweet Sultan (H) *Centaurea moschata* is another of those hardy annuals which dislikes transplanting so should be sown where it is to bloom. Sow thinly in drills 9–10 in apart late in August and thin out the seedlings to 5–6 in. Should the weather be severe place wattle hurdles over the rows, but otherwise the plants require no attention. They come into bloom in July and require no staking. The bloom is cut when just opening.

SWEET PEAS

No annual is more popular, nor so widely grown both for garden decoration and for cutting, whether for market or for home use. It is in fact the perfect cut flower, early to come into bloom, prolific and long lasting. But to be able to grow those large blooms, four to a stem, with long sturdy stalks, the sweet pea must be given attention in all aspects of its culture from the time the seed is sown. Sweet peas may of course be sown where they are to bloom, placing the seed round circles of twiggy sticks or wire netting up which the plants climb and bloom as they wish. Or they may be grown up tall branches to form a hedge. In this way, especially at the back of a border, they are colourful and provide plenty of bloom for the house, but the quality will be far removed from that obtained from plants that are given detailed care from the very beginning.

Preparation of Suitable Position
Most important is the choice of a suitable site for making a trench, without which it is not possible to grow really quality blooms. Owing to the height to which the plants will grow up the canes or netting, whichever is used for training, some form of shelter must be given. This can be a wall which will protect the plants from the prevailing wind and at the same time act as a sun trap. Sweet peas are great lovers of sun and light; the more they can obtain, the stronger and more profusely do they flower. But at the same time, being gross feeders, they must be given a soil enriched with as much manure and fertilizer as possible and they must also be given a mulching of strawy manure during the late summer months.

If there does not happen to be a suitable wall position, then a hedge or wattle hurdling would suffice, though if they are too near a high hedge the hedging plants will take up moisture from the soil which could be utilized by the sweet peas. Almost full sun must of course be afforded the plants—they should be in direct sunlight for at least three parts of the day. Where shelter and sunlight can be assured, the trench (or trenches) should be taken out during the winter months, as soon as possible after Christmas, or even before if the ground is vacant. If space is limited, the growing of only one or two varieties is recommended.

To make a trench take out the soil to a depth of 18 in, then add whatever manure it is possible to obtain. Artificially composted pig or poultry manure, decayed farmyard manure, wool shoddy or spent hops should be placed at the bottom of the trench to a depth of 9 in. On top of this put any decayed green stuff it is possible to procure—old sprout tops or the outer leaves of cabbages—and this should occupy another few inches. Now add a layer of soil and allow the whole to settle for two or three weeks to become well pulverized by the frosts. A small quantity of wood ash and a little bonemeal should be worked into this layer of soil and then the trench should be filled to ground level with the previously removed soil.

One more point. I have always found that it is an excellent plan to place a layer of ground lime either on top of the green stuff or mixed in with the top few inches of soil. Sweet peas are great lovers of lime and this should not be neglected.

Trenches prepared in this manner will provide the plants with an abundance of food throughout their life and will produce cut bloom of most excellent quality.

Sowing the Seed The best results are obtained by treating the sweet pea as a biennial, sowing the seed in a cold frame early in August and wintering the young plants under lights in the same way as for antirrhinums. During winter the plants continue to build up a sturdy constitution and with the advent of the first warm summer weather are ready to make vigorous growth.

An alternative method is to sow in gentle heat early in the new year, growing the plants as sturdy as possible and never allowing the temperature to rise above 50°F (10°C). Far too many sweet pea plants are sold through the post in early summer which have been grown under almost forcing condition and have not been sufficiently well hardened off. Such plants, almost yellow in colour, will never stand up to the rigours of a northern climate and in any case take several weeks to recover from their early set-back. If sowing in heat, maintain just sufficient warmth to enable the plants to keep growing without any tendency to forcing conditions.

The plants may be sown in a cold frame in early March, when they will come later into bloom; or sow over a mild hot-bed, planting the seed in pots which are pressed into the hot-bed. So that the plants grow as 'hard' as possible, plenty of ventilation should be given.

Many varieties possess a hard seed skin which should be slightly chipped before sowing to encourage more rapid germination. Seeds may be sown in pans or boxes. I always use the latter, for this method is more economical and produces as good a plant in every way for the commercial grower. A few specialist growers use thumb-size pots in which they place only one seed and transplant the growing plant into the open ground directly from the pot. If sowing in boxes place between 40 and 50 seeds in each. Watering is easier in boxes as the compost does not dry out as quickly as it does in earthenware pots. Whichever method is used, plant the seed $\frac{3}{4}$ in deep and see that the seedlings receive as much light as possible. Partly diffused light will only encourage a tall thin seedling, which will be of little use as a bearer of choice bloom.

When sowing is done early in August the boxes or pots should be carefully watered and placed in well-ventilated frames covered with clean lights. At this time of the year germination takes only four or five days and as soon as the plants have formed a second leaf joint they should be pinched back to encourage a bushy habit. By early October they will have formed sturdy plants and all watering should then be left off for the duration of the winter months, otherwise the plants may damp off. A little ventilation should be given, but when severe frosts occur the lights should be covered with sacking or canvas.

When sowing is done in a heated glasshouse in January, the temperature should be between 45°F and 50°F (7–10°C), never higher, for too high a temperature only encourages weak growth. In early April remove the plants to cold frames where they are to harden in readiness for transplanting in the prepared trenches in early May, or mid-April in the south.

There is little to choose between the two methods as to sturdiness of plant and time of flowering. If the frames are not in use in July or August, it would be more economical in space to sow the sweet peas in them and to use the heated house for more tender subjects.

The seed-sowing compost should consist of a friable loam containing a little peat, some coarse sand and a very small quantity of one of the sweet pea fertilizers which are made up in compound form by several firms. At all times great care must be taken with the watering. Water only when the soil is dry and the seedlings appear to need moisture. Over-watering causes more trouble than anything else in the growing of sweet peas.

Planting Out When transplanting to the open ground choose a moist day—one on which there are no cold spring winds blowing. If there are ground frosts about, delay planting until conditions are more favourable. Set the young plants 12 in apart and plant as firmly as possible. Where netting is being used it is better to stagger them on either side of the line, thus:

A few twigs should be placed near each plant to encourage it to twine and from there they will readily take to whichever form of support is to be used.

Staking methods cause more discussion among amateur growers than anything else. Some contend that a good bloom can only be achieved when the plants are trained up bamboo canes and they scorn any other method. Canes are excellent for training and supporting the plants, but I have had equally good results when using wire or string netting, which is easier to use and much less expensive to buy. Branches containing a large number of twigs may also be used, but this method does not simplify picking the blooms. The most economical method in every way is netting. The tendrils rapidly wind themselves round the netting and the plants

It is worth using a straight line or piece of wood to space annuals regularly

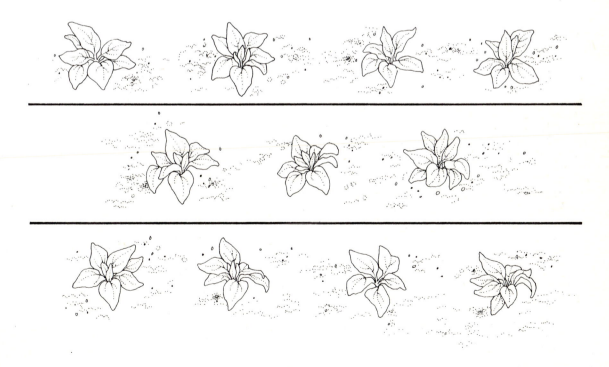

make great headway provided they are kept moist during a dry period.

Care and Attention Until the plants have climbed at least 4 ft they should not be allowed to form flower stems and the buds should be removed almost daily. If the plants come into flower too easily they will take away the nourishment required to build up a strong plant.

Mulching should be commenced in June, decayed grass mowings and strawy manure being highly suitable. Care should be taken to see that whatever form of staking is used is made as firm as possible and this should be inspected throughout the summer. There is nothing more annoying than to find the plants (and supports) lying on the ground just when they have reached full bloom, having been blown over by a high wind.

During the summer months the plants benefit greatly from waterings of either poultry or farmyard manure. This prolongs the flowering period and greatly enhances the colour of the bloom.

The bloom should be cut with as long a stem as possible and as soon as the buds are breaking into colour.

Varieties

'Air Warden' Vivid orange-cerise, an unusual colour and quite sun-proof. Very widely grown for exhibition.

'Blue Bell' A true bluebell colour, most popular on the market and exceedingly prolific.

'Edith' The colour is rich salmon-pink on a deep cream ground, the blooms being large and of beautiful form.

'Elizabeth Taylor' A magnificent variety, the mauve blooms very large yet refined, having frilled petals and long sturdy stems.

'Fairy' This is a most unusual sweet pea with large frilled flowers of a lemon-yellow colour, flushed with pink at the centre and an attractive wire edge of salmon-pink.

'Gigantic' A huge frilled white with a long sturdy stem. Excellent for 'making-up' purposes.

'Great Britain' The large blooms are of rich cream overlaid with apple-blossom pink.

'Leamington' The large frilly blooms are of deep lilac-mauve, with a delicious scent.

'Mavis' This is a most unusual and beautiful sweet pea, being of a rich salmon colour overlaid with tangerine.

'Mrs C. Kay' A beautiful mauve of large size, excellent formation and carrying a large number of blooms per stem.

'Myosotis' Of a mid-blue colour quite unusual in sweet peas. Sweetly scented and bearing an average of 4–5 blooms on long wiry stems. One of the best varieties yet introduced.

'Patricia Unwin' Possibly the best salmon-pink. A most striking colour similar to the famous 'Picardy' gladiolus.

'Red Crusader' The huge frilled blooms are of deep rose shaded with crimson.

'Red Velvet' The red-crimson colour with its velvet sheen is almost a replica of the 'Ena Harkness' rose. Long lasting in water.

'Welcome' A rich bright crimson, quite the best of its colour. Bears huge blooms on long stems.

'What Joy' This is a sweet pea which should be more widely grown. A rich cream colour and perfect in form.

ANNUALS SOWN WHERE THEY ARE TO BLOOM

The following list includes annuals which resent root disturbance and those that, for one reason or another, are generally sown directly in the open as soon as the weather and condition of the soil permit.

These are in addition to the many cut-flower annuals cited in the previous list which are happier sown where they are to bloom.

Adonis (H)   With its anemone-like flowers and serrated foliage, this plant should be more widely grown. There are both summer- and autumn-flowering species, but as the former, *A. aestivalis*, is slow to germinate, its seed should be sown in late August the previous year and this may mean that it should be confined to southern gardens. Seed of *A. autumnalis* is sown early in April. Thin out the plants to 10 in apart. They reach a height of 12 in.

Alonsoa (HH)   This lovely annual may be raised in gentle heat or sown late in April where it is to bloom. The dainty flower spikes resemble miniature sidalceas. The best form is *A. warscewiczii compacta*, which grows to a height of 15 in and should be allowed the same distance between plants to mature. Pinch back the growing point to make a bushy plant.

Anchusa (H) The annual form *A. capensis* 'Blue Bird' makes a bushy plant 15 in tall and covers itself with brilliant blue flowers resembling forget-me-nots. Sow early April for it is completely hardy.

Brachycome (HH)   *B. iberidifolia*, known as the swan river daisy and a native of Australia, enjoys a light, dry soil and a sunny position. It attains a height of only 9 in and bears its blue, purple and lavender blooms from mid-June until October. Sow early in May and thin to 6 in. Blue Star hybrids are the best.

Cacalia (H)   The tassel flower, a native of Africa, should be given a position of full sun and a dry soil. *C. coccinea* bears tassels of bright scarlet, whilst there is an equally striking golden form *C. aurea*. Seed is sown late in April in the open or late March in gentle heat as this plant trans-

plants readily. As it grows to a height of 18 in, it should be thinned to 12 in apart.

Candytuft (H)   The most easily grown of all annuals and much loved by children. The heads, like large pennies on 10 in stems, appear throughout summer in profusion. It flourishes in any soil and may be used at the front of a shrubbery or almost anywhere. Obtainable in crimson, rose and lilac, the best strain is the Giant Hyacinth-flowered.

Clary (H)   Annual salvia, *Salvia scalarea* 'Oxford Blue', a charming plant, growing to a height of 18 in and bearing masses of deep blue flowers from mid-July until late September. There is also a lovely shell-pink form, 'Pink Gem'. Sow early April and thin out to 12 in apart.

Collinsia (H)   *C. bicolor* 'Salmon Beauty', flourishes anywhere, producing masses of dainty salmon-pink flowers from June till the end of August on 12 in stems. If the seed is sown thinly in early April, or in early autumn in a sheltered garden, no thinning will be necessary.

Convulvulus (H)   For quickly covering a fence or trellis at the back of a border *C. major*, the morning glory, with its beautiful trumpets in shades of blue and mauve is most effective. For the front of a border *C. tricolor* in its various forms, making a compact plant 10 in high, is equally striking. Sow early April and thin to 10 in apart.

Dimorphotheca (H)   Though a native of South Africa, the Star of the Veldt is almost completely hardy and may be sown mid-April where it is to bloom or a month earlier in gentle heat. The plants grow to a height of 12 in and bloom throughout late summer. *D. aurantiaca* bears flowers in shades of orange and yellow. Needs a sunny situation and a light sandy soil.

Echium (H)   *E. plantagineum*, at its best in a poor, dry soil. 'Blue Bedder', which makes a compact plant 15 in high and in bloom from June to September, is a valuable plant and is so free flowering that it may be used for bedding. Sow early April, spacing the plants to 15 in apart.

Eschscholzia (H) Like the echium, the Californian poppy is a most colourful plant for a poor, dry soil. Sown early in April the seed germinates rapidly and the plants, growing to a height of about 10 in bear a profusion of flowers throughout summer. Amongst the best varieties are: 'Dazzler', flame; 'Enchantress', rose and cream; 'Orange King'; and 'Crimson Queen'. Sown in groups about a shrubbery the plants add rich colouring and thrive in poor soil.

Felicia (H) *F. bergeriana*, with its sky-blue star-like flowers borne on 6 in stems, is a plant deserving of greater popularity. Like all South African plants, it should be given a sunny position and a dry soil. In bloom from June until October, it makes a valuable and original edging plant.

Gilia (H) The hardy annual species of this plant bear heads of star-like flowers on 18 in stems and are excellent either for border display or for cutting. *G. capitata* bears blue flowers. The seed may be sown either in early autumn or early in spring, the plants being thinned to 12 in apart.

Godetia (H) Deservedly amongst the most popular of all annuals which are sown where they are to bloom. There are tall-flowering varieties like the orange 'Kelvedon Glory', and the salmon-pink 'Sybil Sherwood', which attain a height of 2 ft; intermediate varieties such as the crimson 'Firelight' and the snow-white 'Purity', so lovely together; and the dainty dwarf 'Lavender Queen' and 'Crimson Glow' which make compact plants less than 12 in in height.

No annual will provide a more vivid display than Godetia if it is given a sunny position and a soil containing a little humus. Sow early in April and thin to 9–12 in apart, depending upon the height of the variety.

Helianthus (H) *H. annuus*, the sunflower, is a valuable annual for hiding an unsightly wall and may also be sown at the back of a border. There are single and double forms bearing rich golden blooms and attaining a height of 8 ft in a single summer. Not quite so tall is the striking 'Sutton's Red', the yellow bloom having a wide mahogany circle round the centre. Seed is sown early in April and the seedlings thinned to 2 ft apart.

Jacobaea (H) This hardy plant, often listed as *Senecio elegans*, is now obtainable in a double form, in crimson, purple, white and rose. The seed is sown at the end of March and as the plants attain a height of 18 in they should be thinned to 12 in apart.

Senecio arenarius is the annual cineraria, of similar height, which bears sturdy flowers through summer.

Lavatera (H) *L. trimestris* is the annual mallow. The deep rose-pink 'Loveliness', growing to a height of 3 ft and forming a dense bush-like plant, is the best variety. Requring a moist soil, the seed is sown early in April and thinned to 2 ft apart. The mallow is at its most splendid during August and September, a delightful plant for the back of the border.

Layia (H) This native of California is at its best in a dry, sandy soil and should be given a position of full sun. Seed is sown early in April—to the front of the border for the plants grow only 10–12 in high—and the plants bear most of their bloom during August and September. The variety of *L. elegans* known as tidy tips has dainty yellow flowers edged with white and is a most attractive plant.

Leptosiphon (H) For edging, this is a lovely little plant, which comes quickly into bloom from an early April sowing. The new French hybrids, only 4–5 in high, cover themselves in star-like flowers embracing all the colours of the rainbow. Coming into bloom early in June, they remain colourful until mid-September. Do no thinning.

Leptosyne (H) *Coreopsis maritima*, valuable both for cutting and garden decoration. With its semi-double marguerite-like flowers of golden-yellow, 'Golden Rosette' grows to a height of 18 in. The bloom is held on long, wiry stems and borne from mid-June until September from a late March sowing. Thin to 10 in apart.

Limnanthes (H) Should be used like leptosiphon, for an edging. The plants are sweetly scented and highly attractive to bees. *L. douglassii* grows to a height of 5 in and bears yellow and white flowers. Do no thinning and sow the seed late in March.

Linaria (H) *L. maroccana*. The flowers of the Fairy Bouquet are like miniature antirrhinums, produced in profusion on 7 in stems throughout mid-summer. The colour range is enormous: white, ruby, rose, purple, yellow, the spikes being neat and compact. Sow in any soil towards the end of March. No thinning is necessary if the seed is sown thinly.

Linum (H) Grows to 12–15 in and bears dainty flowers of the most brilliant colour. Continuity may be achieved if the first sowing is made towards the end of March, and a second early in May. Thin to 6 in apart. *L. grandiflorum caeruleum* bears bloom of brightest blue; *L. grandiflorum rubrum* has flowers of vivid crimson, borne in great profusion.

Lupin (H) Extremely hardy and growing strongly in the poorest of soil, *Lupinus hartwegii* reaches a height of 2½ ft and may be obtained in white, deep blue and rose.

Nigella, one of the cornflower family, with blue flowers and inflated seed pods

Seed is sown at the end of March and is sufficiently large to be planted individually about 15 in apart. *L. nana* is the Tom Thumb lupin, growing to a height of only 15 in and useful for the front of a border or shrubbery.

Malope (H) Very similar in form and habit to the lavatera, *M. trifida* makes a bushy plant 3 ft tall. The bloom is of various shades of crimson and rose, and at its best from August until late October. Sow at the back of the border early in April and thin to 20 in apart.

Matthiola (H) This is the night-scented stock, so much appreciated if sown beneath a window which can be left open during a summer evening. *M. bicornis* grows to a height of 10 in, covering itself in tiny flowers of palest lilac. Sow early April. No thinning is necessary if the seed is sown thinly.

Mentzelia (H) The large golden-yellow blooms of *M. lindley* (formerly known as *Bartonia aurea*), with their numerous fluffy stamens give this flower a most charming appearance. This is a valuable plant for a dry, light soil and has a long flowering period, mid-June until late September. Sow early April and thin to 1 ft apart, for the plants attain a height of 18–20 in.

Mignonette (H) This is one of those annuals which is especially valuable for sowing in a limy soil; it is in fact as great a lover of lime as the dianthus. It also likes a soil containing some humus. Though sweetly scented, the mignonette, *Reseda odorata*, has never until recently been conspicuous for the quality of its flowers. With the introduction of the large-flowered varieties, this plant has now become attractive as well as fragrant. The lovely deep yellow 'Golden Goliath', the richly coloured 'Crimson Giant', and the bright-flowered 'Red Monarch' all grow to a height of 12 in and make large branching plants—a great improvement on the old mignonette. Sow in early April to bloom mid-June till mid-August; and to continue the display, make a second sowing in May.

Nasturtium (H) Most colourful in a dry, sandy soil where it does not make excessive foliage, no hardy annual provides more colour over so large an area in such quick time. The Tom Thumb varieties growing to a height of 10 in may be used for bedding, spacing the large seeds 9 in apart and sowing early in April. Outstanding is 'Ryburgh Perfection', with its vivid scarlet flowers and silver foliage.

Almost as compact are the Dwarf Double Hybrids, comprising lemon, salmon, rose, orange and crimson shades and a host of intermediate colours.

For a terrace or for covering a bank, the Gleam Hybrids are very striking, being semi-double and sweetly perfumed. Notable among them is the new Fiery Festival, with blooms of luminous scarlet. All come into bloom mid-June and continue until early November.

Nemophila (H) Enjoying a cool, moist soil and a position of partial shade, there is a semi-climbing species *N. aurita*, bearing deep mauve flowers; and *N. menziesii*, Baby Blue Eyes, which bears pale blue flowers with a striking white centre. Growing to a height of only 6 in and coming into bloom in mid-May from an early April sowing, this is an attractive edging plant.

Oenothera (H) It is *O. bistorta* which is the annual. It grows to a height of 20 in and bears large golden-yellow flowers, similar to those of the biennial form, the evening primrose. Seed is sown early in April, the plants coming into bloom late in July and remaining colourful until the end of September. Thin to 15 in apart.

Omphalodes (H) *O. linifolia* is an attractive plant for the front of a border, its tiny cream-coloured flowers and attractive grey foliage providing a striking contrast to the more richly coloured subjects. Sow at the end of March and thin to 6 in.

Papaver (H) It is *P. rhoeas*, the Shirley poppy, which is so valuable sown where it is to bloom, for the new double-flowered strain embracing shades of plum, slate-blue, crimson, scarlet and many more, adds a richness to a border or shrubbery equalled by few other plants. Seed is sown early in April to bloom from July until late October, and a sowing may also be made in a sheltered border in early September to bloom mid-May until mid-August. This is one of those valuable annuals which may be sown in a poor clay or sandy soil, but for an autumn sowing the ground should be well drained. Sow thinly and thin the plants to 12 in apart.

Phacelia (H) Producing its pinnacles of harebell-like flowers of a rich mid-blue, on 9 in stems and coming into bloom early in June from an early April sowing, *P. campanularia* is one of the most colourful of all edging plants for a dry, sandy soil. Thin to 4 in.

Rudbeckia (H) Growing to a height of 2 ft, *R. bicolor*, the annual form of the better-known perennial, is an excellent plant for the back of the border and also for cutting. The two best varieties are 'My Joy', large golden-yellow, and 'Kelvedon Star', yellow blooms with a striking bronze disc. Seed is sown towards the end of March, the young plants being thinned to 15 in apart when they will then make a riot of colour.

The plants may also be treated as biennial and sown in early September, but as they are naturally so late to come into bloom, there is little to be gained

Two attractive annuals for every garden—Cosmea and the annual chrysanthemum

by this. The rudbeckia is valuable in that it is at its best during late autumn, when most other annuals are past their prime.

Specularia (H) Venus's looking glass, as *S. speculum* is often called, is a delightful edging plant. From an early April sowing it bears deep violet bell-shaped flowers on 9 in stems from mid-July until September. The plants sow themselves as readily as forget-me-nots.

Tropaeolum (H) There are two annual species of the climbing nasturtium: *T. lobbianum*, obtainable in crimson, orange, scarlet and gold; and *T. canariense*, the golden Canary creeper. Both will cover a trellis in a single season and both are happy in any soil. Sow at the end of March, 15 in apart.

Ursinia (HH) With their orange daisy-like flowers and the bushy habit of the plants the ursinias lend distinction to any border. They may be sown at the end of April where they are to bloom, or raised in heat for they will readily transplant. *U. anethoides* and its hybrids in shades of ruby and purple, bloom on 12 in stems; the orange-flowered 'Golden Bedder' is rather more dwarf. Allow 10 in between the plants.

Virginian Stock (H) *Malcomia maritima*. Growing to a height of 5–6 in and obtainable in shades of crimson, mauve, white and blue, these dainty little plants are delightful for edging a border. Sow at the end of March. No thinning is necessary if sown thinly.

Viscaria (H) Any garden soil suits this plant but it does like an open situation. *V. oculata* and its hybrids reach a height of 15 in and may be obtained in shades of blue, mauve and deep pink. The Tom Thumb hybrids, in white, rose and blue, flower on only 6 in stems. Seed is sown early in May and the plants thinned to 6 in apart.

Above Bergenia purpurescens.
Below *the dwarf* Kniphofia modesta

KNIPHOFIA
MODESTA

Chapter 8

HARDY BORDER PLANTS

As with other plants, the hybridist has during the past decade concentrated on introducing hardy border plants suited to modern conditions. The small garden demands a plant of compact habit which will be in proportion to its surroundings, whilst shortage of labour for the garden means that all plants must be as labour-saving as possible. Those massive herbaceous borders in spacious gardens, which demanded so much time and expense in the staking and tying of the 4–7 ft plants, are now rarely to be seen. Instead, we have plants that are generally no more than 4 ft in height, capable of blooming over a long period with the minimum of attention.

The compact, upright habit of the modern border plant makes it possible to plant a herbaceous border in the smallest of gardens, using plants which grow no more than just over 3 ft. Three rows should be used: plants 9–18 in in height at the front; $1\frac{1}{2}$–$2\frac{1}{2}$ ft in the centre; and those around 3 ft tall at the back. The length of the border will depend upon the ground at one's disposal, but the width

Top left Eucomis bicolor.
Right Schizostylus coccineus.
Below foliage plants on a patio

should be no more than 3 ft, less than half that of the herbaceous borders of old. This will permit the back-row plants to be attended without treading the ground. Such a border, using plants of neat compact habit, can be made in the most exposed garden. It will be necessary to select plants that bloom over a long period, because of the restricted size of the border and to achieve the maximum colour at one time. By careful selection the border can be made colourful from May until almost the end of November, when the plants should be cut back to 6 in of their base and the ground forked between them. If at the same time the soil is enriched with a little decayed manure, used hops or some peat, the border should not require disturbance for at least four years.

PREPARATION OF THE SOIL

Much may also be done to bring various soils into a condition in which most border perennials will flourish. If the border is to be made in a town garden, where the soil is generally of an acid nature caused by deposits of soot and sulphur, it should be given a good dressing with lime. If the soil is sticky and contains

143

a high proportion of clay particles, it is desirable to break up the particles so that the soil will be better aerated and drained and there will be less likelihood of the plants decaying through excess moisture collecting about the roots during winter. Unhydrated or caustic lime should therefore be incorporated as the soil is being dug over, to a depth of at least 15 in. The action of moisture on the lime will cause it to disintegrate, at the same time breaking up the soil.

The work should be done early in autumn, the ground being cleared of all perennial weeds at the same time. Early in November some humus should be incorporated and almost any humus-forming materials will be suitable—decayed garden refuse, well-rotted manure, seaweed, peat, and used hops, which are generally obtainable from a local brewery. If it is not possible to obtain any manure, fork in some peat and give a dressing of bonemeal, 2 oz per sq yd. It is advisable to allow the ground ten days in which to settle down before planting so that there will be no air pockets about the roots after planting. It should be said that a light, sandy soil will require more humus than will a heavy soil, to enable it to retain moisture during dry summer periods. Hardy border plants are copious drinkers and heavy feeders and if they are to have a long life and bloom over an extended period they must never lack moisture at their roots.

PLANTING

Where the soil is light and friable, planting is best done during the third week of November. If it is delayed until spring such a soil may suffer from lack of moisture, dry periods often being experienced during spring and early summer, and this makes it difficult for the plants to become established. Where the soil is heavy and not too well drained, planting is best delayed until the end of March. From autumn planting, however, a much better display of bloom may be expected the first summer.

Plants are best set out in groups of three so that there will be a liberal splash of colour from each variety. Odd plants set here and there about a border will never make a pleasing display, neither will plants that are set out too formally. Ample space should be allowed between each group rather than between each plant, though the plants should be spaced within the groups according to their vigour and habit. It is also important to arrange the colours to provide pleasing contrasts, planting, for example, those that bear yellow or orange flowers near those bearing blue or purple bloom. Pink contrasts well with blue, likewise red with white. And whilst it is desirable to use plants that have as long a period of flowering as possible, not all will reach their full beauty at the same time and so care must be taken to see that there are no ugly gaps about the border, devoid of colour for long periods. Near plants which come early into bloom, the lupins and delphiniums of dwarf habit, plant those which bloom late in the season, the heleniums and perennial asters. Then in front of these plant the early-blooming lupins and monardas. Near the May-flowering doronicum plant the August-flowering phlox. About the border plant several groups of those very long-flowering plants such as *Achillea eupatorium*, and *Poterium obtusum* with its attractive pink blooms like bottle brushes.

Before ordering the plants and before any planting is done, the border should be carefully planned, selecting long-flowering plants of compact habit which require the minimum of attention. Set out the plants when the soil is friable and quite free of frost, make them quite firm, then rake over the ground between the plants. As a guide to planting, rings of sand may be made on the surface of the soil and small labels placed in each on which has been written the name of the plant, colour of the bloom and flowering time, following the plan previously made on paper. This permits the plants to be set out without delay, at the correct distance apart and exactly as planned.

BACK-ROW BORDER PLANTS (3–4 ft)

Acanthus Its place of origin was southeast Europe, and the complicated pattern of the long crinkled leaves was used by the builders of ancient Greece as a motif in their decorative carving. The plants bloom in July and August and thrive in a well-drained loam and in semi-shade. Plant in spring, 3 ft apart.

A. mollis latifolius has very large leaves and sends up flower spikes of pinky-blue to a height of 3 ft, whilst *A. spinosa* forms rosettes of spiny leaves and bears purple and white flowers on erect stems 3–4 ft tall.

Achillea *eupatorium* With its beautifully 'cut' silver-grey foliage, strongly aromatic, and bearing flat heads of brilliant yellow from July until late October on 3 ft stems, this is a magnificent border plant. 'Coronation Gold' and 'Flowers of Sulphur', both well named, are outstanding new varieties. Plant near the Michaelmas daisies at 18 in apart. Two plants together make a fine display.

Aconitum Happy in a heavy soil and in semi-shade, these plants should have their tuberous roots planted 2 in deep and 2 ft apart. As with all blue-flowered plants, spring planting is best.

'Bressingham Spire' grows 3 ft tall, the spikes being densely packed with violet-blue flowers. 'Blue Sceptre' grows only

2 ft, its flowers being half-purple, half-white. Both bloom July–September.

Anemone *japonica* In bloom from early August until November, this is a lovely plant for growing near the Michaelmas daisies and like them it enjoys a moist soil. 'Max Vogel' has its semi-double blooms of clear pink, 'Louise Uhink' is pure white, and 'Herzblut' rose-red. Each of them bloom at a height of just under 3 ft. Plant 18 in apart.

Aster *novi-belgii* No border is complete without the liberal use of these Michaelmas daisies, in bloom from early September until mid-November. Plant them with the rudbeckias, 15 in apart and use those flowering on 3 ft stems to the back of the border. 'Ada Ballard', 'F. M. Simpson', 'Marie Ballard' and 'The Sexton' bear very large blue blooms on 3 ft stems. In pink shades, the brightly coloured 'Schoolgirl', 'Orchid Pink' with its attractive golden centre, 'Lassie' and 'Charmwood' are among the best. Outstanding in the crimson shades are: 'Crimson Brocade'; 'Winston Churchill', beetroot-red; 'The Rector', claret-red; and 'Red Sunset'. As a contrast, 'Chorister' is a lovely pure white. Among the purple-violet colours three of the best are: 'Flying Enterprise' with plum-purple flowers; 'Festival', orchid-purple; and 'Petunia', violet.

For the back row of a very small border there are several very fine Michaelmas daisies, including: 'Fontaine' with its large tawny-pink bloom with an orange centre; 'Tapestry', double rose-pink; 'Violet Lady', deepest purple; 'Winsom Winnie', rose-red; 'Melbourne Belle', crimson-red; and 'Chequers', violet-mauve. All grow to a height of a little over 2 ft.

Astilbe *arendsii* For a moist, peaty soil these are valuable plants and if several varieties are planted together, bloom may be enjoyed from early July until mid-

September. 'Erica' with feathery spikes of clear pink is the first to bloom, followed by 'Fire', with its plumes of salmon-red. Then comes 'Dusseldorf', bright salmon, and lastly 'Jo Orphorst', which bears its ruby-red spikes well into September.

Astrantia *carnolica* Grows to a height of 3 ft and requires a moist, humus-laden soil and a position of partial shade. During July and August it bears nodding starry white flowers tinted with pink. They are surrounded with green bracts which turn purple with age. Plant in November.

Baptisia *australis* A little-known border plant, long-living in ordinary soil and is most free-flowering. Plant in spring 2 ft apart and it will soon form a dense clump. In June and July it sends up its flower spikes of indigo-blue, like small lupins, on 3 ft stems. The blooms are enhanced by the handsome grey-green foliage.

Bocconia *cordata* Known as the plume poppy, it is a most striking back-of-the-border plant which bears large panicles of coral-pink flowers on 5 ft stems from July until September. *B. cordata* 'Bee's Flame' bears plumes of salmon-orange above bronzy scalloped leaves and is at its best during August.

Plant in November, 3 ft apart and increase by root division every three or four years.

Campanula They should be planted in spring but are amongst the easiest of border plants to manage, flourishing in any ordinary well-drained soil. *C. persicifolia*, the peach-leaf campanula, grows 3 ft tall, making a spreading clump of small glossy leaves, and in June and July bears cup-shaped flowers of lavender-blue; there is also a pure white form. *C. macrantha* is a stately plant growing to 4 ft with spikes of pendant violet flowers. 'Loddon Anna', a variety of *C. lactiflora*, grows just less than 3 ft and bears flowers of a lovely shade of cool lilac-pink.

Centranthus *ruber* This, the valerian, often found naturalized on old walls, will flourish in poor soils and in a sun-baked situation. Forming a thick woody taproot, difficult to divide and re-establish, it is best raised from seed sown in spring, the plants being moved to their flowering quarters before they become too large. Once established, they will be almost indestructible. Allow 2 ft between the plants and give them a light soil if possible. The best form is *C. atrococcineus* which bears flowers of deep crimson; *C. albus* bears white flowers. They are effective when planted together.

Cimicifuga They bear their long tapering spikes, like those of the eremurus, on 5 ft stems and are at their best in September and October. With their rich creamy-white blooms they are a pleasing foil for the red and purple Michaelmas daisies

Delphiniums, traditionally blue, are also available in whites, yellows and reds

and *Lobelia cardinalis*. They require a rich loamy soil which is well drained in winter. Plant in spring or late autumn, allowing 3 ft between the plants.

C. cordifolia has heart-shaped leaves and bears tapering spires of creamy-white whilst *C. racemosa* bears its long feathery racemes a month earlier. The form 'White Pearl' bears a spike of purest white.

Coreopsis Flowering from early June until September, this is a most colourful plant and the blooms last well in water. These attractive flat blooms are borne on 3 ft stems. 'Badengold', pure golden-yellow, is most showy. Excellent, too, is 'Astolat Variety', the golden blooms having a crimson blotch. Plant 18 in apart.

Delphinium The most stately flowers of the border, many grow 7–8 ft tall with their flowering spikes almost half that height. They require a rich well-drained soil and spring planting; and so that they will be long living, remove the flower spikes as soon as they begin to die back. Plant 2–3 ft apart. Each spike should be well supported as it grows.

Of many lovely varieties, 'Alice Artindale' with its centre rosette of purple against outer petals of pale blue is outstanding whilst 'Garter Knight' is heliotrope and cobalt-blue with a jet 'eye'. 'William Richards' is electric blue and is one of the first to bloom whilst 'Swanlake' is white and enhanced by the black centre.

It is the dainty 'Belladonna' hybrids that are suitable for a very small border for they bloom at a height of only 3 ft. They have a far more feathery habit than the tall large-flowered varieties and make a charming display during June and July. Planting should take place in March, about 20 in apart. 'Orion', medium blue and 'Capri', with its sky-blue flowers are extremely compact, also the new white,

'Elstead White'. Plant with it 'Wendy', with its blooms of gentian-blue or 'Pink Sensation' (*D. × ruysii*), with its spikes of delicate salmon-pink.

Dictamnus *fraxinella* Requires a well-drained, sandy soil and should be planted 2–3 ft apart. It bears its spikes of marshmallow-pink flowers in July on erect stems 3 ft tall; but the plant has additional interest in that its ash-like leaves exude a volatile oil which surrounds the plant, and if ignited burns with a blue flame. The plant is known as the burning bush.

Dierama *pulcherrima* Native of South Africa, is known as the wand flower, for its drooping claret-purple bells appear during August and September on cane-like stems 5 ft tall which sway in the gentle breezes. Its montbretia-like foliage gives additional charm to the plant, which to be hardy and long living requires a rich but well-drained soil. Plant 2–3 ft apart and do not disturb for ten or more years when the clumps may be lifted and divided in spring.

There are some lovely hybrids named after birds; of these, 'Nightingale' bears flowers of fuchsia-pink and 'Ringdove' a lovely shade of soft shell-pink.

Digitalis This hardy plant, the foxglove, is common to Britain and grows so readily from seed that it is always propagated in this way. Seed is sown early in spring in boxes or pans in a frame and the young plants moved to prepared beds where they are grown on until large enough to move to the border in autumn. They will bloom the following year and do well in ordinary soil and in semi-shade. The biennial hybrids raised by the Reverend Wilks produce their finger-shaped blooms all the way up a 3–4 ft stem but even more arresting is *D. × mertonensis*, a true perennial which bears flowers of a lovely shade of strawberry-pink whilst *D. lutea* bears bright yellow flowers. Plant 18 in apart and *D. purpurea*, the ordinary fox-glove, will usually propagate itself from self-sown seed.

Doronicum So valuable in that it comes into bloom before the end of April, bearing its large yellow daisy-like flowers above pale green foliage and is quite happy in partial shade. Very compact and free flowering is 'Miss Mason', orange-yellow; whilst 'Bunch of Gold', with its canary-yellow flowers is slightly later to bloom and is of similar habit. Plant 18 in apart. The flowers last well in water.

Echinacea *purpurea* It is one of the best late-flowering plants for the back of the border, growing 4 ft tall and in bloom from early August until October. It requires a rich soil but well drained in winter. Plant in autumn 2–3 ft apart. The variety 'The King' grows to 4 ft and bears large crimson-purple flowers with a central cone of dark brown; 'Robert Bloom' bears rosy-purple flowers on 3 ft stems.

Echinops The globe thistles require full sun and a light, well-drained soil. They are mostly back-row plants where their thistle-like foliage of grey-green shows to advantage against the brilliant red of *Lychnis chalcedonica*. Plant in spring 3 ft apart and 3 in deep.

'Taplow Blue' grows 4 ft tall, its ball-like heads of steely-blue appearing in July and August. 'Veitch's Blue' is more compact, its globular heads of electric blue remaining colourful for several weeks.

Eremurus Growing to a height of 6–9 ft, the fox-tail lilies are amongst the most handsome of all border plants and should accompany the delphiniums, preferably planted with them in a small border to themselves for they require the same rich humus-laden soil and protection from winds. As they come early into bloom, plant in November, 3 ft apart and spreading out the tuberous roots. Only

just cover the crown, as for paeonies, sprinkling sand or peat around it before covering. If the soil is heavy, plant on a mound of sand, spreading out the roots, as for asparagus, and it may be advisable to leave the crown just above soil level.

E. himalaicus is the first to bloom, before the end of May. It bears a massive spike 8–9 ft tall, studded with hundreds of white star-like flowers. Then follows *E. bungei* which grows to only half the height, its golden flowers having orange anthers. *E. olgae* bears its fragrant spikes of apricot-pink during July and August.

Eryngium The sea hollies grow from 2 to 4 ft tall and require an open sunny situation and a well-drained soil containing some humus. The flowerheads consist of a centre cone of florets surrounded by spiny bracts. If cut just before fully open, they will keep through winter and make attractive indoor decoration. Plant in spring and when established, leave well alone.

E. alpinum grows 3 ft tall, its large grey cones surrounded by feathery bracts. The hybrid Amethyst is equally fine, both the flowers and stems being of deep violet, whilst *E. varifolium* is most striking with violet flowers surrounded by a ring of white spines. They bloom in July and August.

The American species *E. agavifolium* has saw-edged leaves and bears cone-shaped flowers.

Helenium Most of them come into bloom in July and remain colourful until late autumn, their daisy-like blooms with attractive dark cone centres being borne in large sprays. Many are too tall for the small border, but several of the newer varieties are ideal. The old 'Crimson Beauty', with its crimson-brown flowers, grows to a height of only 2½ ft, likewise 'July Sun', its large golden flowers being flushed with orange, whilst 'Wyndley' bears a bloom of similar colour and has the same habit. These are really better for the middle of the border. Excellent for the back row is the new 'Goldlackzwerg' which bears blooms of gold flecked with crimson on 3 ft stems, whilst 'Butter-pat', late flowering, bears a bloom of butter-yellow.

Iris The German or bearded iris rhizomes should be planted in July immediately after flowering has ended, which may not be a suitable time to disturb the border and for this reason irises are often planted in a border to themselves. They require an open, sunny situation and a well-drained soil containing plenty of lime rubble (mortar) for irises fail to bloom more through lack of lime than for any other reason. Irises do not like manure but some leaf-mound or clearings from ditches will help to lighten

Dividing an iris. Use a sharp knife and make sure each section has leaves

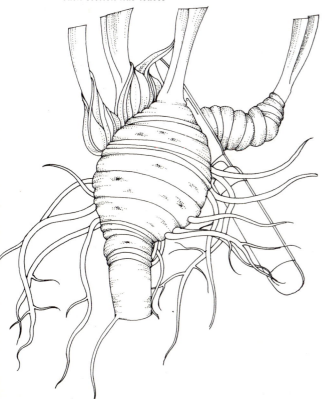

the soil and old mushroom-bed compost will be all that is necessary by way of fertilizers. The iris is one of the best of plants for a town garden, being tolerant of deposits of soot and sulphur, but it should be given a dressing of lime rubble each autumn. Remember that if the rhizomes are allowed to remain undivided for more than four or five years they will bear fewer and fewer flowers for each year they are left untouched.

From the ends of the rhizomatous roots the sword-like leaves appear and from the central portion are borne the flowers. The rhizomes must be so divided (using a sharp knife) that each group of leaves contains a portion of the root. A long-established plant will divide into six or more plants. When planting, allow the top or upper part of the rhizome to rest on the surface of the soil with the fibrous roots on the underside in the soil. Allow 2 ft between the plants and tread them firmly.

The modern bearded irises are amongst the most beautiful plants of the garden and especially attractive are the new pinks amongst which 'Croftway' and 'Ester Fay' are outstanding, the blooms being of deepest pink with an orange beard. Striking, too, is 'My Honeycomb', honey and tan with white fall petals edged with gold and tan. 'Limelight' is a gorgeous lime-yellow self. 'Lady Ilse', sky-blue, and 'Dancer's Veil', cream edged with royal mauve, should be in every collection and so should 'Brasilia', its blooms being of an unusual shade of luminous henna-brown veined with purple.

Kniphofia No small border will be complete without these lovely old plants, generally known as red-hot pokers, though now there are also pure whites and yellows. 'Yellow Hammer' bears spires of golden-yellow from July until September and grows to rather less than 3 ft,

whilst 'Maid of Orleans', of similar habit, bears spikes of pure ivory-white. Plant near them the compact and long-flowering 'Lord Roberts', with its pokers of orange flame. Planting should be done singly, allowing the plants 3 ft in which to grow.

Ligularia Valuable plants for moist clay soils, to associate with the heleniums and golden rods. They grow from 3 to 4 ft tall and bloom in July and August. Plant in autumn 2 ft apart.

Othello, a form of *L. clivorum*, has handsome deep purple foliage and bears its dark orange flowers on sturdy 4 ft stems whilst Greynog Gold bears pyramidal spikes of rich golden-orange flowers.

Lupin The wonderful creations of George Russell of York during the 1930s brought about a new interest in this stately border plant, for the old thin spikes of purple or white gave way to

Red-hot pokers come into their own in late summer and early autumn

thick tapering 3 ft spires of brilliant red and gold, pink, crimson and yellow shades which gave new interest to the border in early summer. Ordinary soil suits this plant, and it requires little or no manure but rarely does well in a limestone soil.

Always plant lupins in November (with paeonies) and allow 2–3 ft between the plants. Propagation is by root division at this time but the hard woody roots are difficult to divide and a better method is to take cuttings in May when 3 in high. Root them in a frame, around the side of pots containing a sandy compost.

Amongst many lovely varieties are: 'Flaming June', both bells and standards being of orange-red; 'Gladys Cooper', with sky-blue bells and standards of dusky pink; 'Tom Reeves', deep yellow; 'Betty Astell', both bells and standards being of soft shell-pink. 'Riverslea' is a deep crimson self-growing 4 ft tall, but 'Rita', also crimson, grows only 2 ft tall and with the pink and gold 'Mrs Micklethwaite' is right for the small border, usually towards the middle.

Lychnis *chalcedonica* Flowering from June until early September on 3 ft stems, this plant with its flat heads of flaming scarlet gives a splash of rich colour to any border. Plant 18 in apart. There is a double-flowering variety, *L. rubra plena*, which grows to a height of only 2 ft and should be used at the middle of the border. *L. coronaria* grows only to 15 in and is a more difficult plant to establish. It requires a well-drained soil and sunny position. Plant it in spring 15 in apart.

Phygelius *capensis* The Cape figwort, closely related to the pentstemon, grows 4–5 ft tall and may not be entirely hardy in the most exposed gardens. It may be cut down by a hard frost but will come again in spring and during autumn, bearing its large crimson tubular flowers with their orange throats. Plant 2 ft apart and in a light, well-drained soil, preferably in an open sunny position. If there is no frost damage allow the foliage to remain on the plants until early spring to give protection. Propagate by cuttings, taken in May.

Rudbeckia A new series of dwarf varieties of this late summer- and autumn-flowering plant has taken the place of those which bloom on 6 ft stems. Outstanding is 'Goldsturm' and equally valuable is 'Goldquelle', both of which bear fully double blooms of golden-yellow on 3 ft stems. The former blooms from early July until mid-September, the latter from early September until late in November, so plant two or three together for a succession of bloom.

Salvia With their attractive grey foliage, several of the salvia species are superb plants for the back of a small border. *S. × superba* bears dainty spikes of violet-purple on 3 ft stems for a period of at least ten weeks, whilst a very dwarf form, *S. compacta*, is a lovely mid-row plant. Likewise, for mid-border is *S. haematodes*, which bears silvery-lilac blooms on branched stems from July until October. Plant 20 in apart in spring.

Sidalcea *malvaeflora* With their marsh-mallow-like flowers in shades of pink, a number of the new sidalceas are of sufficiently compact habit for a small border. They prefer a sunny position and should be planted 18 in apart. Revealing quite a new colour-break is the compact 'William Smith' with large blooms of a warm shade of salmon-pink. A charming variety is 'Dainty', its shell-pink blooms having an attractive white centre. 'Loveliness', too, is very compact, with spikes of glowing pink.

Solidago The golden rod has been greatly improved of recent years, the plants now being short and compact with their plumes of yellowish-green possessing more substance and remaining colourful over a much longer period. The plants do well in partial shade and in any soil. Growing to a height of less than 3 ft is 'Golden Shower' with its arching sprays, whilst the earliest to bloom is 'Lineralis', with plumes of bright yellow. Excellent for the front of a border is the new 'Queenie', which bears its dainty sprays on only 12–14 in stems.

Thalictrum The meadow rues enjoy a cool, moist soil, one containing some humus rather than clay. Plant in autumn, setting the crowns 3–4 in deep and 2 ft apart.

T. aquilegifolium has grey-green foliage and in May and June bears purple flower-heads on 3 ft stems. *T. glaucum*, with glaucous foliage, grows to 5 ft and bears masses of fluffy yellow flowers. But the finest of all is *T. dipterocarpum*, 'Hewitt's Double', growing 3–5 ft tall and flowering in July and August when an established plant will present a billowing mass of rosy-mauve, a superb sight.

Verbascum With graceful 4 ft flower spikes this is one of the loveliest plants for the back of the border, flowering in July and August. Mulleins require a light, well-drained soil for a long life, and they will then form large rosettes from which arises the flower spike. Plant in spring 2 ft apart.

'Cotswold Beauty' bears branching spikes of buff-coloured flowers whilst 'Pink Domino' bears flowers of a lovely shade of buff-pink. 'Royal Highland' is apricot and gold and 'Gainsborough' lemon-yellow, this being the most difficult variety to establish.

MID-BORDER PLANTS
($1\frac{1}{2}$–$2\frac{1}{2}$ ft)

Anchusa These require a light well-drained soil and an open sunny situation and should always be planted in spring, spaced at 18 in apart. 'Loddon Royalist' makes a bushy plant 2 ft tall and during June and July bears masses of royal-blue flowers. 'Little John' grows to only half that height and bears its rich blue flowers until late in August.

Aquilegia The new McKeana Hybrids from America with their huge bi-coloured blooms and so easily raised from seed, will bring the columbine a new popularity. The plants are especially happy in a shaded position and bloom in April and May.

Centaurea Better known as the perennial cornflower, it has handsome hairy silvery foliage. *C. montana purpurea* flourishes in ordinary soil, the flowers appearing from early May until July, borne on stems 18–20 in long. The thick

fleshy roots are best propagated by root cuttings, pieces 1 in long being placed in boxes or pans and just covered with soil. They will root within a month if kept moist. In the border, plant 20 in apart. This plant will prove difficult to eradicate once the roots take hold.

Of other species, *Centaurea pulchra major* bears bright pink flowers above grey-green foliage, and *C. dealbata* with its 'white-washed' leaves bears cerise-pink flowers from July until November.

Chrysanthemum The Korean and Pompon members of this large family, which grow to a height of no more than a little over 2 ft, are ideal mid-border plants and may be left undisturbed for several years. During early autumn they produce a more brilliant mass of colour than almost any other plant and are of course excellent for cutting. Plant in spring 10 in apart. Outstanding for its large double orange blooms is 'Carlene'; 'Polly Peachum' bears a bloom of a lovely shade of peach-pink; also of compact habit is 'Sunny Day', the canary-yellow blooms having a delicious perfume; 'Tapestry Red' bears a double crimson bloom. In the Pompon section, 'Bob' covers itself with tiny buttons of vivid scarlet; 'Denise', with golden-yellow blooms; 'Titania', with orange-bronze; and 'Little Dorrit' with a delicate shade of shell-pink.

Chrysanthemum *maximum* This is a valuable long-flowering perennial and cut flower, the varieties 'Esther Read' and 'Jennifer Read' bearing their fully double pure white blooms on 2 ft stems throughout summer; 'Horace Read' grows 4 ft tall. The plants are happy in ordinary soil which must be well drained in winter. Plant 15 in apart in groups of three.

Erigeron The modern varieties do not hang their heads like those of old, and the blooms are of richer colours. Growing to a height of about 20 in, the new 'Foerster's Liebling' bearing semi-double flowers of pure pink is a good mid-border plant; 'Dimity', which grows only to 12 in and covers itself with orange-pink flowers is excellent for the front of a border. Plant 12 in apart in spring.

Euphorbia Tolerant of semi-shade but equally happy in full sun, the euphorbias or spurges are valuable border plants if only for the rich autumnal colourings of their foliage. Growing 2–3 ft tall, small groups planted about the border will provide rich orange and bronze tints to offset the purples and reds of the Michaelmas daisies. In addition, they bloom during early summer, bearing yellowish-green heads for several weeks.

E. corallina grows nearly 2 ft tall and bears its flowers on wiry stems. In autumn, the plant becomes a mass of flaming orange as it dies back. *E. griffithii* grows 3 ft tall and bears orange flowers in early summer, amidst bronze-tinted foliage. It is suitable for the back of the border.

The spurges require a soil containing some humus but one that is well drained in winter. Plant in spring 18 in apart and propagate by root division.

Hemerocallis Known as the day lily because its richly coloured blooms last for only twenty-four hours before others take their place. This is a fine mid-border plant, the very dwarf varieties blooming on 2 ft stems. Their dahlia-like tuberous roots are best planted in autumn, 18 in apart in groups of two or three. Possibly the three best for a small border are: 'Viscountess Byng', orange; 'Royal Sovereign', golden-yellow; and 'Radiant', orange-red.

Hesperis *matronalis* 'Dame's violet' it is called because of its deep purple blooms which have a pronounced scent in the evening, though it more resembles the

Day lilies have been much improved in recent years and the colour range increased

stock than the violet. It is amongst the most desirable of border flowers—though it is now rarely seen in gardens. Also known as the sweet rocket, *H. matronalis* grows 30 in tall and blooms during early summer, bearing its flowers in terminal sprays. The double form, *H. flore-pleno* is a delightful plant. It requires ordinary soil and is propagated by division of the roots or by cuttings taken in May and rooted in a sandy compost. Plant 18 in apart.

Hosta Previously classified as *Funkia*, these are the plantain lilies, long-lived plants with broad-ribbed foliage in various shades of green and sometimes showing gold and silver variegations. They do well in semi-shade and may be planted in the shade of a northerly wall. Growing 1–2 ft tall, they give subdued colour to the border or shrubbery where, in a moist humus-laden soil, they increase to form thick clumps. Propagation is by division every four or five years. During July and August, they form graceful spikes of white or lilac-grey flowers.

H. albomarginata has dark green leaves with a silver-white band round the edge whilst the leaves of *H. aurea*, especially in early summer, are golden-yellow edged with dark green. *H. undulata* is also effective, having curled foliage with a white band at the centre.

Inula With its compact habit, its grey-green foliage and large-rayed flowers of bright golden-yellow, this is a valuable but little known perennial. The blooms are borne on upright 20 in stems and remain colourful from June until early September. *I. royleana* bears striking

Peony 'Bowl of Beauty', palest pink with golden stamens—a truly lovely flower

orange-rayed flowers; *I. oculis-christi* has bright yellow blooms of similar form.

Lysimachia *punctata* Bearing upright whorls of golden-yellow flowers on 2 ft stems and of compact habit, this is an excellent plant where space is limited and it does well in any soil. Plant 18 in apart. It blooms from mid-June until the end of August.

Lythrum With its bushy habit and bearing masses of thin pencil spikes from July until September, this is a fine mid-border plant. Possibly the two best varieties for a small garden are 'Robert' and 'The Rocket', both of which bear spikes of pure rose-pink. 'The Beacon', with crimson-red flowers, is rather taller growing but could be used for the back of the border.

Monarda The bergamots are excellent plants with their pungent foliage and upright flower stems and are happy in full sun or partial shade. Plant 15 in apart in groups of three. The new 'Prairie Glow', bearing its salmon-red blooms on 2 ft stems is very showy; 'Adam', crimson, and 'Cambridge Scarlet' have a similar habit and richness of colour.

Meconopsis Natives of the lower Himalayas, and though most are monocarpic (ie they die after flowering once), *M. baileyi* and *M. cambrica* are true perennials and are readily raised from seed sown in boxes or pans in a frame in spring. The plants, however, should not be allowed to bloom their first year, not until thoroughly established. They require a rich, leafy soil which does not dry out in summer. They also like to be in semi-shade. Plant in spring 2 ft apart and preferably from pots.

M. baileyi, the blue poppy, requires perpetual moisture at its roots when growing. In July it bears large sky-blue flowers with golden anthers, above rosette-like foliage. *M. cambrica*, the Welsh poppy, bears pale yellow flowers from July until September on 2 ft stems and, unlike most species, is happy in ordinary soil and full sun.

Paeony Most valuable in the border for it is happy in partial shade and will remain vigorous for fifty years in a rich, humus-laden soil. Plants, containing three 'eyes', are best planted in October and November, the only time when they are really dormant. Plant 2 ft apart and not too deeply. Certain varieties are taller growing than others, but of those that are reasonably dwarf 'Duchess de Nemours' (white) and 'Sarah Bernhardt' (silvery-pink) are the first to bloom, followed by 'Elizabeth Stone' (satin-pink) and 'Peter Brand' (crimson); the shell-pink 'Pure Delight' is one of the last to bloom. Each possesses a distinct fragrance.

Phlox The recent introductions, noted for their compact habit, are also less troubled by eelworm than the older varieties. The lovely Symons-Jeune phloxes are rather too vigorous for the tiny border but the Regal phloxes are of suitably compact habit. 'Sandringham', with its large trusses of cyclamen-purple, 'Glamis', rich pink, and 'Windsor', carmine-red, all bloom on $2\frac{1}{2}$ ft stems. With lovely new 'Blue Lagoon' and the pure white 'Rembrandt', of similar habit, they should be planted in groups 12 in apart.

Poterium *obtusum* This so neglected plant is one of the longest flowering of all perennials; from June until October it bears fluffy pink blooms like bottle brushes and is one of the loveliest of all plants. It grows to a height of $2\frac{1}{2}$ ft and should be planted 18 in apart.

Scabiosa *caucasica* A lover of lime, the scabious is one of the longest flowering of all perennials, coming into bloom in mid-summer and remaining colourful until almost the year end. The flat blooms, with their cushion centres are borne on

Scabious, with its pale blue flowers, is one of the most striking border plants

2 ft stems which are almost leafless. Plant in spring, 20 in apart. Still one of the best is 'Clive Greaves', with its large mauve-blue blooms and great freedom of flowering. Also lovely is 'Imperial Purple', with its bloom of deepest purple, and 'Rosalind' bearing flowers of a new shade of wistaria-blue.

Trollius Extremely valuable in that it blooms early in summer when there is little colour in the border. The globular flowers are borne on erect 2 ft stems, the plants being set out 18 in apart in groups of two or three. The three best varieties are possibly 'Alabaster', a new variety from Germany which bears ivory blooms; 'Salamander', fiery orange; and 'Canary Bird', primrose-yellow.

155

FRONT-ROW BORDER PLANTS (9–18 in)

A number of very charming junior editions of the more robust perennials may now be obtained and these are very suitable for making up miniature borders for the smallest of gardens.

Aster The dwarf forms of *A. novi-belgii* are indispensable plants for autumn flowering, remaining colourful from early September until November and making compact mounds 9–12 in high. 'Little Blue Baby' and 'Lilac Time' do not grow more than 6 in tall and are lovely for a small rockery. Other charming varieties are: 'Queen of Sheba', lilac-pink; 'Peter Pan', clear rose-pink; 'Midget', pale blue; 'Victor', light blue; and 'Little Red Boy'.

Anaphalis A charming border plant of everlasting type with handsome grey woolly leaves and bearing its fluffy white flowers throughout summer. A hardy plant, it does best in a sandy soil and is propagated from root cuttings in May. Plant 15 in apart. Anaphalis is a pleasing foil for plants with red flowers.

A. nubigena bears its papery-white flowers in clusters from July until October and retains its silver-grey foliage until Christmas. *A. triplinervis* grows 12 in tall and has broader leaves whilst *A. yedoensis* bears its branched flowerheads on 2 ft stems.

Bergenia Related to the saxifrage family, the plants are of value in that they readily adapt to a dry, sun-baked situation and bloom during March and April when few other border plants are in bloom. They are shade tolerant and evergreen, the large round leaves providing shelter for other plants from cold spring winds. Growing 12–15 in tall, the flowers are borne on short thick fleshy stems. Plant in November, 18 in apart, and propagate from pieces of the root.

B. cordifolia has deep pink flowers and heart-shaped leaves whilst *B. delavayi* has bronze foliage and flowers of even deeper pink. There are also two fine hybrids, 'Abendglut' which bears crimson flowers, and 'Delbees' which has shiny bright green leaves and bears rosy-red flowers.

Campanula *lactiflora* The new variety 'Pouffe' is one of the few border campanulas to bloom over a long period. It forms a tiny mound 9 in high and covers itself in masses of light blue flowers from June until early September.

Convallaria *majalis* The lily-of-the-valley is a native of deciduous woodlands and enjoys similar conditions in the garden, ie semi-shade and a leafy soil. Planted in small groups about a border, it quickly spreads to form a thicket of sheathing leaves from which arise the dangling white bells on 6 in stems.

Plant the crowns in November, 12 in apart and 3 in below soil level, and divide every four or five years to keep the stock vigorous. They will appreciate a mulch of decayed manure and leaf-mould in winter.

The best form is 'Fortin's Giant' which in June bears creamy-white bells but also lovely is *C. majalis rosea* which bears rosy-lilac bells a week or so earlier.

Cynoglossum *nervosum* The hound's tongue, so called from the shape of its leaves. A plant that is long living in a well-drained soil, it grows 2 ft tall and from mid-June until the summer ends it provides a splash of true blue on the border canvas. It bears its flowers in clustered sprays, like an anchusa. As with most blue-flowering plants, it is advisable to plant in spring, 20 in apart.

Dianthus In addition to the rock garden pinks, there are hardy carnations and pinks growing 12–20 in tall which are valuable as border plants or for bedding on their own. They are excellent as cut flowers, lasting well in water and do not drop their petals.

These plants require an ordinary soil but one well drained in winter, and they need a liberal amount of lime in their diet. Like scabious, they can be top dressed with mortar or hydrated lime every spring without over-doing it. They resent manure and leaf-mould. An open, sunny situation is essential to their successful flowering.

Plant in spring, preferably from pots, spacing them 12–15 in apart and do not plant too deeply. Propagation is by layering or by removing the un-flowered shoots in July, pulling them away with a gentle tug. The shoots are called 'pipings' and root easily in sandy compost in a frame. Move to small pots when rooted and plant out in spring. After flowering, remove all dead blooms to prevent seeding, which weakens the plant.

To grow border carnations for exhibition, the side shoots and buds must be removed as they form, to allow the plant to concentrate its energies on a single bloom per stem. This may require support by means of a small stake and galvanized ring. Borders are best propagated by layering the un-flowered shoots. The following are well-tried favourites: 'Beauty of Cambridge', perfectly symmetrical blooms of pure sulphur-yellow; 'Bookham Grand', free-flowering large blooms of bright crimson-red; 'Ebor', a 'fancy', the chocolate-coloured blooms being flaked with red; 'Harmony', a 'fancy' of great beauty, the French-grey ground being suffused cerise-red; 'Kathleen Davis', of perfect form, the white ground attractively marked with crimson; 'Leslie Rennison', large refined blooms of deep lavender shot with cerise-pink; 'Madonna', like a pure white camellia; 'Pink Model', dainty flowers of pure salmon-pink; 'Scarlet Fragrance', large

flowers of brilliant nasturtium-red with a rich clove perfume.

Of the many lovely pinks, the Allwoodii strain, raised by the late Montague Allwood, enjoy a long period of flowering and are admirable for cutting. 'Blanche' bears double blooms of ivory-white; 'Doris', double blooms of salmon-pink with a shell-pink centre; 'Phoebe' is salmon-red; and 'Edward' is rose-red flushed cherry-red.

The lovely old garden pinks should be in every collection. 'Black Prince' bears flowers of darkest red; 'Mrs Sinkins' is white with fringed petals; and 'Dusky' a lovely shade of smoky-pink. 'Montrose Pink' bears scarlet blooms, and 'Earl of Essex' double blooms of deep pink.

The laced pinks are also handsome and have an interest all their own. 'Dad's Favourite' bears white flowers, heavily edged with chocolate-brown; and 'London Glow' has a pale mauve ground with thick lacing of crimson-black.

Dicentra Growing 1–2 ft high, the plants enjoy semi-shade and a moist leafy soil. They have much-divided foliage and bear heart-shaped flowers in May and June, before the larger number of border plants come into bloom. *D. spectabilis*, the bleeding heart of cottage gardens, bears its dangling bells on graceful arching stems whilst the hybrid 'Bountiful' has bluish-grey foliage and from May until September bears deep pink bells. Plant in November 18 in apart and propagate by division of the roots.

Epimedium Plants of the Berberis family, the leaves remaining through winter to protect next season's buds. In spring they are replaced by new leaves. The plants enjoy semi-shade and a cool, leafy soil. They bloom in April and May, bearing sprays of four-petalled flowers on wiry stems 9 in tall. In November plant

9 in apart and they will soon cover the ground with their creeping roots.

E. macranthum 'Rose Queen' is perhaps the finest form, with bronze-tinted foliage and bearing long-spurred flowers of rosy-mauve. '*E. pinnatum colchicum*' bears bright yellow flowers and the hybrid 'Warleyense', rich orange flowers. The foliage of these plants takes on rich bronzy colourings in autumn.

Geranium *endressii* The variety 'Wargrave Pink' is one of the longest flowering of all perennials, from May until November. It forms a bushy plant 15 in tall and should be planted 2 ft apart. It bears small cup-shaped blooms of a beautiful clear pink. The hybrid, 'Johnson's Blue', of similar habit, bears bloom of clear blue. Plant one of each of these crane's-bills together.

Geum The two best varieties are the yellow flowered 'Golden West' and 'The Opal' with its intense flame-coloured blooms. Both form compact little plants, flowering on 15 in stems from the end of May until the end of August, almost twice as long as the other geums. Plant 9 in apart.

Heuchera Excellent plants for a dry sandy soil, the new hybrids bear their graceful clouds of bloom on arching stems 18 in tall. 'Red Spangles', the best of all, bears sprays of deepest crimson, whilst 'Shere Variety' bears vivid scarlet flowers.

Nepeta The catmint *N. mussinii*, so called because cats love to roll about in its foliage, is, with its informal habit, ideally suited to plant at the front of the border. With its grey-green foliage and purple flower spikes, it presents a picture of misty loveliness during early summer.

Spring is the time to plant, 15 in apart, and a soil that is well drained in winter is necessary. The plant grows well in a gravelly soil. Only 12–15 in tall, it blooms from late in May until the end of summer.

After flowering, cut off the dead blooms but not the stems, which will provide winter protection. Propagate by root division in spring. The smallest pieces will soon form a dense clump. If it can be obtained, the new variety Violacea bears flowers of deep purple.

Oenothera This, the perennial form of the lovely evening primrose, is a lovely plant, in bloom from mid-June until September. The 'Yellow River' variety of *O. fruticosa* bears its large yellow cup-shaped blooms on 18 in stems and is happiest in a sunny position.

Omphalodes Enjoys partial shade and a moist soil rich in humus and is a useful plant in that it blooms in May, together with coreopsis and doronicum. *O. cappadocica* bears dark blue forget-me-not flowers on 12 in stems, its dark green foliage adding to its attractions.

Planting is best done in June immediately after flowering when the plants may be divided and replanted. The variety 'Anthea Bloom' which bears pale blue flowers above grey-green foliage is an admirable plant.

Onosma *echioides* It is generally thought to be rather too tall for a rockery and slightly too dwarf for the herbaceous border, so it is rarely seen and we miss much for it is one of the loveliest plants of the garden and also extremely hardy. It likes a well-drained soil and a sunny situation, where from mid-June until late in August it bears its rich golden tubular flowers in pendulous form on 8–9 in stems. The blooms also carry a delicious almond fragrance.

Papaver *orientale* For long the oriental poppies, with their habit of falling along the ground if not well supported, have been grown in borders, but for the small

Fritillaria meleagris, *the snake's head fritillary: subtle rather than dramatic*

garden, plant the lovely 'Peter Pan' of upright habit. The larger salmon-scarlet blooms are borne on 12 in stems. Another bearing its bloom on erect stems 20 in long and suitable for mid-border position is the double crimson-red 'Border Beauty'.

Physostegia The variety 'Vivid' bears its almost square spikes of rosy-pink flowers on 12 in stems and blooms from early July until September.

Platycodon *grandiflorus mariesii* This is an unusual and charming plant for a small border, bearing balloon-like flowers of pale blue on 12 in stems from July until September.

Polygonum *affine* A lovely plant with spikes of crimson-red on 12 in stems during August and September. In autumn the leaves turn an attractive golden colour.

Potentilla The small rounded blooms, similar to those of the geum, remain colourful from June until September. 'Gibson's Scarlet' and the semi-double 'Yellow Queen' are the smallest of the dwarf varieties being held on 12 in stems.

Prunella Through June and July the variety 'Pink Loveliness' bears its dainty spikes of clear pink flowers on 12 in stems above attractive dark foliage. It likes a rich soil and a sunny position.

Pulmonaria *augustifolia azurea* Valuable for the front of the border. Its gentian-blue flowers, borne in clusters, appearing in April, before the leaves begin to unfurl. The variety 'Munstead Blue' has deep blue flowers and 'Pink Dawn' flowers of rose-pink enhanced by silver-spotted leaves.

Plant in November 12 in apart and in a well-drained soil. It does well in semi-shade.

Pulsatilla *vulgaris* It used to be classi-fied as *Anemone pulsatilla*, and is known as the Pasque flower because it blooms at Easter—though in most gardens rather later. It does well in a light chalky soil and is difficult to establish unless planted from pots when young. When once established, it must not be disturbed. Plant in the border or alpine garden 12 in apart. Its large purple flowers with their golden anthers are followed by silky seed heads.

Sedum *spectabile* The border stonecrops growing 1–2 ft tall are admirable plants for a dry border, flourishing in ordinary well-drained soil. They bloom from August until October, the flattish flower-heads of dusky rose-red being enhanced by the glaucous green fleshy leaves. Plant 18 in apart in spring and propagate by root division.

'Meteor' bears large rosy-red flower-heads on 15 in stems; 'Ruby Glow' has similarly coloured flowers and blue-green leaves; 'Autumn Joy' grows twice as tall and is suitable for a mid-border position. It bears its dusky red flowers during late autumn. All are frequently visited by late-summer butterflies.

Stachys *lanata* Known as donkey's ears on account of its handsome, long, silvery-grey leaves, it is a most pleasing plant bearing spikes of bright tubular pink flowers clustered together.

Stokesia *laevis* In bloom throughout late summer and early autumn, the large lavender-blue flowers borne on 12 in stems. Plant 12 in apart in spring.

Tradescantia *virginiana* Quaint in that the propeller-like flowers are backed by a long leaf, these natives of Virginia remain in bloom from June until late in August. 'J. C. Weguelin' bears a bloom of pretty sky-blue; 'Osprey', a white bloom; whilst 'Gayborder Violet' is deepest purple. Plant in groups of three or four, 9 in apart. They grow to 18 in.

Left   the common monkshood— beautiful but poisonous.
Right   a butterfly gladiolus

LIST OF BORDER PERENNIALS

Name	Colour	Height	Season
Acanthus mollis	pinky-blue	3 ft	July–Aug
Acanthus spinosa	purple and white	3–4 ft	July–Aug
Achillea eupatorium	yellow	3–4 ft	July–Oct
Aconitum 'Bressingham Spire'	violet-blue	3 ft	July–Sept
Anaphalis nubigena	white	15 in	July–Oct
Anaphalis triplinervis	white	12 in	July–Oct
Anchusa 'Loddon Royalist'	royal blue	2 ft	June–July
Anchusa 'Little John'	mid-blue	12 in	July–Aug
Anemone japonica	white/pink	3 ft	Aug–Oct
Aquilegia	various	3 ft	April–May
Aster novi-belgii	blue/pink/red	2–4 ft	Aug–Nov
Astilbe × *arendsii*	white/red/salmon	2–3 ft	July–Sept
Astrantia carnolica	white and pink	3 ft	July–Aug
Baptisia australis	indigo blue	3 ft	June–July
Bergenia cordifolia	pink	15 in	March–April
Bergenia delavayi	rose	15 in	March–April
Bocconia cordata	coral-pink	5 ft	July–Sept
Campanula lactiflora	pale blue	9 in	June–Sept
Campanula 'Lodden Anna'	pink	3 ft	June–July
Campanula macrantha	violet	4 ft	June–July
Campanula persicifolia	white/blue	3 ft	June–July
Centaurea dealbata	cerise	18–20 in	July–Nov
Centaurea montana	purple	18–20 in	May–July
Centaurea pulchra major	pink	18–20 in	May–July
Centranthus ruber	white/crimson	3 ft	July–Sept
Chrysanthemum, Korean	crimson/yellow/orange	3 ft	July–Dec
Chrysanthemum maximum	white	2–5 ft	July–Sept
Cimicifuga cordifolia	creamy-white	5 ft	Sept–Oct
Cimicifuga racemosa	creamy-white	5 ft	Aug–Sept
Convallaria majalis	white	6–9 in	June–July
Coreopsis 'Badengold'	yellow	3 ft	June–Sept
Cynoglossum nervosum	mid-blue	2 ft	June–Aug
Delphinium	blue	2–6 ft	June–July
Delphinium × *ruysii*	pink	2 ft	June–July
Dianthus (pink)	crimson/pink/white	15 in	June–Aug
Dicentra spectabilis	crimson	18 in	May–June
Dictamnus fraxinella	pink	3 ft	July–Aug
Dierama pulcherrima	purple/pink	4–5 ft	Aug–Sept
Digitalis lutea	yellow	3–4 ft	July–Aug
Digitalis × *mertonensis*	dusky pink	3–4 ft	July–Aug
Doronicum	yellow	3 ft	April–June
Echinacea purpurea	crimson-purple	5 ft	Aug–Oct
Echinops ritro	electric blue	4 ft	July–Aug
Epimedium macranthum	rosy-purple	9 in	April–June
Epimedium pinnatum	yellow	9 in	April–June

Name	Colour	Height	Season
Eremurus bungei	yellow	4–5 ft	May–July
Eremurus himalaicus	white	8–9 ft	May–July
Eremurus olgae	apricot-pink	5–6 ft	July–Aug
Erigeron	violet/blue	2 ft	July–Aug
Eryngium alpinum	violet-blue	3 ft	July–Aug
Euphorbia corallina	yellow	2 ft	May–July
Euphorbia griffithii	yellow	3 ft	May–July
Geranium endressi	pink	12 in	May–Nov
Geranium 'Johnson's Blue'	violet-blue	15 in	May–Nov
Geum	yellow/scarlet	18 in	June–Aug
Helenium	bronze/yellow	3–4 ft	July–Oct
Hemerocallis	crimson/yellow/pink	2 ft	July–Aug
Hesperis matronalis	violet/white	2–3 ft	May–July
Heuchera sanguinea	crimson	18 in	June–Aug
Hosta (Funkia)	white/lilac	2 ft	July–Aug
Inula oculis-christi	yellow	2–3 ft	June–Aug
Inula royleana	orange	2–3 ft	June–Aug
Iris germanica	various	3–4 ft	June–July
Kniphofia	orange/yellow	2–4 ft	Aug–Sept
Ligularia clivorum	orange-yellow	4 ft	July–Aug
Lupin	various	3–4 ft	June–July
Lychnis chalcedonica	scarlet	3–4 ft	June–Sept
Lychnis coronaria	cerise	15 in	July–Aug
Lysimachia punctata	yellow	2–3 ft	June–Aug
Lythrum	red/rose	2–3 ft	July–Sept
Mecanopsis baileyi	sky blue	2–3 ft	July–Aug
Mecanopsis cambrica	yellow	2 ft	July–Sept
Monarda didyma	crimson/pink	2–3 ft	July–Sept
Nepeta mussinii	violet-blue	15 in	June–July
Oenothera fruticosa	yellow	18 in	June–Sept
Omphalodes cappadocicus	blue	12 in	May–June
Onosma echioides	yellow	9 in	July–Aug
Paeony	crimson/white/pink	2–3 ft	May–July
Papaver orientale	red/pink	1–2 ft	July–Aug
Phlox decussata	purple/red/pink/white	2–3 ft	July–Sept
Phygelius capensis	crimson	4–5 ft	June and autumn
Physostegia	rose-pink	12 in	July–Sept
Platycodon	pale blue	12 in	July–Sept
Polygonum affine	crimson	12 in	July–Sept
Potentilla	scarlet/yellow	12 in	July–Sept
Poterium obtusum	pink	2–3 ft	June–Oct
Prunella 'Loveliness'	pink	12 in	June–July
Pulmonaria	blue	18 in	April–May
Pulsatilla vulgaris	purple/pink	6 in	April–May
Rudbeckia	yellow	5–6 ft	July–Sept
Salvia haematodes	silvery-lilac	3 ft	July–Oct
Salvia × superba	violet-purple	3 ft	July–Oct

Name	Colour	Height	Season
Scabious caucasia	violet/blue	2 ft	July–Oct
Sedum spectabile	rose-red	18 in	Aug–Oct
Sidalcea malvaeflora	pink/salmon	3–4 ft	July–Aug
Solidago canadense	yellow	3–5 ft	July–Nov
Stachys lanata	pink	18 in	July–Sept
Thalictrum aquilegifolium	purple	3 ft	May–July
Thalictrum dipterocarpum	rosy-mauve	4–5 ft	July–Aug
Thalictrum glaucum	yellow	4–5 ft	May–July
Tradescantia	violet/blue	18 in	June–Aug
Trollius	orange/yellow	2–3 ft	May–June
Verbascum	buff/pink	4 ft	July–Aug
Veronica spicata	pink	15 in	July–Sept
Veronica teucrium	blue	15 in	July–Sept

Chapter 9

BULBS IN THE GARDEN

Bulbs are among the most versatile plants, and certainly among the most labour-saving. Once planted they require little or no attention but continue to increase year by year. For a small garden they provide more colour for the amount of ground they occupy than almost any other plant and as their foliage dies back each year after flowering, they are never troubled in a town garden by the deposits of soot and sulphur which harm so many plants.

Bulbs may be used to give colour to corners of the garden where few other plants would flourish, beneath shrubs and trees, and in dark corners where tall buildings cast their shadow. But whereas spring-flowering bulbs are planted in profusion, those bulbs which bloom at other periods of the year remain sadly neglected, with the result that much beauty is missing from our gardens. Most of the autumn- and winter-flowering bulbs may be classed as miniature and so are very suitable for the small garden. Plant them about a rockery which would otherwise be devoid of colour at this time, or use them as an edging to a path or shrubbery. Set them around ornamental trees, or in short grass, though only those which bloom during winter should be planted in the lawn, for it is essential that they have time to die back before the lawn is given its first summer cut and with it the foliage of the bulbs.

Wherever possible, plant bulbs where they will not be disturbed and where they may be left for years to increase, both by self-sown seed and offsets. The bulbs will benefit from an occasional mulch of peat and decayed manure, old mushroom-bed compost being ideal, but they will require no other attention. This is much more labour-saving than the use of, say, tulips and hyacinths for bedding when lifting and planting have to be done each year.

An important factor in the culture of small flowering bulbs is to ensure that they are planted in a well-drained soil; excess moisture remaining about the bulbs during the dormant period will cause them to decay. For the same reason do not plant too deeply. The miniature bulbs, with few exceptions, should be covered with only 2 in of soil. They are best planted in groups of half a dozen, placing the bulbs on a layer of peat and sand to encourage adequate drainage. The autumn- and winter-flowering bulbs

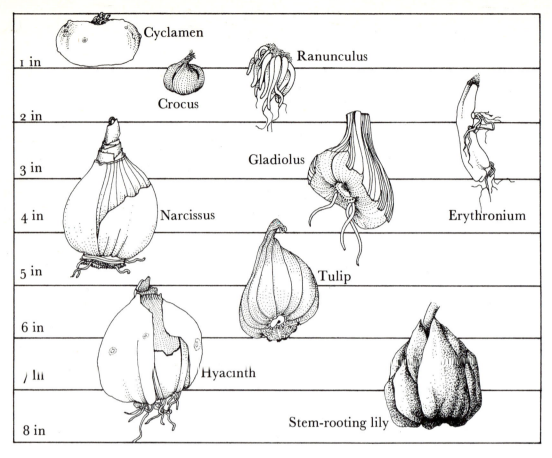

1 in — Cyclamen

2 in — Crocus — Ranunculus

3 in — Gladiolus

4 in — Narcissus — Erythronium

5 in — Tulip

6 in

7 in — Hyacinth

8 in — Stem-rooting lily

A diagram showing correct planting depths for various bulbs and corms

should be planted during June and July, and the spring- and early summer-flowering bulbs during October and November. Many of the small flowering bulbs seed themselves profusely and what may originally have been a dozen bulbs will in a few years' time become a mat of vivid colour over a wide radius. There are few gardens that will not be made more beautiful throughout the year by at least a few groups of these lovely small flowering bulbs with their glorious colourings; at no time is their brightness more appreciated than during the winter.

WINTER-FLOWERING BULBS

Aconite There are several lovely forms of the eranthis or winter aconite which, when planted in drifts about a shrubbery,

around the base of trees, or along a path, will give a welcome splash of colour during February and March, their beautiful golden cups nestling amongst bright green, fern-like foliage. The foliage provides a valuable ground cover long after the blooms have faded. *Eranthis hyemalis* bears in February its brilliant golden cups amidst foliage of emerald green, and in March *E. cilicica* comes into bloom. Its flowers have broader petals and are of a deeper shade of gold, whilst the foliage is tinted with bronze. Plant in groups, spacing the bulbs 5–6 in apart.

Crocus Because several species bear their flowers during the darkest days of winter, the winter-flowering crocus is one of the most valuable of all plants. The corms should be planted in generous drifts where the winter sunshine can reach the flowers, otherwise they will not open sufficiently well to reveal their full beauty. The flowers only open in sun.

There are several species which come into bloom during November and by planting a number of these there will be colour until the end of March, when the large-flowered Dutch hybrids take over the display. In bloom before the end of November is the hardy *Crocus longiflorus*, its sweetly scented lilac tubes having a brilliant scarlet stigma. The Galilee crocus, *C. ochroleucus*, comes into bloom at the same time; this has creamy-white flowers with an attractive orange base. Though the bloom is only small, it gives bright colour during dull November days. Then comes the early December-flowering *C. laevigatus fontenayi*, with fragrant, lilac-buff blooms feathered with purple. It seeds freely. Plant near it *C. tournefortii*, which has large blooms of a lovely warm lilac-rose, but is rather tender and should be confined to a sheltered garden.

Then, coming into bloom early in the new year, whenever the ground is free from snow and hard frost, *C. imperati* gives of its beauty. The inner petals are violet, the outside fawn and feathered with purple, and the flowers are richly fragrant. The blooms of *C. sieberi* follow, soft lavender-blue with a striking golden base. In bloom at the same time is a particular favourite of mine, *C. fleischeri*, which bears small white flowers. These have scarlet stigma which can be seen through the petals. The blooms appear to be so frail though they are really extremely hardy.

In February comes *C. ancyrensis*, with its small flowers of deepest orange. These, like the blooms of *C. fleischeri*, are more

Crocus chrysanthus '*Snow Bunting*', *a very choice crocus with wide-open flowers*

star-like when open than any other crocus flowers. The lovely *C. korolkowi* also blooms early in February, deep gold stippled with grey on the outside.

Iris A genus of about 300 species, native to the north temperate regions. There are irises to bloom at all seasons of the year. They may be divided into two distinct groups: those having a rhizomatous rootstock amongst which are the flag or German irises which are usually planted in the border; and the bulbous irises derived from *I. xiphium* and including the Dutch irises, grown commercially for their cut bloom. In turn, the bulbous irises comprise three main groups: (1) those of the Reticulata group which bloom in winter and spring on 3–6 in stems; (2) those of the Xiphium group which includes the Dutch irises; and (3) the Juno irises of Bokhara and Afghanistan, with deeply channelled leaves enclosing the stem at the base. They are the most difficult to manage.

For window box or trough, for the rockery or for planting in grass or along a path, there are no plants as hardy or so easy to grow as the delightful little *Iris reticulata* and several other dwarf species. They come into bloom with the first warm rays of the spring sunshine, towards the end of February or in early March, and making almost no foliage, and with their upright habit, require only the minimum of room to display their charms. Like the hardy cyclamen, the dwarf irises do well in a soil containing lime rubble, but enjoy a more open situation. Plant in October 2 in deep, and to produce a rich display plant circular groups of six bulbs, spacing them 2–3 in apart

Iris reticulata *'Cantab', a very early-flowering pale blue bulbous iris*

The first of these dwarf species to bloom and most charming is *I. danfordiae*, which bears its bright golden blooms before the end of February. Then comes *I. histrioides major*, the quite large blooms of which are borne on 6–8 in stems. The purple-blue flowers have a conspicuous white blotch on the fall petals.

In March *I. reticulata* comes into bloom, its sweetly fragrant flowers borne on 8–9 in stems. The blooms are deep violet-purple, with a striking yellow blotch on the fall. Possibly lovelier is the new variety 'Cantab', which has pale blue standards and rather deeper coloured fall petals attractively marked with a golden crest. As a companion, 'Royal Blue', which may be described as being a pure Oxford-blue colour is equally lovely, the fall petals having the same conspicuous golden blotch.

Irises of the Xiphium group may be planted in the border in groups of 6–12, or in beds for cutting for home decoration. Make the bed 3–4 ft wide, dig in some humus and give a liberal dressing of lime. When the soil is friable, tread the ground and plant the bulbs like shallots, pressing them into the soil 4 in apart each way. This should be done in early autumn and close planting will enable the stems to support each other. They will be ready for cutting early in May or will provide colour in the border when few other plants are in bloom.

Amongst the best are 'Blue Champion', with flowers of clear cornflower blue having a yellow blotch on the fall petals; 'Golden Harvest', deep yellow; and 'Lemon Queen'.

If a 7–8 cm bulb is planted, instead of the usual 6–7 cm size, and in a soil enriched with some decayed manure, a second crop may be expected the following year though the blooms will be smaller.

The Juno irises require plenty of

moisture when beginning to grow but very little when resting in winter. They are native of lower mountainous slopes and come into bloom soon after the melting snow provides them with their correct moisture requirements. They form thick stems with long leaves clasping at the base, like leeks, and bear their flowers from the axils of the leaves in spring and early summer. *I. bucharica* bears white and yellow flowers; and *I. orchioides*, the orchid iris, has flowers with pale yellow standards and deep yellow falls.

The large fleshy bulbs are planted in a sunny corner in autumn. Handle them with care for the fleshy roots which grow below the bulbs should not be broken. Plant 2 in deep, into a soil containing plenty of leaf-mould and decayed manure and during dry weather in spring and summer water copiously. They should be left undisturbed for years.

Eranthis hyemalis the spring aconite. One of the earliest bulbs to flower

Snowdrop This is the galanthus, everybody's favourite. On a low grassy bank, about a lawn or shrub border, indeed anywhere, no bloom is more welcome when with the melting of the snow their beauty is displayed. They can be left undisturbed, to reproduce themselves from seed, or they may be lifted immediately after flowering and be divided and replanted. Each of the species is lovely, and outstanding is *Galanthus imperati atkinsi* which bears its large, snow-white tubes on 8 in stems soon after Christmas. At its best during February is *G. nivalis*, the familiar green-tipped snowdrop. The double form, *flore plena*, is rather later to bloom. For March flowering *G. elwesii* is an excellent variety, bearing attractive grey foliage and large flowers with vivid green inner segments held on 6–7 in stems.

Squill The hybrid *Scilla tubergeniana* which comes into bloom before the end of February and is a valuable addition to the winter garden. Plant 4 in apart, for when established each bulb will produce three to four stems each with up to a dozen blooms. It grows 6 in tall, the pale blue flowers having dark blue stripes down the petals.

SPRING-FLOWERING BULBS

Anemone Rarely are the poppy anemones used for bedding, yet they provide a brilliance of colour over a longer period than most other plants. Their fern-like foliage and cup-like blooms borne on 6–8 in stems make them an ideal plant for a small garden and, if planted 6 in apart, they will quickly cover the ground with their bright green foliage. From an early autumn planting they come into bloom early in summer and continue until the following autumn. They then have a period of rest and if the ground has been well enriched with humus, will bloom again in spring. A hundred corms of the 2–3 cm size, which is the best to use for bedding (the smaller corms being more vigorous), cost very little indeed and give masses of bloom for indoor or garden decoration. They are completely hardy, and are extremely tolerant of the soot-laden atmosphere of a town. Plant the corms in early October, 1 in deep and do not plant too close together for they quickly form masses of roots and make an abundance of foliage.

By using separate varieties, some delightful colour schemes may be enjoyed. Among the single or de Caen anemones, 'His Excellency' bears a bloom of velvet-red with a striking white ring round the centre; this variety is particularly attractive planted with 'The Bride', pure white with a black centre. Or plant with them, in circles, the purple-blue 'Mr Fokker'. Among the double or St Brigid anemones, 'The Governor' bears a bloom of brilliant pillar-box red; 'Queen of Brilliance' is cherry-red; 'Lord Lieutenant', navy-blue; and 'Mount Everest', pure white.

The beautiful anemone species, too, remain sadly neglected yet are an inexpensive method of providing masses of rich ground colour during spring and early summer. For a mass carpeting for daffodils the rich blues of several of the species make an exquisite picture. They thrive particularly well in a chalky soil. In well-drained soil plant during late autumn, but where the soil is unduly heavy it is better to delay until mid-March.

One of the first to bloom is *Anemone apennina*, which may easily be raised from seed or by root division immediately after flowering, though the most usual method is to plant tubers late in autumn. This is a charming plant for a shrub border or rockery, for the plants love the protection of stones. Its fern-like foliage appears as soon as the snow has gone, its single bright blue flowers with their golden centres appearing early in April on 6 in stems.

Equally hardy is *A. blanda*, the Grecian windflower, which bears its deepest blue flowers on 4 in stems during the first sunny days of spring. It is at its loveliest planted beneath silver birch trees, or on a bank of short grass beneath tall trees where the sunshine may reach it. Possibly a miniature dell would suit it even better, for, like all anemones, it does not like cold winds. With the blue-flowered *A. atrocoerulea* plant the equally lovely *A. rosea*, which bears delicate rose-pink flowers.

Another beautiful plant is the silky

windflower, or pasque flower, so named by the Elizabethan writer Gerard because it is usually in bloom for Easter. It also enjoys similar conditions to the Grecian windflower, being at home in a pocket about a rockery where it can form a long taproot. As it does not like disturbance, planting is best done from small pots in October where the soil is light, or in March where the ground is heavy. Propagation is by root cuttings, though the plants may readily be raised from seed in the same way as *A. alpina*, the last of the species to come into bloom. As these are plants of the alpine regions, seed is sown during October in an outdoor bed enriched with leaf-mould and some lime, and left entirely to the elements. Germination takes place in spring, and the seedlings should be potted in autumn or transplanted to flowering positions the following spring, at all times keeping the seedlings moist.

One of the loveliest varieties of *A. pulsatilla* is 'Letchworth Seedling', which bears a bloom of rich burgundy-red. Equally lovely is 'Budapest', found in Hungary, which bears a bloom of vivid lilac, whilst 'Rosea', which received an award of Merit in 1953, bears a bloom of strawberry-pink. The blooms are equally lovely in the bud stage, the outsides being covered with golden hairs.

A most handsome species is the cyclamen-leaf anemone, which has large polished leaves and bears its handsome golden cup-shaped bloom during May. The plant prefers a position of full sun, but must have its roots in moisture so appreciates a deep humus-laden soil. An equally fine plant is *A. vernalis*, called the lady of the snows, though in Britain it does not bloom until May. It has finely cut foliage, its buds being violet-tinted, covered in golden hairs, and opening to silvery-white bloom.

All anemones are delightful plants for many positions about the small garden and, once established, they should be left for years to give of their beauty.

Crocus   To continue the display from *Crocus ancyrensis* and *C. korolkowi* comes the beautiful *C. corsicus*, its handsome cream-coloured blooms feathered with purple. It is, however, expensive, and does not increase readily. A more accommodating plant is the 'Snow Bunting' variety of *C. chrysanthus*, which is similar in colouring. Lovely, too, are 'Cream Bunting', without any trace of feathering, and 'Blue Pearl', its pearl-blue flowers having an attractive golden base. Blooms of the *C. chrysanthus* section are large and refined.

For late March flowering, plant *C. aureus*, which was known to Gerard in 1597, bearing pale yellow flowers. Also *C. vernus* 'Haarlem Gem', which has lilac-blue flowers. Both bloom together. Lastly comes *C. olivieri*, with its attractively pointed petals of vivid orange making it the brightest crocus of all.

Crown Imperial   It was introduced into Europe by Charles de l'Écluse (Clusius) in 1576, and reached England shortly afterwards, possibly through Sir Francis Drake for he was on friendly terms with the botanist, to whom he sent plants collected in the New World. Shakespeare mentioned it and it grows in his New Place garden at Stratford-upon-Avon, flowering in April on 3 ft stems. The flowers are borne in a circular cluster of orange or yellow bells which hang down to protect the organs of fertilization. At the base of each petal there forms a drop of liquid (nectar) which defies the laws of gravity. At the end of the stems is a tuft of leaves.

Suitable for the spinney or dell, for its home is the deciduous woodlands of Asia Minor, the plant requires a soil containing some decayed manure and either peat or leaf-mould. Plant the bulbs early in spring, on a layer of sand and placing each bulb slightly on its side to prevent moisture forming in the hollow at the top. If growing in an exposed position, the stems may need staking for they carry a considerable weight when in bloom. Plant 6 in deep and 12 in apart. The plants will live longer if the dead flower-head is removed without delay.

Daffodil Botanically this is narcissus but plants with the large trumpet flowers are usually called daffodils whilst those with a small crown are known as narcissi. Both are of the same genus, named by Linnaeus in honour of the youth of Greek mythology who was changed into this flower. Among the most beautiful flowers of springtime, they are also of extreme hardiness and will grow almost anywhere but nowhere are they lovelier than in short grass in an orchard or spinney where they can be left undisturbed for years, increasing from bulblets annually. Their stems are strong and they require no staking, not even in the most exposed garden. But they should be grown inform-ally, in small groups of five or six bulbs, 5 in deep and 10 in apart. The smaller species should be planted only 2 in deep.

If planting in grass, cut out a square to the width of a spade and remove the turf to a depth of 2 in. Then work into the soil some decayed manure or used hops before planting the bulbs and replacing the turf, treading it firmly into position. 'Double-nose' bulbs will produce several flowers from each, but 'rounds' of good quality are cheaper and quite as good for garden culture. It was the opinion of Mr Guy Wilson, raiser of so many lovely varieties, that even a good-sized offset could produce a top-quality bloom. The skin of the bulbs should be light brown, clean and quite smooth, and the bulbs should feel firm when pressed. Plant daffodils early, in September, and tulips late, and do not remove the foliage until it has turned brown and died back. This will be from 2–3 months after flowering has ended. To remove the foliage too soon weakens the bulbs.

Of the yellow-trumpet daffodils 'Dutch Master' is outstanding, with overlapping petals of deepest yellow and a large serrated trumpet, whilst 'Kingscourt' has a smooth perianth of immense breadth and a perfectly balanced bell-mouthed trumpet. In bi-colours, 'Trousseau' has a pure white perianth and a trumpet of palest yellow, whilst 'Spellbinder' has these colours in reverse, the perianth petals being lemony-green with a white trumpet shaded lemon at the edge.

Amongst the pure white daffodils, 'Mount Hood' forms a large beautifully proportioned bloom; 'Cantatrice' and 'Broughshane' are equally fine.

In large-cupped narcissi, 'Adamant' has a perianth of saffron-yellow and a deep orange cup whilst 'Carlton' has both perianth and cup of soft, clear yellow. 'Air Marshall' is also striking, the perianth being of deepest yellow with orange-scarlet cup. The early-flowering 'Fortune' should be in every collection, the perianth of clear yellow being enhanced by a cold crown of coppery-orange. 'Louis de Coligny' is most attractive with its pure white perianth and dainty trumpet-shaped crown of apricot-pink. Another lovely 'pink' is 'Wild Rose', aptly named for its cup is shaded wild rose-pink to the base; 'Rose of Tralee' has a crown of deep apricot-pink.

Of the small-cupped narcissi, 'Edward Buxton' has broad perianth petals of lemon-yellow and a deep yellow cup margined with orange. 'Dreamlight' is white throughout with a cerise edge to the cup.

Double narcissi are long lasting, both when cut and in the garden. 'Santa Claus' is pure white throughout and 'Mary Copeland' has white and orange interlacing petals.

Lovely though these large-flowered daffodils are, for the small garden, and for planting beneath young trees, or about a shrubbery or on a grassy bank, the small-flowered or miniature daffodils possess a charm all their own.

The earliest and smallest of the dwarf daffodils is surely *Narcissus minimus*, which bears its tiny yellow trumpets on only 3 in stems and comes into bloom before the end of February. Almost as early is *N. minor*, with a yellow-lobed trumpet on a 5 in stem early in March. At the same time blooms *N. cyclamineus*, the cyclamen-flowered daffodil, so called because its golden trumpet is reflexed like a cyclamen bloom; it grows to a height of 6 in. 'February Gold' is a lovely hybrid with a lemon-yellow perianth and frilled orange trumpet. It is rather taller-growing, but another hybrid, 'Beryl', which has a pale yellow perianth and orange cup, blooms on 8 in stems.

One of the loveliest of the miniatures is *N. canaliculatus*, a tiny polyanthus narcissus, which towards the end of March bears four sweetly scented flowers to each 6 in stem, and above erect blue-green foliage. At the same time the hoop-petticoat daffodil, *N. bulbocodium*, is in bloom, its little rounded flowers of golden-yellow borne on 6 in stems above the rush-like foliage. The angel's tears daffodil, *N. triandus albus*, also bears its cluster of drooping, globular, creamy-white blooms towards the end of March; it is of a similar height. Towards the end of April *N. tenuior* is in bloom. It is known as the silver jonquil and bears two or three deliciously fragrant blooms of cream and yellow on 8 in stems. Last to bloom is

Erythronium dens-canis *the dog's tooth violet. The name refers to the curious tubers*

N. gracilis, one of the loveliest of all, though it grows to 12 in. It bears as many as five pale yellow jonquil-like blooms to each stem during the last days of May, and is richly fragrant.

Dog's Tooth Violet There is no more beautiful plant for planting about the roots of trees, in those pockets of soil where the blooms are protected from cold winds, than *Erythronium dens-canis*, which likes a soil containing plenty of leaf-mould. The dainty little blooms, in colours of rose, purple, or white, hover like moths above the beautifully mottled foliage, held on stems only 4 in long. They bloom for weeks, being little troubled by cold weather though they do appreciate some protection from cold March winds.

When planting, prolonged exposure to sunlight or wind causes the tubers to shrivel; for this reason they are usually sent out in bags of sawdust or peat in which they should be kept until the time of planting.

Plant in October, 3 in deep and 6 in apart, setting the tubers, in shape like a dog's tooth, on a layer of peat or sand. Do not disturb for several years, though the plants will appreciate a mulch each year after flowering.

Of several handsome varieties, 'Pink Perfection' has flowers of soft clear pink, and 'Lilac Wonder' purple flowers with a brown spot at the base of each segment.

Two lovely species bearing lemon-yellow flowers are *E. grandiflorum*, native of Idaho and Washington, and *E. citrinum*, native of the Deep Creek Mountains of Nevada where it blooms in April. The first of these has deep green unmottled leaves; the second, lance-shaped leaves mottled with brown.

Glory of the Snow The chionodoxas are some of the most brilliantly coloured flowers of the spring and should be planted as profusely as possible, and then left undisturbed to reproduce themselves. Unlike the crocus, they do not close up at the slightest breath of cold wind, whilst they remain quite untroubled by sleet showers.

Chionodox sardensis is the first to come into flower, blooming early in March, when it bears loose sprays of rich gentian-blue flowers with their vivid white centres on 4–5 in stems. Then at the end of the month blooms *C. luciliae*, of similar habit, with brilliant blue flowers and glistening white centre. Not without good reason is it called the glory of the snow. There is also a pure white form, *C. luciliae alba*, and a rose-pink form, *C. luciliae rosea*, whilst the new 'Pink Giant', flowering on 6 in stems and bearing flowers of cycla-men-pink, is enchanting. For April, *C. gigantea* with large lavender-blue flowers on 5 in stems is very lovely.

Grape Hyacinth This is the muscari, which has dainty 'hyacinth' spikes made up of dozens of tiny grape-like blooms. For naturalizing with the yellow blooms of the dwarf daffodils and wild primrose they make a charming contrast. If left undisturbed, the muscari will rapidly increase and form dense purple-blue carpets from March until the end of May. The first to bloom is *Muscari azureum* with spikes of bright Cambridge-blue on 6 in stems. Plant together with the equally lovely pure white form, *album*. The well-known free-flowering hybrid 'Heavenly Blue', which is slightly taller-growing and bears fragrant gentian-blue flowers throughout April, is also very attractive. This is followed by the new hybrid 'Cantab', of similar habit and bearing pleasing pale blue flowers. The latest to bloom is *M. polyanthum album*, which bears handsome spikes of pure white bells on 6 in stems, remaining more than a month in bloom.

Hardy Cyclamen Like the dog's tooth violet, which it greatly resembles, the hardy cyclamen is excellent for use about the roots of mature trees, or on the rockery. Or it may be planted at the base of a wall where it will delight in protection from cold winds. The plants may be divided into two groups, those which bloom in autumn, and those which bloom early in spring.

In bloom in March is *C. coum*, which has dark green leaves and bears on 6 in stems the deep rose-red flowers with the reflexed petals which make the cyclamen so attractive. There is also a blush-white form, *album*. *C. repandum* blooms during May. It has beautiful silver marbled foliage and bright crimson flowers. The corms require shallow planting, no more than 1 in deep, and like the dwarf irises they appreciate liberal quantities of lime rubble in the soil.

Hyacinth An excellent bedding plant for late spring display for it remains long in bloom and is of neat, upright habit whilst its balsamic fragrance is appreciated by everyone. It bears some 10–50 bell-shaped flowers, packed tightly together on a leafless scape 10–12 in high.

For bedding, a bulb of 16 cm circumference is large enough, but 18–20 cm should be used for pot culture indoors. The bulb should possess a silvery sheen and be quite firm when pressed at the base. A humus-laden soil should be provided and the bulbs planted 12 in apart in October. Their rather stiff habit will be relieved if Juliae primroses, forget-me-nots or winter-flowering pansies are planted with them. After flowering, remove the dead blooms and lift the bulbs with their foliage. They should be placed in shallow boxes and the foliage allowed to die back before it is removed. Store the bulbs in peat until planting time again.

Amongst the finest varieties are: 'Lady Derby', salmon-pink; 'City of Haarlem', creamy-yellow; 'Ostara', dark blue; and 'Jan Bos' which bears a spike of ox-blood red.

Lebanon Squill *Puschkinia scilloides* is a charming April-flowering plant which grows only 6 in tall. The blooms are white striped with pale blue, and several are borne at the end of each stem. It requires much the same culture as the scillas and a position where the bulbs will receive some sunshine to ripen, without which they will not bloom well. William Robinson, the Victorian authority on flowers, described this as 'one of the prettiest plants of the garden'.

Plant in October 3 in deep and 4 in apart, in groups of 12–20 for maximum effect. They increase rapidly from offsets.

Spring Meadow Saffron What a delightful plant is this little-known bulb *Bulbocodium vernum*, which bears in March star-shaped flowers of bright rose-purple, which appear before its leaves. It greatly resembles the autumn crocus, growing only 6 in high and so hardy that it can be planted anywhere. Plant in autumn, 3 in deep and 4 in apart.

Spring Snowflake This is *Leucojum vernum*, a most interesting little plant, excellent for massing on the rockery, in the shrubbery, and in short grass. In a sheltered position, where it may receive some sunshine, it will bear its drooping bell-shaped blooms before the last day of March. These white blooms are attractively tipped with green. In a soil containing plenty of humus the bulbs will multiply rapidly. Plant in autumn, 3 in deep and 6 in apart.

Spring Star Flower This is *Tritelia uniflora*, which during April bears on 6 in stems lavender star-like flowers with a violet stripe down each petal. The bulbs should be planted 3 in deep to protect them from frost; the plant prefers a permanent position.

Squill This is the spring-flowering scilla, bearing its tiny spikes at a height of only 4 in, which is suitable for a trough, rockery or shrubbery. It likes a more sunny position than the English and Spanish scillas—the bluebells. The first to bloom is *Scilla bifolia*, in blue and shell-pink forms, followed by *S. sibirica*, towards the end of April. This Siberian squill bears short spikes of blue or white flowers. The Dalmatian species should not be neglected. This is *S. amethystina*, which produces spikes or deep purple-blue flowers on 6 in stems towards the end of May. The squills should be planted 3 in deep and in a soil containing some humus.

Tulip It takes its name from 'tulbend', the Turkish for turban which the flowers resemble in shape and colouring. The first species to reach Europe was brought from Constantinople by Conrad Gesner in 1559 and named *Tulipa gesneriana* after him.

For spring and early summer display in the garden, the tulip stands supreme. The smallest of the dwarf Kaufmanniana hybrids and the single and double tulips may be used in window boxes and tubs, and the Darwin and Cottage varieties for large beds, perhaps inter-planted with polyanthuses or winter-flowering pansies or with wallflowers and forget-me-nots to give ground cover and to relieve the bareness of the tulip stems. For outdoor planting use a 9–10 cm bulb—though the 10–12 cm size will produce a bloom of top quality. Plant 4–5 in deep (half that depth for the species) and about 9 in apart. Circles of contrasting colours make for an effective display, or the bulbs may be planted about the border or shrubbery in groups of a dozen of the same variety.

Tulips enjoy a heavier soil than most bulbs but it should be well drained, so incorporate some decayed manure and peat or leaf-mould. Used hops or old mushroom-bed compost is also suitable. Plant the bulbs in November, though it is permissible to plant tulips until Christmas. As for all large bulbs, use a wide-nose trowel so that the base of the bulb will be in contact with the soil at the bottom of the hole.

It is usual to lift tulips after flowering. Remove the dead head and place the bulbs with stems and foliage attached in trays in an airy room to die back gradually. Then remove the stems and store the bulbs in boxes of peat until ready to use again. If 10–12 cm bulbs were originally obtained, these should give a second flowering but after that they are discarded and new bulbs purchased.

Single early tulips These are invaluable for wind-swept gardens on account of their dwarf habit, and come into bloom early in spring. They are right for planting in small beds, spaced 6–8 in apart and growing 12–15 in tall. Amongst the loveliest are: 'Apricot Beauty', a lovely shade of rosy-apricot; 'Bellona', golden-yellow; 'Dr Plesman', glowing scarlet; 'Keizerskroon', scarlet flowers with a broad edge of yellow; and 'Peter Pan', deep pink, shading to cream at the petal edges.

Double early tulips Growing only 10–12 in high, their paeony-like blooms retain their colour for several weeks, longer than any other tulips. They bloom shortly after the singles. Some of the finest are: 'Aga Khan', yellow, shading to orange at the petal edges; 'Dante', ox-blood red (plant it with the white Schoonoord for a striking display); 'Jan Vermeer', cardinal-red edged with gold; 'Peach Blossom', rose-pink; and 'Tearose', primrose-yellow flushed with apricot, very large flowers.

Cottage tulips From 20 to 30 in tall, they have egg-shaped blooms and are at their loveliest in May, usually accompanying wallflowers or early-flowering pansies. Plant them 9–10 in apart. Outstanding are: 'Bond Street', yellow flushed with orange; 'Fortune's Gift', rose-pink shaded with orange; 'G. W. Leak', geranium-red; 'Royal Porcelain', white-edged red; and 'Louis XIV', royal purple.

Darwin tulips The 'kings' of all tulips, bearing almost square-shaped blooms on 3 ft stems. They are at their best early in June. Some of the finest are: 'Charles Needham', ox-blood red with a velvety sheen; 'Golden Hind', intense yellow as if painted with gold leaf; 'Magier', white with purple shading at the edges; 'Flying Dutchman', cherry-red; and 'The Bishop', deepest purple.

Lily-flowered tulips The result of crossing the hybrid *T. retroflexa* with a Cottage tulip. *T. retroflexa* was evolved from an original crossing of *T. gesneriana* and *T. acuminata* which has elegant pointed petals. They are May flowering; the blooms have pointed, slightly recurving petals and are carried on 2 ft stems. Among the best are: 'Aladdin', crimson with yellow edge to the petals; 'China Pink', well named; 'Ellen Willmott', primrose-yellow; 'Sidonie', of port wine colouring; and 'Queen of Sheba', scarlet-bronze edged with yellow.

Parrot tulips So called from the fringed feather-like petals and the intermingling colourings of red, orange, yellow, steely blue and green. They are Darwin 'sports' and bloom at the same time as Darwins. Most striking are 'Fantasy', the first modern Parrot, its creamy-white blooms feathered with green; 'Orange Favourite', the orange blooms feathered with apple-green; and 'Texas Gold', yellow flowers feathered with green.

Multi-flowered tulips These grow 2–3 ft tall and bear 3–6 flowers which branch from the main stem. Plant 12 in apart to make a colourful display. The most economical of tulips for bedding. 'Claudette' has ivory-white flowers edged with cerise; 'Emir' is oriental red and 'Georgette' red with a wire edge of gold.

Triumph tulips Raised from the Darwin and Single Early tulips, they bloom early in May on 2 ft stems, the cone-shaped flowers being of many unusual pastel colourings not found in any other group. 'Mary Housley' is yellow, shaded with apricot; 'Garden Party', white with a broad edge of carmine-pink; and 'Rose Korneforus', heather-pink shading to silvery-mauve at the petal edges.

Tulip species All the tulips, including the large-flowering Dutch hybrids, are suitable for the smallest of gardens—for no plant gives a more brilliant splash of colour during April and May and even into June. But many of the species, the earliest of which comes into bloom in March, will prove particularly suitable, with their dainty habit, for planting about a rockery, as an edging to a path, in the shrubbery, or in short grass. There, unlike the large-flowering Dutch tulips, the bulbs may be left down for many years, and rather than deteriorate they will multiply each year to provide a more and more attractive display. They are first-rate bulbs for the small garden.

One of the first to bloom, and making a plant of dainty habit, is *Tulipa turkestanica* which bears cream-coloured flowers, flushed with bronze and green, on short-branched stems. In a sunny position it is in bloom from early March. In bloom shortly after is *T. pulchella*, a beauty amongst miniature flowers. It bears, on 5 in stems, charming urn-shaped flowers of deepest purple. Early in April blooms *T. clusiana* on 8 in stems, the outer petals cherry-red and the inner petals white. The bulbs should be planted 6 in deep, close to crazy paving or rockery stone. In bloom at the same time is another gem for the rock garden, *T. dasystemon*, which bears numerous canary-yellow blooms to each 6 in stem. Towards the end of April *T. chrysantha* comes into bloom, its deep yellow flowers shaded cherry-red on the outside. One of the most colourful of the species is *T. praestans*, which is rather taller-growing and bears three or four brilliant orange flowers to each stem.

There are a number of May-flowering species which will prolong the season into the first weeks of summer. Flowering on only 6 in stems, the dainty *T. linifolia* bears glowing scarlet blooms which have a purple centre; *T. persica*, the smallest of all tulips, bears its brilliant yellow fragrant blooms on only 3 in stems.

The brilliantly coloured early *T. kaufmanniana* is outstandingly beautiful. A native of central Asia, it opens its huge polished blooms before the end of March and remains long in flower. The species bears a creamy-white bloom with broad petals which are shaded with red on the outside. It grows to a height of only 6 in and bears as large a bloom as do the Darwin and Cottage tulips. An even dwarfer form of exquisite beauty is the variety 'Gaiety', whose deep cream-coloured blooms, striped with red on the outside, almost rest on the ground. Outstanding, too, is *T. kaufmanniana aurea*, the blooms being like cups of golden-yellow with outsides of deepest scarlet. Beautiful and of dwarf habit is the variety 'Shakespeare', a blend of apricot and salmon, whilst *T. coccinea* bears a bloom of deepest crimson. Just two or three planted together will provide rich colouring in the garden when there are few other brightly coloured flowers.

Striking too, is *T. fosteriana* which blooms in April, its grey-green leaves enhancing the scarlet flowers held on 12 in stems. Of a number of beautiful hybrids, 'Red Emperor' (also known as 'Madame Lefèbre') bears globular flowers of vermilion with black and yellow basal markings, whilst 'Golden Eagle' bears yellow flowers which have a scarlet 'flash' on the outside of each petal.

Several of these hybrids are the result of crossing *T. fosteriana* with *T. greigii* which has also produced a series of hybrids from crossings with varieties of *T. kaufmanniana*. They have the unusual and exquisite purple and pink leaf markings of *T. greigii*. 'Cape Cod' grows only 8 in tall and has yellow flowers, shaded with apricot and striped with scarlet; 'Salmon Joy' is azalea-pink edged in white; 'Red Riding Hood' has vermilion flowers enhanced by grey-green foliage.

SUMMER-FLOWERING BULBS

Alpine Hyacinth An attractive and valuable little plant for it is extremely hardy and bears its amethyst-blue flowers on only 6 in stems. *Hyacinthus amethystinus* blooms during May and early June and is charming on the rockery or for edging. Plant in autumn 2 in deep and 4 in apart.

Californian Hyacinth Another charming little plant, requiring a warm sheltered garden where, during May and June, it will bear its pretty bright blue flowers at a height of 6 in. *Brodiaea grandiflora* is delightful used by the side of a path.

B. coccinea is most arresting and is known as the Californian firecracker. It has narrow leaves and bears drooping crimson-red flowers tipped with green on a 2 ft stem.

Camassia Native of British Columbia and Oregon, it is the American counterpart of the bluebell of Britain to which it is closely related. Camassias grow well in partial shade and in ordinary soil, and in mid-summer bear their purple-blue flowers in loose racemes. They are excellent for cutting and do well in an orchard or spinney. Plant in autumn, 3 in deep and 6 in apart, placing the bulbs on a layer of sand.

C. esculenta is the best known. The flowers are mid-blue veined with deeper blue, and up to twenty are formed on a single stem.

Flowering Garlic The alliums are rarely planted by the modern gardener, yet with their large flowerheads are most attractive. The very dwarf may be used on the rockery, the others being valuable for naturalizing and for planting in a shrubbery. They grow well in ordinary soil and should be planted 6 in apart.

For the rockery, *Allium ostrowskianum*, growing less than 6 in tall, is excellent, bearing its rosy-red flowerheads during June. For the shrubbery, *Allium moly*, the golden garlic, is a most colourful plant, bearing during May and June lemon-yellow umbels in profusion and on 12 in stems. In bloom at the same time is *A. neapolitanum*, which bears graceful white flowers on 15 in stems.

Gladiolus Mostly of South African origin, it is one of the most popular of summer flowers, grown in large numbers by the commercial and cut-flower growers. Of easy culture and well adapted to the cool summer climate of Britain and North America, the gladiolus stands supreme as a late summer and early autumn flower, bearing its handsome funnel-shaped blooms on 3–4 ft stems. When cut and in water, it will retain its beauty for ten days or more.

It requires a rich friable loam and a sunny situation. Plant the corms in early April 3 in deep and 10 in apart, preferably on a layer of sand or peat to assist drainage. The corms should have a high crown and be firm and plump rather than be thin and shallow. For exhibition, plant a 12–14 cm corm; but for ordinary garden display, a 10–12 cm corm is large enough. Smaller corms will prove disappointing though the Primulinus and miniature forms make a smaller-sized corm. Water copiously during dry weather, and in a wind-swept garden it will be advisable to stake the flower spike when 2 ft long.

If growing for garden display, remove the dead flowers but not the foliage, which should be allowed to die back before lifting the corms in October. At the base of the old corm a new one will have formed and this is carefully detached and placed on a tray to dry, before storing in boxes of sand and in a frost-free room.

Allium moly, golden garlic, yellow flowers and grey foliage. Easy in any soil

To guard against thrip, which will feed on the corms during storage, reducing them to a cork-like tissue, treat the corms with naphthalene flakes (1 oz for 100 corms) before storing.

Of many lovely varieties of the Large-flowered gladiolus, the following are to be recommended: 'Adorable' which opens eight florets at a time, creamy-yellow with an amber blotch in the throat; 'Arisctocrat', one of the best 'smoky' gladioli, the strawberry-red flowers shaded with grey; 'Athlone', buff-pink; 'Circe', tangerine with a 'tongue' of cream on the lower petal; 'Connecticut Yankee', deep pink; 'Eridge', mauve-blue; 'Flower Song', golden-yellow; 'Sans Souci', fiery scarlet; and 'Redcoat', red with ruffled petals.

In the Butterfly strain which in all respects grow to only half the size of the Large-flowered, 'Blue Goddess' is silvery-blue; 'Chinatown', tangerine; 'Ice Follies', ivory-white; and 'Melodie', salmon-pink. In the Miniatures, raised in Canada by Mr Leonard Butt, 'Bo-Peep', buff-pink with attractive ruffled petals, 'Lavender & Gold', which is mauve with a yellow throat, and 'Toytown', scarlet, are most pleasing.

Of the Primulinus varieties with their hooded upper petal chiefly developed by Unwins of Histon, Cambridge, 'Atom' is orange-red with a white edge, 'Chinese Lantern', orange with a yellow throat, and 'Primrose Dame', pale yellow. Striking, too, is 'Richard Unwin', of chestnut colouring with a cream stripe on the fall petal.

Ixia Natives of South Africa, the ixias are not completely hardy in Britain or North America and in exposed gardens should not be planted until April, when they will bloom in July. They produce five or six erect leaves and salver-shaped flowers, borne in a loose spike. Plant the corms 3–4 in deep and 6 in apart in a sandy compost containing lime rubble, and in an open, sunny position otherwise the blooms will not open.

I. maculata is the hardiest species. It is known as the golden ixia and bears 5–17 flowers of the deepest golden-yellow to each spike. *I. odorata* bears pale yellow flowers which are scented like freesias.

Lily Probably no race of flowering plant is as versatile as this, nor perhaps one so long in cultivation. The white Madonna lily, *Lilium candidum*, native of the Near East, is known to have been cultivated since earliest times. The chief areas of distribution are North America, and from

A stem-rooting lily. These need to be planted deeper than ordinary lilies

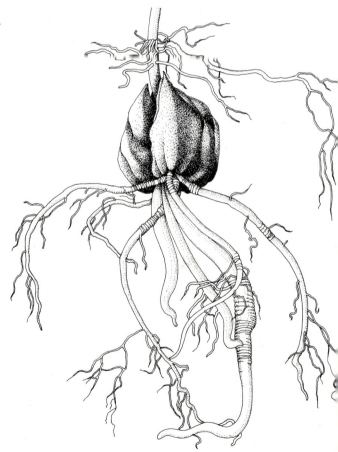

Asia Minor to the Himalayas, and farther eastwards to China, Japan and the Philippine Islands.

Lilies have large bulbs with overlapping scales and bear their gorgeous flowers in terminal umbels on a leafy scape. The flowers droop or are upright or horizontal, the perianth funnel- or bell-shaped, with six spreading or recurving segments. Their outdoor flowering season extends from May until late September, and there are species for full sun or partial shade, and for a calcareous or acid soil. They may be planted in the shrubbery and herbaceous border, or in the wild garden and left there to take care of themselves when they will bloom year after year.

Where the soil is heavy, plant lilies on a bed of sand and cover them with sand or peat before filling in with soil. As a rule, those flowering early should be planted in autumn, and those flowering late in summer should be planted in spring. Depths vary: the stem-rooting species need to be 6–8 in deep and the basal-rooting, 1–2 in deep. In general, plant lilies two to three times deeper than their diameter, and 12–18 in apart depending on habit.

At first, the bulbs will form basal roots but as the stem grows, roots form from that part which is below ground. Later, roots form above soil level and so most species require top dressing as they grow. This should consist of leaf-mould or peat together with a little decayed manure. If in an exposed situation, the stems of the taller varieties will require staking. After flowering, remove the dead blooms as they die back but not the stem and leaves as these will provide nourishment for the bulb until they die down in autumn.

Species	Height	Flowering time
Shade-loving species		
L. amabile	2–3 ft	July–Aug
L. auratum	6–8 ft	Aug–Sept
Bellingham hybrids	5–6 ft	July–Aug
L. canadense	3–4 ft	July–Aug
L. davidii	4–5 ft	July–Aug
L. hansonii	3–4 ft	June–July
L. henryi	5–6 ft	Aug–Sept
L. martagon	3–4 ft	June–July
L. pardalinum	4–5 ft	July–Aug
L. regale	3–4 ft	July–Aug
L. speciosum	4–6 ft	Aug–Sept
L. superbum	5–6 ft	July–Aug
L. tigrinum	4–5 ft	Aug–Sept
Sun-loving species		
L. brownii	3–4 ft	July–Aug
L. chalcedonicum	3–4 ft	July–Aug
L. dauricum	2–3 ft	July–Aug
L. pomponium	3 ft	June
L. pumilum	1–2 ft	May–June

Species	Height	Flowering time
Lime-loving species		
L. amabile	2–3 ft	July–Aug
L. canadense	3–4 ft	July–Aug
L. candidum	3–4 ft	June–July
L. cernuum	1–2 ft	June–July
L. chalcedonicum	3–4 ft	July–Aug
L. croceum	3–4 ft	June–July
L. davidii	5–6 ft	July–Aug
L. hansonii	3–4 ft	June–July
L. martagon	3–4 ft	June–July
Mid-century hybrids	2–3 ft	June July
L. monadelphum	3–4 ft	June–July
L. pumilum	1–2 ft	May–June
L. pyrenaicum	2–3 ft	May–June
L. regale	3–4 ft	July–Aug
L. testaceum	4–5 ft	July
L. tigrinum	4–5 ft	Aug–Sept
These lilies prefer a lime-free soil		
L. amabile	2–3 ft	July–Aug
L. auratum	6–8 ft	Aug–Sept
L. pardalinum	4–5 ft	July–Aug
L. superbum	5–6 ft	July–Aug
These are suitable for the wild garden		
L. canadense	3–4 ft	July–Aug
L. hansonii	3–4 ft	June–July
L. henryii	5–6 ft	Aug–Sept
L. pardalinum	4–5 ft	July–Aug
L. pyrenaicum	2–3 ft	May–June
L. rubellum	12–15 in	June
L. speciosum	4–6 ft	August
L. testaceum	4–5 ft	July

Asiatic or *Mid-century Hybrids* Mostly raised by M. Jan de Graaf at the Oregon Bulb Farm, USA. They are of easy culture and do well under ordinary garden conditions. Among the best of those with upright flowers are: 'Cinnabar' which bears its funnels of cinnabar-red on 2 ft stems; 'Enchantment', nasturtium-red; and 'Joan Evans' which bears on each stem eight or nine yellow trumpets spotted with maroon. These hybrids bloom in June and July and are stem-rooting.

Of those which have flowers facing outwards, 'Brandywine' bears flowers of orange-red spotted with maroon and 'Corsage' has flowers of creamy-yellow shading to pink at the petal edges.

Of those bearing their flowers in pendant fashion, 'Amber Gold' has trumpets of buttercup-yellow spotted with maroon; 'Pink Charm' is clear shell-pink and 'Panamint' has flowers of greenish-yellow speckled with red.

Aurelian Hybrids Raised by de Graaf from *L. henryii* and the Aurelianense crosses of M. Debras. They bear elegant trumpets in yellow, apricot and white, one of the finest being 'Limelight', its long trumpets of soft yellow being shaded with lime-green. When fully open, the flower measures 6 in across. They are stem-rooting and are in bloom in August.

Bellingham Hybrids These are mostly base-rooting lilies, happy in full sun or semi-shade and raised in the USA from *L. parryi* and *L. pardalinum*. Growing to 6 ft they need a sheltered corner. The flowers have gracefully reflexing petals and up to twenty are borne to each stem. They are obtainable in shades of garnet, maroon, orange, and yellow spotted with maroon. 'Buttercup' is one of the best of all the yellow lilies. 'Shuksan' which grows only 3 ft tall has orange flowers flushed with scarlet.

Oriental Hybrids Derived from *L. auratum* and *L. speciosum*, the two most important lilies of the east. August-flowering, they grow 3–4 ft high and are stem rooting. They require an open, sunny situation and a soil containing leaf-mould. They bear flowers of great beauty. 'American Eagle' is pure white, spotted red in the throat and shaded green on the reverse and with delicious perfume. 'Empress of India' bears flowers of crimson, shaded deep pink on the reverse. The petals curl back at the tips in a pleasing way.

L. amabile Bears 2–6 reflexed scarlet flowers on each 2–3 ft stem in July, the flowers being spotted with black. A shade-lover. Plant 6 in deep as it is stem-rooting.

L. auratum The golden-rayed lily of Japan which will not tolerate excessive moisture about the roots in winter. Plant in March, in a well-drained soil. The glistening white blooms have broad golden bands at the centre of each petal and are borne 10–30 to a 6 ft stem in August.

L. brownii One of the finest of the trumpet lilies but the scales are brittle and the bulbs must be carefully handled. It requires a lime-free soil and partial shade. The trumpets are satiny white and 7–8 in long. The plant itself grows 3–4 ft, flowering in July and August.

L. canadense A lily of the deciduous woodlands of eastern North America, it bears its orange-yellow flowers in July on long pedicels. It requires a lime-free soil and dappled shade. Grows 3–4 ft tall.

L. candidum The June-flowering Madonna lily, depicted so often in the paintings of the old masters and incorporated in the arms of the borough of Marylebone. It is base-rooting and requires shallow planting, placing the bulb on its side so that excess moisture will readily drain away. The satiny glistening white flowers have a delicious scent. Grows 3–4 ft high.

L. cernuum Grows only 18 in tall and in June bears 2–6 nodding Turk's cap flowers of lilac-pink, with a sweet perfume. It requires a leafy soil and no lime.

L. chalcedonicum The scarlet Turk's cap lily of the east and one of the first to reach the west. Once it grew in every garden but is now rare. Plant 4 in deep for it forms basal stem roots. Nothing in the garden is more brilliantly scarlet than this. The flowers, which appear in July, are glossy, like sealing-wax. Grows 3–4 ft high.

L. davidii Growing 5–6 ft tall, its stems run underground before turning upwards. Though stem-rooting, plant only 3–4 in deep. The flowers are orange and are borne in July and August, 10–20 to a stem on long pedicels.

L. hansonii Long living and happy in most soils, it is one of the best garden lilies, bearing its orange martagon-type flowers on 3–4 ft stems. Plant in autumn for it comes early into growth.

L. henryi An outstanding lily, tolerant of lime but needing to be planted 8 in deep. It blooms late in August, bearing up to 50 large Turk's cap blooms on a 5–6 ft stem; they are golden-orange, enhanced by long green stamens.

L. kelloggii A lily of Pacific North America which is base-rooting and should be planted only 2 in deep in dappled shade. The flowers have reflexed petals and open white, turning pink with age.

L. martagon The common Turk's cap or martagon lily which became naturalized in Britain many centuries ago. Best grown in the wild garden, it blooms in July, bearing to each stem 10–30 flowers of claret-red, spotted with purple. It will seed itself and spreads rapidly.

L. michiganense Found in damp meadows of eastern North America. It bears 4–6 orange-red flowers of Turk's cap style on 3–4 ft stems. It requires a lime-free soil and the bulbs should be planted 4 in deep.

L. pardalinum The panther lily, found in deciduous woodlands of Pacific North America. Its orange-red flowers are spotted at the centre and borne in a raceme of 20–30 on a 5 ft stem. Plant 4 in deep and lift and divide the bulbs every five or six years. In bloom June and July.

L. parryi Its funnel-shaped flowers of brilliant yellow are sweetly scented and are borne 20 or more to each 5 ft stem. Plant in autumn 4 in deep in a soil containing plenty of peat or leaf-mould.

L. philadelphicum Known as the red lily, it is a native of the eastern United States and bears its flowers of reddish-orange in whorls of 2–5 on a 2 ft stem. Difficult to establish, it should be lifted and divided when in full bloom.

L. pomponium Native of southern Europe, its Turk's cap flowers are borne 2–10 on a 2 ft stem in June and are brilliant scarlet but with an unpleasant foxy smell. It grows best in poor soil containing some lime rubble but may take three years to come into bloom. Plant 4 in deep.

L. pumilum (syn *L. tenuifolium*) Native of Siberia, it is a martagon-type lily bearing 2–6 coral-red flowers on an 18 in stem in May. Stem-rooting, the bulbs are planted 4 in deep. 'Golden Gleam' is a yellow-flowering form.

L. pyrenaicum Native of the Pyrenees, it blooms in May, bearing 3–12 drooping flowers of greenish-yellow heavily spotted with black, and with scarlet anthers. Plant 4 in deep. It is in no way particular as to soil. Grows 2–3 ft.

L. regale One of the most popular species for it does well under average cultural conditions. Growing 5 ft tall, it bears in July 20 or more funnel-shaped flowers of glistening white to each stem, arranged horizontally and in wheel fashion. It is lime-tolerant and will withstand many degrees of frost. Plant 6 in deep and in a sunny position. It comes early into leaf and should be protected from cold winds.

L. rubellum Bears 1–4 funnel-shaped flowers on an 18 in stem clothed in dark green leaves which set off the pink flowers to advantage. Plant the small white bulbs 6 in deep, into a lime-free soil containing peat or leaf-mould. It blooms in may.

L. superbum Native of Pacific North America where it is known as the swamp lily because it likes plenty of moisture whilst growing. The Turk's cap flowers are of vivid orange shading to red at the petal tips, and with red anthers. Plant the bulbs 2 in deep in a peaty soil. It grows 5–6 ft and blooms in August.

L. tigrinum The tiger lily, its orange bell-shaped flowers marked with black are borne 20 or more to a 4 ft stem. Plant 6 in deep in a lime-free soil. A bulb of 16–18 cm will bloom the first season. It is autumn flowering.

Morea An interesting and not quite hardy plant in the British Isles though *M. spathulatum* will tolerate several degrees of frost. Plant the corms in autumn, in a sunny sheltered corner, 4 in deep and 6 in apart and cover with cloches or ashes to give frost protection. The bright yellow flowers are borne on 3 ft stems and are followed by handsome seed 'pods' which may be used for floral decoration.

M. pavonia is known as the peacock iris for at the base of each petal of the snow-white flowers is a circle of peacock-blue surrounded with purple, like the 'eyes' on a peacock's tail.

Ranunculus *R. asiaticus* is native of Turkey. It has claw-shaped tuberous roots and, during the hey-day of the old florist's flowers, shared the popularity of the auricula and the striped tulip. In 1792 Maddock listed over 800 varieties. But in most gardens it requires winter protection, or it should be planted in spring and lifted in autumn, the tubers being stored in boxes of peat or sand over winter.

The plants require a rich soil but one that is well drained in winter. Incorporate some peat or leaf-mould and decayed manure and plant the tubers in drills as for anemones, spacing them 4 in apart and planting 3 in deep. Plant claw downwards with the 'eye' at the top, and cover with peat before filling in the drill. When once growth commences, water copiously and

an occasional application of manure water will enhance the quality of bloom.

Like pompon dahlias, the flowers are borne on 12 in stems and are obtainable in all the brilliant dahlia colours whilst the Turban strain has scarlet flowers spotted with gold.

Snakeshead Fritillary This is a most valuable plant, coming into bloom early in May when the spring-flowering bulbs have finished. The drooping bell-shaped flowers, much like a snake's head, are amongst the most beautiful of the garden, dancing at the end of 9 in stems in the early summer breezes; nowhere do they look more attractive than in short grass. In the species *Fritillaria meleagris*, 'Aphrodite', which bears a pure white bell, is very beautiful; a dozen bulbs may be obtained for the price of a packet of

Ornithogalum nutans with green and white flowers is ideal for naturalizing

cigarettes. Plant with it 'Orion', its purple-red blooms attractively chequered. On account of its unusual markings the plant was known to the early garden writers as the chequered daffodil. Delightful plants in every way.

Spire Lily *Galtonia candicans*, and though a native of South Africa it is hardy in all but the coldest areas of Britain and North America. It grows 4–5 ft tall and blooms late in summer. It requires a moist deeply worked soil and should be planted in spring 6 in deep and 12 in apart. After flowering, allow the stems to die back, then cover with a thick layer of peat or ashes to protect the bulbs from frost. The bell-shaped flowers are greenish-white and are borne at the end of the leafless scape on long footstalks. When cut, they remain fresh in water for about ten days.

Star of Bethlehem *Ornithogalum umbellatum* is one of the finest summer-flowering bulbs, bearing umbels of snow-white star-like flowers on 15 in stems during June.

Equally attractive is *O. nutans*, which grows only 10 in high, its spikes of silver-grey flowers shaded on the outside with green. Excellent for naturalizing or for planting about a shrubbery. The bulbs should be planted 2 in deep.

Summer Snowflake The dainty spring snowflake is followed in May by *Leucojum aestivum*, 'Gravetye Variety' being the best form. Its drooping white flowers, tipped with green, are borne on 18 in stems and when cut last long in water.

Tiger Flower The tigridias are natives of Mexico and Peru and are so named because of the spots on the throat of the flower. The large outer petals form a deep cup, before opening flat or horizontal, the three inner petals being small. *T. pavonia* is most striking, the outer segments being violet at the base, scarlet at the tips and with yellow zoning.

In gardens which enjoy a warm winter climate plant tigridias in October, 4 in deep and 6 in apart, and they will bloom early in summer. Where the garden is exposed, plant in April, when they will bloom at the end of summer. To assist with drainage, plant on a layer of sand.

After flowering, lift the corms as for gladioli and store in boxes of peat in a frost-free room.

Tritonia A delightful bulbous plant from the Cape. *Tritonia crocata* is not completely hardy in exposed gardens but it should be grown wherever possible, even if the bulbs have to be protected in winter by covering with ashes. Select a warm, sunny position and plant the bulbs there in April, 3 in deep in a sandy soil. They will not bloom the first season, but the following May and June they will give delight with their branching racemes of glowing salmon-orange flowers on 9 in stems.

Wood Lily Natives of North America, the wood lilies are interesting plants for a wild garden but are often difficult to establish. The finest is *Trillium grandiflorum*, the wake robin, which is also the most free flowering. It enjoys partial shade and leafy soil, as found in its native woodlands from Quebec to North Carolina. The flowers have three outer segments of green and three inner segments of white, veined with green. They bloom in early summer on 15 in stems. *T. undulatum* is the painted wake robin. It is present in open woodlands from Ontario to Georgia, the white flower appearing as if painted with purple streaks and followed by a three-angled bright red berry.

Plant the rhizomes in October in a soil containing plenty of peat or leaf mould, setting them 3–4 in deep and 9 in apart. They are at their loveliest planted in small groups of six or more and they increase rapidly.

AUTUMN-FLOWERING BULBS

Amaryllis This is the belladonna lily (*A. belladonna*, but in the USA *Brunsvigia rosea*) which bears its funnel-shaped blooms of rose-pink on leafless stems in September. Outdoors, it requires a position of full sun, as at the foot of a wall facing due south, and a well-drained soil. Plant the bulbs in spring on a bed of shingle with the nose 6 in below soil level and 15 in apart. Water copiously during summer. In August feed with dilute liquid manure, and after flowering heap ashes or sand over the bulbs for winter protection. The bulbs should not be disturbed for several years.

In September as many as ten funnel-shaped flowers are borne on a leafless scape 2 ft in length, and are followed by strap-like leaves 18 in long. The variety *purpurea major* bears deep rosy-red flowers on 3 ft stems; 'Windhoek' has rose-pink flowers with an attractive white throat.

Autumn Crocus Known as the meadow saffron, *Colchicum autumnale* is a British native plant bearing mauve-pink flowers. It is mostly confined to deciduous woodlands and orchards, away from grazing animals for the plant has poisonous properties. It is in no way botanically related to the crocus.

The plants flower in autumn, the funnel-like blooms having a long slender tube which extends down to the bulb. A flowering-size tuber or bulb should be not less than 20 cm in circumference, and to be successful it requires a soil which is retentive of summer moisture. Plant in spring 3 in deep and 6 in apart. The strap-like leaves appear early in summer and because of their coarse, rather untidy, appearance the plants should be confined to the shrubbery or orchard.

One of the earliest species to bloom is *C. agrippinum*, the mauve-pink blooms being chequered on the outside with purple squares. It blooms in August and is easy to establish. *C. speciosum* is most striking with huge crocus-like flowers of bright carmine-red. There is a pure white form, *album*. The new hybrids are even more beautiful, coming into bloom in September and continuing until mid-November. 'Autumn Queen' bears bright rose-coloured flowers which have an attractive white throat; 'Rosy Dawn' has cup-shaped flowers of bright rose-pink; and 'The Giant', huge blooms of soft lilac-rose which make their appearance when the first two are finishing.

Autumn-flowering Crocus These plants are autumn-flowering species of the true crocus and should not be confused with the autumn crocuses, the colchicums. The first to come into bloom, and this happens before its leaves appear, is *Crocus zonatus*, bearing pale rosy-lilac flowers with a white stigma. It blooms early in September and is followed by *C. speciosus*, the bright violet-blue flowers of which have a striking orange stigma. A new variety, 'Oxonian', which bears deep violet-purple flowers of great size, is most arresting.

Then comes *C. asturicus*, its deep purple flowers having even deeper stripes at the base of the petals. During October blooms the sweetly scented *C. longiflorus*, which has soft lilac flowers and a scarlet stigma. This is followed by the saffron crocus *C. sativus*, with lilac flowers and a blood-red stigma. In bloom during November are *C. ochroleucus*, cream-coloured with an orange base, and *C. niveus* bearing huge snow-white tubes which are most arresting on a November day.

Autumn Cyclamen With their handsome marbled foliage these are amongst the most rewarding of autumn-flowering plants. *Cyclamen neapolitanum* bears masses of rosy-pink flowers during September before the appearance of its foliage. This later provides an attractive background for muscari, scillas, and other bulbs which bloom in spring. The corms may be planted in shade and should never be disturbed. *C. cilicium* is also lovely, making a compact plant with small rounded leaves zoned with silver, the pale pink flowers having a deep carmine eye. The exception to the rule of shallow planting is *C. europeum*, the corms of this species needing to be planted 4–5 in deep. It, too, has pretty silvered foliage and bears sweetly scented crimson flowers.

Babiana The best species is *B. stricta* and its several varieties which in autumn bear flowers of blue, violet and crimson in loose spikes on 12 in stems, like large freesias. They are not frost-hardy in Britain and North America and require a sunny sheltered corner where the corms may be planted 6 in deep in a well-drained soil. After flowering, cover with a deep mulch to give winter protection.

'Tubergen's Blue' bears flowers of soft sky-blue whilst 'Zwanenburg Glory' has alternating blue and white petals.

Sternbergia Grows on barren mountainous slopes in the Holy Land and Asia Minor and may have been the 'lily of the field' of the Bible. Bearing handsome crocus-like flowers, sternbergias bloom well only in a dry, sun-baked soil, as at the foot of a wall facing south. They grow well in a chalky soil, so where lime is not present incorporate some mortar or lime rubble.

Plant the bulbs in early June, 3–4 in deep and 6 in apart and do not disturb for seven or eight years. It is only after two years or so that they begin to flower well, and then the deep golden-yellow chalices of *S. lutea* are a magnificent sight in the autumn sunlight.

Zephyr Flower *Zephyranthes candida* is a most valuable plant in that it is perfectly hardy and bears its crocus-like blooms during September and October. The blooms are pure white with orange stamens, being born amidst rush-like foliage on wiry stems 9 in long. The plants are at their best about a shrubbery and require a well-drained soil.

Botanical name	Popular name	Colour	Flowering time
WINTER			
Crocus ancyrensis	Crocus	orange	Feb
Crocus fleischeri	Crocus	white	Jan
Crocus imperati	Crocus	purple	Jan
Crocus korolkowi	Crocus	gold	Feb
Crocus laevigatus fontenayi	Crocus	lilac/buff	Dec
Crocus longiflorus	Crocus	lilac	Nov
Crocus ochroleucus	Crocus	white	Nov
Eranthis cicilicia	Aconite	gold	March
Eranthis hyemalis	Aconite	yellow	Feb
Galanthus elwesii	Snowdrop	white	March
Galanthus imperati	Snowdrop	white	Jan
Galanthus nivalis	Snowdrop	white	Feb
Iris danfordiae	Iris	yellow	Feb
Iris histrioides major	Iris	purple	March
Iris reticulata	Iris	purple/blue	March
Scilla tubergeniana	Squill	pale blue	Feb

Botanical name	Popular name	Colour	Flowering time
SPRING			
Anemone apennina	Common windflower	blue	April
Anemone blanda	Grecian windflower	blue	March
Anemone coronaria	Poppy anemone	various	April–Sept
Anemone pulsatilla	Pasque flower	crimson/pink	April
Anemone vernalis	Lady of the snow	white	May
Bulbocodium vernum	Spring meadow saffron	purple-red	March–April
Chionodoxa gigantea	Glory of the snow	lavender	April
Chionodoxa luciliae	Glory of the snow	blue/white	April
Chionodoxa sardensis	Glory of the snow	blue	March
Crocus aureus	Crocus	yellow	March
Crocus chrysanthus	Crocus	various	March
Crocus olivieri	Crocus	orange	March
Crocus vernus	Crocus	lilac	March
Cyclamen coum	Hardy cyclamen	rose/white	March
Cyclamen repandum	Hardy cyclamen	crimson	May
Erythronium dens canis	Dog's tooth violet	purple/pink	March–April
Leucojum vernum	Spring snowflake	white	April–May
Muscari azureum	Grape hyacinth	pale blue	March
Muscari 'Heavenly Blue'	Grape hyacinth	deep blue	April
Muscari polyanthum	Grape hyacinth	white	May
Narcissus bulbocodium	Miniature daffodil	yellow	April
Narcissus canaliculatus	Miniature daffodil	gold/white	March
Narcissus gracilis	Miniature daffodil	yellow	May–June
Narcissus minimum	Miniature daffodil	yellow	Feb
Narcissus tenuior	Miniature daffodil	cream	April
Narcissus triandus	Miniature daffodil	cream	April
Puschkinia scilloides	Lebanon squill	pale blue	April
Scilla bifolia	Squill	blue/pink	April
Scilla sibirica	Siberian squill	blue/white	April
Tulipa chrysantha	Tulip	yellow	April
Tulipa clusiana	Tulip	cherry-red	April
Tulipa dasystemon	Tulip	yellow	April
Tulipa kaufmanniana	Tulip	various	March–May
Tulipa linifolia	Tulip	scarlet	May
Tulipa persica	Tulip	yellow	May
Tulipa praestans	Tulip	orange	May
Tulipa pulchella	Tulip	purple	April
Tulipa turkestanica	Tulip	cream	March
SUMMER			
Allium moly	Golden garlic	yellow	May–June
Allium ostrowkianum	Flowering garlic	rose-red	June
Brodiaea grandiflora	Californian hyacinth	blue	May–June
Fritillaria meleagris	Snakeshead fritillary	white/cream	May–June

Botanical name	Popular name	Colour	Flowering time
Leucojum aestivum	Summer snowflake	white	May
Lilium maculatum	Lily	orange/crimson	June
Ornithogalum nutans	Star of Bethlehem	white/green	June
Ornithogalum umbellatum	Star of Bethlehem	white	June
Tritonia crocata	Tritonia	salmon/orange	May–June

AUTUMN

Botanical name	Popular name	Colour	Flowering time
Colchicum speciosum	Autumn crocus	carmine	Sept–Oct
Crocus asturicus	Autumn-flowering crocus	purple	Sept
Crocus longiflorus	Autumn-flowering crocus	lilac	Oct
Crocus niveus	Autumn-flowering crocus	white	Nov
Crocus ochroleucus	Autumn-flowering crocus	cream	Nov
Crocus sativus	Autumn-flowering crocus	lilac	Oct
Crocus speciosus	Autumn-flowering crocus	lilac	Sept
Crocus zonatus	Autumn-flowering crocus	violet	Sept
Cyclamen cilicium	Autumn cyclamen	pink	Sept
Cyclamen europeum	Autumn cyclamen	crimson	Aug–Sept
Cyclamen neapolitanum	Autumn cyclamen	rose	Sept
Sternbergia lutea	Lily of the field	yellow	Sept
Zephyranthes candida	Zephyr flower	white	Sept–Oct

Chapter 10

FLOWERS IN TUBS

Where there is no garden but possibly only a veranda or terrace, a flat roof or a small courtyard, tubs can be made to play a part in the fulfilment of one's desires to have a garden, however small. Indeed, with its depth of soil, considerably more may be done with a tub than with a window box. Cordon and horizontally trained apples and pears may be grown in tubs around a sunny courtyard, also most of the popular soft fruits, including the strawberry and tomato. Tubs may also be used for a climbing plant, a clematis or rose which may be trained about a wall of a house or yard, whilst almost all plants, from the miniatures to the taller-growing trees and shrubs, will be quite happy in suitably sited and well-prepared tubs of the appropriate size.

The size of the tubs and the height of the plants selected will be governed by the size of the yard, roof or terrace, but the most attractive display may be obtained from a tub of fairly wide diameter and not too tall. Cider casks conforming to these dimensions are obtainable from West Country cider firms and though they will have had considerable use in the storing of cider they will give many more years' service in the growing of plants.

The casks, which will have been sawn in two, will be of seasoned oak and will not require treating in any way, though they may be painted on the outside if a more colourful effect is required; they then look very attractive against the colour-washed walls of house or yard.

One of the most pleasing town gardens that I know consists of a tiny courtyard paved with concrete flagstones between which plants of thyme are growing. Around the washed walls tubs are arranged and planted with all manner of summer-flowering plants including those of trailing habit which almost clothe the sides of the tubs. A few moments' attention each week for watering and the removal of dead blooms is all that is necessary. After the summer display has ended the tubs are cleared, the soil refortified with a little peat or hop manure, and then replanted with bulbs and spring-flowering plants, whilst winter-flowering pansies, primroses and *Erysimum linifolium* provide colour through the darkest days of winter.

PREPARATION OF THE TUB

To enable the plants to take advantage of the full depth of soil, the tubs must receive thorough preparation. Holes should be drilled in the base, and a layer or crocks or broken brick to a depth of 2 in placed over them so that in the event of wet weather there is ample drainage. Over the crocks should be placed partially rotted turves and a layer of decayed stable manure. This should just about fill up half the tub. The balance will be of prepared compost, depending much upon the requirements of the plants that are to occupy the tubs. Dahlias, for instance, prefer a soil liberally enriched with decayed manure and peat, whereas geraniums, though having a liking for a little rotten manure, prefer a soil which is drier and contains less humus. As a general rule, the compost should consist of new turf loam; the soil of town gardens, which is frequently inert and extremely acid, is quite unsuitable. As the compost should be left in the tubs for several years, it goes without saying that it should be well prepared. Kettering loam is excellent where it can be obtained, but loam from pasture land which will be fibrous and free from weed spores will be equally valuable. Mix with it some well-decayed manure, preferably cow manure or a quantity of used hops. Peat is also excellent, especially where the soil is of a heavy nature.

A well-prepared soil not only produces a healthy and free-flowering plant but ensures that the plants do not suffer from lack of moisture at the roots. This means that in an open situation, where natural moisture can be taken up by way of dew and rain, the tubs can be left for several weeks without the plants coming to any great harm.

Before filling, the tub should be raised on pieces of wood or crazy paving stone of no more than 1 in thickness and made quite secure so that they cannot tilt. This will greatly prolong the life of the tubs by keeping the base above ground level, providing a circulation of air and preventing the tubs remaining for long periods in pools of rain water.

After the tubs have been filled to the brim with the prepared compost, allow it a full week in which to settle down before planting. It will in fact settle to about 2 in below the top of the tub and this allows for watering and for top dressings later. It also prevents water and soil from being splashed over the sides by heavy rain.

To prevent the soil from becoming sour, it should be given a top dressing with lime (unless planting lime-haters) each year when cleared of the summer-flowering plants. This, together with the careful initial preparation of the compost, should give a life of at least four years before refilling is necessary.

PLANTS SUITABLE FOR TUB CULTURE

Astilbe These are excellent plants for a tub in a sunless position, where, so long as they are given a compost containing plenty of peat to ensure retention of moisture during summer, they will require little or no attention. The soil of the tub should not be limed. The plants will be permanent and if several varieties are planted together a long succession of bloom may be enjoyed.

Coming into bloom in early June, the snow-white 'Irrlicht' and the crimson 'Gertrude Brix' are outstanding when planted together. Two which bear a bloom of soft clear pink are 'Erica' and 'Gloria'. The new 'Red Sentinel' and the bright rose-red 'Federsee' bloom in July. For excellent August flowering choose 'Venus', flesh-pink; 'Jo Orphorst', ruby-red; and 'Fire', salmon-red. With astilbe it is noticeable that the later varieties grow slightly taller than those which bloom first.

Begonia Besides the multiflora types, the large-flowered tuberous begonia is an excellent plant for tub culture, the tubers being started into growth in gentle heat (possibly in a sunny window) in the early spring so that they have formed one or more leaves by the time they are planted out early in June. Tubers of mixed varieties and colours may be inexpensively obtained for this purpose and will give a rich and trouble-free display, though they require more summer moisture than pelargoniums.

Calceolaria On account of the rich colouring of its blooms which are continuously borne until autumn, this is an excellent plant used with salvias or scarlet bedding pelargoniums ('geraniums'). 'Golden Gem' and 'Bronze Beauty' are the two best calceolarias for tub culture.

The time to take cuttings is in September, and only those shoots which have not borne a flower should be removed. Firm side shoots should be selected and these should be inserted into boxes containing a mixture of peat and sand. If kept in a temperature of 60 °F (16 °C) they will root in several weeks, but take longer than most plants because the shoots are hard and shrub-like. Early in spring, when well rooted, the plants should be transferred to 3 in pots containing the same materials as for salvias, and from then onwards should be given the same treatment. As the cuttings show a tendency to damp off, powdered charcoal should be scattered over the compost, and they should be kept dusted with sulphur whilst rooting.

Dahlia Several of the modern dwarf bedding varieties, making bushy plants about 18–20 in in height, are excellent for growing in tubs. They like a soil containing plenty of humus, for they are gross feeders. The tubers may be wintered in boxes of peat or sand in a frost-free

shed or room, and where there is no greenhouse they may be brought into growth in a sunny room by planting in boxes of soil and peat. So that there will be as little delay as possible in the plants coming into bloom, the tubers should be started into growth before planting out in the tubs early in June after the wallflowers and tulips have finished blooming.

Most striking are the Zulu Hybrids, the bloom being of rich deep colouring, the foliage almost a black-green. Excellent, too, is the yellow cactus-flowered variety 'Downham', and the double crimson-scarlet 'Pride of Edentown'. Also valuable are 'Jescot Gloria', with bronzed foliage and golden-yellow flowers, and 'Rothesay Castle', its fully double blooms being of a rich shade of cream overlaid with rose-pink.

Fuchsia The hardier varieties make most charming tub plants and, given the shelter of a wall and a straw or bracken covering around the crowns during winter, a far greater range may be grown in tubs than in more exposed open ground. The plants may occupy the tubs for many years and will greatly benefit from a dressing of peat and decayed cow manure each year when they finish flowering. A fortnightly application of diluted manure water will greatly prolong the season, often until Christmas in a sheltered garden. The plants are copious drinkers when in tubs and in dry conditions should be given a thorough soaking whenever necessary between mid-April and the end of summer.

Hydrangea Excellent for permanent planting in tubs and completely labour-saving in that once planted, apart from the removal of dead blooms after flowering and of any dead wood in April, the plants require almost no attention. The hydrangea is hardy in all parts of Britain. Plant early in April, into a soil containing peat and plenty of decayed manure. Blue flowers may be obtained by watering with aluminium sulphate, 2 oz dissolved in 1 gallon of water. The pink colouring may be accentuated by working in mortar rubble around the roots at planting time. Excellent varieties which will not be too vigorous are: 'Helge', mid-season, of dwarf bedding habit, and bearing, after aluminium-sulphate treatment, a huge deep blue flower; 'Madame Moullière', very early and in all soils bearing a huge pure white bloom of perfect form; 'Miss Belgium', very early with crimson-red (untreated) or deep violet (treated) blooms; 'Parsival', dwarf and early, with huge blooms of deep carmine with attractive serrated petals; almost purple-red when treated.

Marguerite Because of its rather informal habit, it was at one time planted with bedding pelargoniums ('geraniums') and calceolarias; its whiteness, long-lasting qualities, and ability to flourish under all conditions, made it a perfect foil for the brilliant colours and stiff habit of its neighbours. The plant may be classed as almost hardy, yet to propagate it the cuttings should be struck in gentle heat. October is the best time to remove the shoots from the leaf joints, when the plants are being removed from the beds. Insert them in a compost of loam, peat and sand and keep in a temperature of 55°F (13°C), spraying occasionally to prevent flagging. As soon as rooted, the plants should be potted into 3 in pots in a compost containing some decayed manure and some grit. Like the pelargonium, the plants should be given very little water until the sun's rays stimulate growth towards the end of March. During April, as with all these half-hardy plants, heat is necessary only at night, and from 1 May not at all. Early in May move the plants to cold frames and harden off in the normal way for planting in the tub.

Pelargonium This is an excellent tub plant in all its forms. A most pleasing display may be obtained by planting to the centre of a tub the trailing variegated-leaved L'Élegante and training the shoots up small canes. Surround with bedding varieties and around the sides of the tub plant either the smallest of the dwarf types, such as 'Black Vesuvius', or the trailing ivy-leaved pelargoniums, a particularly fine example being 'Mrs W. A. R. Clifton' with vivid green foliage and double rose-bud flowers of vermilion-scarlet. Or plant at the centre the lemon-scented *P. crispum variegatum* of spire-like habit and attractively crinkled leaves of deep green edged with gold. Surround with variegated-leaved varieties of compact habit and edge with trailing lobelia 'Sapphire'.

Salvia Whilst 'Scarlet Pigmy' is the best variety for miniature bedding, those growing to a height of 12–14 in are more suitable for tub culture. Excellent varieties are 'Harbinger', vivid scarlet, and 'Blaze of Fire', crimson-red. They are increased from cuttings taken in early autumn and rooted round the sides of a pot in a temperature of 55°F (13°C). As soon as rooted, the plants should be transferred to small pots to be grown on through winter and spring in a temperature of 50°F (10°C). A stiff loam into which has been incorporated a little decayed manure and some grit will suit them well and though the plants will require little water during the winter months, they will need copious amounts as the sun gathers strength. Plant out early in June after hardening, six plants to a tub and surrounded with white lobelia, ageratum or alyssum for contrast. This makes a striking and long-flowering display.

Besides these, other suitable subjects for tubs are the dwarf roses, Lilliput chrysanthemums, the dwarf Michaelmas daisies and a number of hardy border plants as well as spring-flowering plants such as wallflowers and polyanthuses. Most annuals, too, will flourish in tubs and in addition to those of dwarf habit try the taller-flowering antirrhinums, godetias, calendulas, asters and stocks—indeed almost any compact variety.

An attractive miniature water garden can be made in a water-tight half barrel

BULBS FOR TUB CULTURE

Not only are miniature bulbs quite charming in tubs, but some of the stronger-growing kinds may also be used.

Agapanthus This, the blue African lily, is a valuable bulbous plant for tub culture. *A. campanulatus* is the hardiest species, bearing its blue lily-like flowers during July and August. The pure white form, *alba*, is just as lovely. The plants prefer a soil containing plenty of peat or leaf-mould, and they like a sunny but sheltered position such as is provided by a sunny courtyard. If necessary the tubs should be removed to the shelter of a wall during winter. Only where the roots have become really tub-bound will the agapanthus bloom profusely, so prepare

Planting up a half barrel for use as a miniature garden pool

the soil thoroughly before planting and do not disturb for several years. And do not have the tub too large.

Amaryllis *belladonna* Not quite hardy except in the most favourable districts, the belladonna lily requires similar conditions to the agapanthus: a soil containing plenty of humus and a sunny though sheltered position. In the less favourable districts the tubs should be removed in winter to the protection of a shed or cellar, for the plants do not like root disturbance when once established. Plant the bulbs 6 in deep. From mid-August to early October the lovely pink, nodding, lily-like blooms are borne on leafless stems above green strap-like foliage.

Hyacinth All the large flowering varieties may be used for tub culture, the bulbs being planted in autumn. A most pleasing display which will take away much of their stiffness of habit will be to plant double daisies or the most dwarf of the Juliae primroses as ground cover, also around the side of the tub. With hyacinth 'Blue Danube', the salmon-pink double daisy, 'Dresden China', is extremely pleasing; or with hyacinth, 'Queen of the Whites', plant double daisy, 'Rob Roy', or primrose, 'Dr Molly', with its bronzy-red foliage and crimson-red blooms on short polyanthus stems.

Lily All those lilies which do not grow too tall are suitable for tub culture. If several are planted together, selecting those which are either lovers or haters of lime so that they may be given the most suitable conditions, there will be a continuous display right through summer and autumn.

The following varieties grow best in a soil which is free of lime: *L. pyrenaicum* (May), *L. tenuifolium* (May), *L. hansonii* (June), *L. regale* (July), *L. amabile* (August), *L. tigrinum* (September). All these lilies have also another common characteristic,

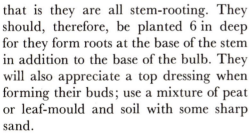

Tubs make versatile containers: a wide variety of plants can be used in striking ways

that is they are all stem-rooting. They should, therefore, be planted 6 in deep for they form roots at the base of the stem in addition to the base of the bulb. They will also appreciate a top dressing when forming their buds; use a mixture of peat or leaf-mould and soil with some sharp sand.

Lilium candidum, the Madonna lily, flowers in June and is not only a lover of lime, indeed it grows badly without it, but it is base-rooting. It should, therefore, be grown on its own—and it makes a fine tub plant. Plant the bulbs 2 in deep and do not disturb for years. Allow the lilies to die down gradually, and if the tub is edged with annuals the display can be continued through summer and autumn.

Tulip No flower is more attractive grown in tubs than the tulip. The dwarf single and double early varieties, the Darwin and Cottage tulips, and the Triumphs with their exotic colour combinations are all equally suitable. The taller varieties, such as Chappaqua and Zina which reach a height of 30 in, need not be included in a tub selection for there is a wide choice of tulips that bloom at a height of 12–24 in. Lovely together are the Darwin tulip 'Charles Needham', with its huge blood-red bloom held on a 24 in stem, and the Cottage tulip

197

'Carrara', which bears a solid pure white bloom on a 20 in stem. Plant six bulbs of each to a tub and edge with red and white double daisies.

TUBS AS WATER GARDENS

Where space is restricted and capital limited, a tub may be made into a most pleasing water garden, to be used as a centrepiece and surrounded by crazy paving or grass, or placed in a corner of a garden. It will be necessary to obtain a tub which is watertight and it may be inserted to its rim in the ground, or placed on a balcony, roof garden or courtyard and planted just as it is. Possibly a tub inserted in the ground is the more attractive and if the rim is allowed to protrude 1 in above soil level, crazy paving may be placed around the tub to a width of about 2 ft. The stones should be set in a layer of cement to prevent weeds from becoming a nuisance. It will be found that when the tub is filled with water the staves will swell; provided a sound tub is obtained there should be no leakage. But before filling with water, the tub must be planted.

No pool, however small, is complete without its water-lily and one of the charming miniatures should be chosen. Lovely is *Nymphaea pygmaea alba*, with its dainty pure white flower, but even lovelier is *N. pygmaea helvola*, which bears a bloom of primrose-yellow. A 3 in layer of soil should be placed at the bottom of the tub and pressed well down, and into this the roots are planted. Around the sides of the tub, which will be 12–15 in deep, stones should be placed to a depth of 6–7 in, and soil pressed into the pockets between them. It is here that the marginal or waterside plants are set for they do not like more than 6–7 in of water over their roots. Plant two or three oxygenating plants to maintain purity of the water and three or four marginal plants to add to the charm of the pool and lend it a natural appearance. The dwarf bullrush *Typha minima* is most attractive and there are several lovely water irises. Plants may be obtained from specialist growers in June, which is the most suitable time to make up a miniature pool. At first, the water will appear muddy but will soon clear and should remain clear, though soil and other material should not be allowed to fall in. The water-lily will bloom from early June until well into October and will be the centre of admiration.

Chapter 11

PESTS AND DISEASES

PESTS OF FLOWERS

Plant	Pest	Treatment
All flowers	Earwig	Spray plant and soil around with Lindex or use Lindex Dust or Gammexane at fortnightly intervals
All flowers	Millipede	Treat soil before planting with Aldrin or Gammexane (1 oz per sq yd)
All plants	Slugs	Treat ground with Slugit; 1 oz in 1 gallon of water will treat 10 sq yd
All plants	Wireworm	Treat ground with Aldrin Dust or Gammexane at rate of 1 oz per sq yd
All plants	Woodlice	Spray with Lindex ($\frac{1}{2}$ oz to 1 gallon of water)
Chrysanthemum	Eelworm	Treat ground before planting with Jeyes Fluid at strength of 2 tablespoons to 1 gallon of water
Gladiolus	Thrip	Before planting dip corms for 2 hours in solution of Lysol or Jeyes Fluid
Lily	Bulb mite	Dip bulbs before planting into a solution of 1 oz sulphide of potassium to 3 gallons of water
Lily	Thrip	Dust plants with Lindex from early June
Narcissus	Eelworm	Place bulbs in clean sack and immerse in tank of water for 3 hours, heated to and kept at 110 °F (40 °C)

Plant	Pest	Treatment
Narcissus and Amaryllidaceae	Narcissus fly	As precaution, dip bulbs in autumn before planting in solution of 1 pint liquid BHC and $\frac{1}{4}$ pint of spreader (Agrol LN) to 20 gallons of water
Rose	Cock chafer Rose chafer Garden chafer	For each, spray with liquid derris containing a spreader or with Sybol (based on gamma-BHC and derris) at intervals of 3 weeks
Rose	Greenfly	Spray in May with Abol-X (1 fl oz to 2 gallons of water); this will give immunity for 2 months, then repeat treatment
Rose	Thrip	Causes malformation of flowers so spray the plants with Sybol at fortnightly intervals from mid-May

DISEASES OF FLOWERS

Plant	Disease	Treatment
Anemone	*Botrytis cinerea* *Puccinia pruni-spinosae* *Schlerotinum delphinii* *Urocystis anemone* Winter browning	Dust with Shirlan AG No known cure Dust corms with Lindex No known cure No known cure
Antirrhinum	*Puccinia antirrhini* Rust	Spray with weak Bordeaux Mixture
Begonia	*Botrytis cinerea* Grey mould *Spaerotheca pannosa* Powdery mildew	Spray with Bordeaux Mixture Dust with flowers of sulphur
Chrysanthemum	*Phragmidium mucronatum* Rust *Septoria chrysanthemella* Blotch *Spaerotheca pannosa* Powdery mildew	Spray with potassium sulphide or lime-sulphur Spray with Bordeaux Mixture Dust with karathane or flowers of sulphur
Colchicum	*Urocystis colchici*	No known cure
Crocus	*Fusarium oxysporum* *Rhizoctonia crocorum*	No known cure No known cure
Cyclamen	*Bacterium carotovorum* *Botrytis cinerea* *Corticium solani* *Thielaviopsis basicola*	No known cure Spray with Shrilan AG Water with Cheshunt Compound No known cure

Plant	Pest	Treatment
Dahlia	*Sphaceloma* Leaf spot	Spray with Bordeaux Mixture
Delphinium	*Pseudomonas delphinii* Black blotch	Spray with weak Bordeaux Mixture
Dianthus	*Didymellina dianthi* Ring spot	Spray with weak Bordeaux Mixture
	Uromyces dianthis Rust	Spray with potassium sulphide
Freesia	*Didymellina macrospora*	Spray with Bordeaux Mixture
	Fusarium bulbigenum	Dip corms in 0.5% formalin
	Mosaic	No known cure
	Sclerotinia gladioli	Dip corms in 0.1% mercuric chloride solution
	Septoria gladioli	Spray with Bordeaux Mixture
Fritillaria	*Sclerotium tuliparum*	Treat soil with 2% formalin solution
Galanthus	*Botrytis galanthus*	Dust with flowers of sulphur
	Urocystis galanthi	No known cure
Gladiolus	*Bacterium marginatum*	Spray with Bordeaux Mixture
	Botrytis gladiorum	Spray with Bordeaux Mixture
	Fusarium bulbigenum	Dip corms in 0.5% formalin
	Fusarium oxysporum	Dip corms in 0.5% formalin
	Rhizopus necans	No known cure
	Sclerotinia gladioli	Dip corms in 0.1% mercuric chloride solution
	Septoria gladioli	Spray with Bordeaux Mixture
	Urocystis gladiolica	No known cure
Hemerocallis	*Didymellina macrospora*	Spray with Bordeaux Mixture
Hyacinthus	*Bacterium carotovorum*	No known cure
	Botrytis hyacinthi	Spray foliage with Shirlan AG
	Sclerotinia polyblastis	Spray with weak Bordeaux Mixture
	Xanthomonas hyacinthi	No known cure
Iris	*Bacterium carotovorum*	No known cure
	Botrytis convoluta	Spray with Shirlan AG
	Didymellina macrospora	Spray with Bordeaux Mixture
	Mosaic	No known cure
	Mystrosporium adustum	No known cure
	Puccinia iridis	No known cure
	Sclerotium tuliparum	Treat soil with 2% formalin solution
Lachenalia	*Mystrosporium adustum*	No known cure
Lily	*Botrytis elliptica*	Spray with Bordeaux Mixture
	Corticium solani	Water with Cheshunt Compound
	Cylindrocarpon radicicola	Dip bulbs in 0.5% formalin solution
	Mosaic	No known cure

Plant	Disease	Treatment
	Phytophthora parasitica *Rhizopus necans*	Water with Cheshunt Compound Add bleaching powder to potting compost
Lily-of-the-valley	*Dendrophoma convallariae* *Puccinia sessilis* *Sclerotium denigrans*	Spray with copper fungicide No known cure No known cure
Matthiola (stock)	*Botrytis cinerea* Grey mould *Corticium solani* Black leg	Dust with flowers of sulphur Water with Cheshunt Compound
Montbretia	*Mystrosporium adustum* *Sclerotinia gladioli*	No known cure Dip corms in 0.1% mercuric chloride solution
Narcissus	*Botrytis narcissicola* *Cylindrocarpon radicicola* *Didymellina macrospora* *Fusarium bulbigenum* *Ramularia vallisumbrosae* *Sclerotinia polyblastis* *Stagonospora curtisii*	Dip bulbs in 0.5% formalin Dip bulbs in 0.5% formalin Spray with Bordeaux Mixture Dip bulbs in 0.5% formalin Spray with Bordeaux Mixture Spray with Bordeaux Mixture Spray with Bordeaux Mixture
Paeony	*Septoria paeoniae* Leaf blotch	Spray with copper fungicide
Pelargonium	*Botrytis cinerea* Grey mould *Phythium spendens* Black leg	Dust with flowers of sulphur Water with Cheshunt Compound
Rose	*Botrytis cinerea* Grey mould *Diplocarpon rosae* Black spot *Phragmidium mucronatum* Rust *Spaerotheca pannosa* Powdery mildew *Sphaceloma rosarum* Leaf spot	Dust with Orthocide Spray with Tulisan or Orthocide Spray with Tulisan or Fungex Spray with karathane or Bordeaux Mixture Spray with Fungex
Scilla	*Sclerotium tuliparum*	Treat soil with 2% formalin solution
Sinningia	*Phytophthora parasitica*	Water with Cheshunt Compound
Tulip	*Botrytis tulipae* *Phytophthora cryptogaea* *Pythium ultimum* *Sclerotium tuliparum*	Spray or dust with Shirlan AG Treat soil with 2% formalin solution No known cure Treat soil with 2% formalin solution

INDEX